Best walks in the Peak District

By the same author

Rambling complete (Kaye and Ward, 1978)
Adventure walking for young people (Kaye and Ward, 1980)
The complete rambler (Granada, 1980)
Great walks of North Wales (Ward Lock, 1982, 1986)
Great walks of the Yorkshire Dales (Ward Lock, 1983, 1986)
Best walks in the Lake District (Constable, 1986)

Best walks in the Peak District

Frank Duerden

Constable London

First published in Great Britain 1988
by Constable and Company Limited
3 The Lanchesters, 162 Fulham Palace Road,
London W6 9ER

Reprinted 1991, 1994
ISBN 0 09 468360 3
Set in Linotron Times 9pt
by Rowland Phototypesetting Ltd
Bury St Edmunds, Suffolk
Printed in Great Britain
by The Bath Press Ltd, Avon

A CIP catalogue record for this book
is available from the British Library

To our first granddaughter, Charlotte Emma, who arrived during the final days of preparation of this book.

Contents

Illustrations

(Photographs taken by Frank Duerden)

Maps and diagrams

(Maps drawn by Frank Duerden)

Acknowledgements

An extremely large number and variety of sources were used during the preparation of this book to provide the background information. It would not be practicable to mention each of these individually, but I would nevertheless like to acknowledge my debt to them.

In particular, I must thank Roland Smith, Head of Information Services, and his colleagues at the Peak District National Park Authority who scrutinised my preliminary list of walks at an early stage, provided information and answered queries as I went along and finally read through the draft manuscript; Peter Roworth, Head Warden, South Peak Estate, and his colleagues at the National Trust who checked my information on Trust properties in the Peak District; Peter Gregory of the North West Water Authority; the proprietor of Blue John Cavern; the Custodian of Peak Cavern; Peter Harrison of Treak Cliff Cavern; R. J. Harrison of Speedwell Cavern; a doctor who checked my entry on the plague; Mr Penrose, Agent Derbyshire Estates, and Mr Day, Keeper of the Collections, of Chatsworth; Mr Greig, Sherwood Forest District of the Forestry Commission; my colleague, Dr Yvonne Williams, who once again looked through the entries with any 'geological' content; Ken Lee for information about Harry Bagshaw; and finally, three friends from the Long Distance Walkers' Association – Brian Adcock, John Corfield and John Feist – who looked through my list of walks and made many useful suggestions.

Some information was taken from the Landranger and Outdoor Leisure maps of the Peak District by permission of the Ordnance Survey; the Countryside Access Charter was included with the permission of the Countryside Commission and the Code of Conduct near Mines by permission of the Peak Park Joint Planning Board. The maps were prepared largely from original material but were based upon maps of the Ordnance Survey and John Bartholomew & Son Ltd.

Finally, I must thank my wife, Audrey, for a great deal of help with proof-reading and for providing her support at those moments of crisis and despair which seem – at least for me – to be part of the process of authorship. For the first time with a book I have no typists to thank, unless I pay tribute to my word processor with whom I am now on fairly good terms.

Introduction

This guide to the walks of the Peak District is based upon exactly the same lines as the first volume in the series, *Best walks in the Lake District*, which was published in the spring of 1986.

The aim has been to select and describe about thirty walks which are the best that the Peak District National Park can offer. I hope that this statement does not sound arrogant, for arrogance was certainly not the spirit in which I approached the task. My list is based upon a great deal of reading, a lot of walking, endless perusal of large-scale maps and finally many discussions and much correspondence with walkers who know the area well. In the end, of course, it was up to me to make the final choice of walks, which I did on the basis of all the information available to me. I hope that I got it right. But if you think that I didn't, then please let me know. I would be very happy to hear from you, via my publisher, if you think that you can improve the list by a substitution or by a modification of any of the routes given.

As before, the routes were selected upon a framework provided by several 'ground rules'. These were: (1) The routes were to be taken from all areas of the Park so as to reflect its varied landscape – although naturally the final coverage was not likely to be even as some parts of the Park are indisputably more attractive than others; (2) They had to vary in length and in difficulty, from short easy strolls to long tough fell walks – in that way the guide would be useful to as wide a range of walkers as possible; (3) Wherever possible the routes were to be circular, so as to avoid problems with transport; (4) They had to pass through good viewpoints or near features of interest such as caves, castles, old mines, etc. – because for me, and I am sure other people, those things make a walk much more interesting; (5) The walking had to be of good quality and generally over firm ground – although I recognised that some people (a minority) are never happy unless they are ploughing about in peat bog, and they also had to be catered for.

All the routes were walked and carefully surveyed specifically for this guide, however many times they had been walked previously and however well I thought that I knew them. The time required for each route was estimated on the basis of Naismith's Rule and they were then placed in order of increasing length. Finally, the list was examined and where necessary modified to take account of difficulty of terrain. The final list therefore should give the walker an idea of the challenge that he faces if he attempts a particular route.

I feel that I should take this opportunity to express my appreciation of the work of the Peak Park Joint Planning Board and its staff, whether full-time, part-time or voluntary. No other Authority has been so energetic in negotiating access agreements with landowners and their creation of three superb railway trails – in conjunction with Derbyshire County Council – deserves the highest praise. A great deal of praise and support should also go to the National Trust who acquired its first property in the Peak District some eighty years ago – Winster Market House – and now looks after 36,000 acres (14 500 ha). As a walker I feel very confident in the stewardship of these two organisations.

The Peak District holds a special and very important place in the history of both walking and climbing. The Dark Peak moorlands may lack height – compared, for example, to those in the Lake District, Snowdonia or elsewhere; even the mountains of the Yorkshire Dales are higher – but are unequalled for sheer toughness of terrain. In no other area has the cult of 'hard walking' been developed to the same extent. If you can hold your own as a walker in the Dark Peak then you can hold your own anywhere. Much the same can be said of rock climbing. The gritstone edges of the Peak possess qualities that make them ideal for the development of sound technique. No other rock has had a greater influence upon the development of British rock climbing than has gritstone. Finally, the Peak District has been at the centre of the battlefield over which the ramblers' right to freedom of access to mountains and moorlands has been fought.

For my own part, my walking days in the Peak District have been very happy ones – with the possible exception of one or two moments on the High Peak Marathon! I hope very much that your days are as happy.

Frank Duerden, 1987

The Peak District National Park

The National Parks and Access to the Countryside Act of 1949, through which the National Parks of England and Wales were established, was the culmination of some twenty years of debate, reports and campaigns. Under its authority a National Parks Commission was set up which was responsible for the creation of Parks in suitable areas. Ten of these were established between 1950 and 1957, of which the Peak District National Park was the first and the Brecon Beacons National Park was the last.

In 1968 the National Parks Commission was replaced by the Countryside Commission which thereby took over responsibility for the Parks. A further change came under the Local Government Act of 1972; under this Act a separate Authority was set up for each National Park which would be responsible for its administration (except for the Peak and Lake Districts where separate Authorities were established at the start). In the Peak District National Park the Authority is called the Peak Park Joint Planning Board.

The Peak Park Joint Planning Board has thirty-four members, of whom twenty-three are appointed by the constituent authorities whose areas form part of the Park; the remaining eleven members are appointed by the Secretary of State for the Environment after consultation with the Countryside Commission. It operates as the planning authority for the area of the Park, with the same planning powers as are normally held by County and District Councils augmented by special powers appropriate to National Parks and to the Peak District in particular. As it is concerned with a National Park it may apply those powers that it has more rigorously. Other functions, however, such as housing, transport and education, remain the responsibility of the County and District Councils within the Park.

The Board's objectives are: (1) To protect both the natural features and the traditional, historical and cultural qualities which make up the distinctive character of the Park; (2) To provide for

The Peak District National Park: the map shows its boundary and the main towns and villages in and around the Park.

FIGURE 1

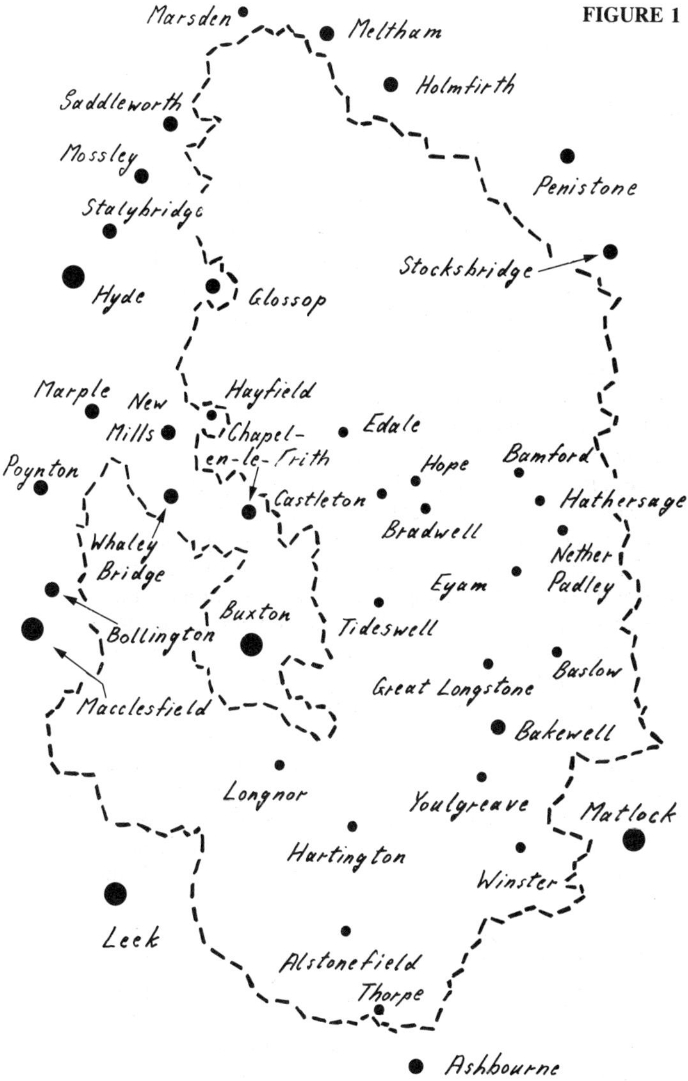

Marsden
Meltham
Holmfirth
Saddleworth
Mossley
Penistone
Stalybridge
Stockshridge
Hyde
Glossop
Marple
New Mills
Hayfield
Chapel-en-le-Frith
Edale
Hope
Bamford
Poynton
Castleton
Hathersage
Bradwell
Whaley Bridge
Nether Padley
Eyam
Bollington
Buxton
Tideswell
Baslow
Macclesfield
Great Longstone
Bakewell
Longnor
Youlgreave
Matlock
Hartington
Winster
Leek
Alstonefield
Thorpe
Ashbourne

FIGURE 2

1. Ashwood
2. Back
3. Horseshoe
4. Deep
5. Great Rocks
6. Monk's
7. Darn
8. Hay
9. Peter
10. Tideswell
11. Tansley
12. Cressbrook
13. Monsal
14. Upperdale
15. Miller's
16. Chee
Longdendale
Alport
Derwent
Woodlands valley
Vale of Edale
Hope valley
Dale of Goyt
Dove
Lathkill
Manifold valley
Beresford
Wolfscote
Dove
Hamps valley
17. Deep
18. Kirk
19. Water-cum-Jolly
20. Long
21. Gratton
22. Biggin
23. Long
24. Cales
25. Middleton
26. Wensley

visitors and ensure that they appreciate and understand the area, but do not damage it; (3) To support and encourage farming and woodland management, which are amongst the best means of maintaining the distinctive character of the area; (4) To consider carefully the social and economic needs of the area. It will be obvious that on some occasions these objectives will be in conflict and the Board will have the difficult task of reconciling the various interests involved.

The Board works in a number of different ways to achieve its ends. It has, first of all, its own budget which it can use, for example, for repairing footpaths and in providing facilities for visitors such as Information Centres. It can use its planning powers not just to prevent damaging development within the Park, but also to redirect development along more desirable lines. Finally – and this is probably the most important – the Board maintains close liaison with a wide variety of other organisations so that it can influence their decision-making processes. The Board therefore achieves most of its objectives by co-operation rather than by compulsion.

About a half of the total expenditure of the Board comes from the Government in the form of a grant, about one quarter is provided by the County Councils from their rates and most of the remaining quarter is from the sale of publications and other activities of the Board.

The headquarters of the Board are at Bakewell where the main administrative functions are carried out. In addition, there are six Information Centres (plus a mobile one), a National Park Study Centre, a Youth Hostel at Hagg Farm, several campsites and a number of car-parks and picnic sites. It is also responsible for the management of several estates and about 34 miles (55 km) of trails over disused railway lines.

The visitor to the Park will meet staff at the Information Centres and is also likely to see some of the Authority's Rangers out in the field. The Ranger Service is headed by a Chief Ranger who is assisted by four District Rangers and about twelve Area Rangers.

The principal dales of the Peak District National Park.

All of these are full-time workers, but there is also a strong group of Volunteer Rangers. The main purpose of the Service is to help visitors and to deal on the ground with some of the problems that arise.

It is usually necessary to clear up one common misconception, which is that the land in a National Park is somehow 'owned' by the nation. Nothing could be further from the truth! In the Peak District National Park about three quarters of the land is privately owned. Of the remainder the Water Authorities own 13 per cent and the National Trust 10 per cent, leaving a mere 4 per cent for the Peak Park Joint Planning Board. This is in stark contrast to most other countries of the world where National Parks are owned by the nation.

Information Centres are situated at:

Bakewell: (062 981) 3227
Castleton: (0433) 20679
Edale: (0433) 70207
Fairholmes (Upper Derwent Valley): (0433) 50953

In addition there are two information points, open during the summer weekends, at Torside (Longdendale valley) and Hartington (old station on Tissington Trail).

Some facts and figures about the National Park

Designated: 28 December 1950 (confirmed on 17 April 1951). The Peak District National Park was the first British National Park to be designated, followed by the Lake District and Snowdonia in that order.
Area: 542 sq miles (140 377 ha). Of the ten National Parks four others are larger, i.e. Lake District, North York Moors, Snowdonia and Yorkshire Dales.

Gateway to the Peak. A millstone is the emblem of the Peak District National Park.

PEAK DISTRICT
NATIONAL PARK

Emblem: An annular millstone on a rectangular base. Millstones have been placed on main roads leading into the Park.
Administrative area: Parts of three Shire Counties (Derbyshire, Cheshire, Staffordshire), four Metropolitan Districts (Kirklees, Sheffield, Barnsley, Oldham) and five Shire Districts (High Peak, Derbyshire Dales, Staffordshire Moorlands, North East Derbyshire, Macclesfield).
Population: 38,370. But there are another 17 million living within 50 miles (80 km) in the great conurbations of Manchester, South Yorkshire and the West Midlands! Probably more than half of the population of England live within a two-hour drive of the Park.
Visitors: About 20 million visitor-days each year, equalled only by the Lake District.
Footpaths and bridleways: It has been estimated that there are approximately 5000 miles (8047 km) of footpaths and bridleways withing the area of the Park.
Land use: The total area of the Park may be divided roughly as follows:

Designated open country	37 per cent
Reservoirs and lakes	1 per cent
Under crops	2 per cent
Under grass	46 per cent
Woodland	5 per cent

The remainder is built up.

The Dark Peak takes up about 74 per cent of the area and the White Peak the remaining 26 per cent (i.e. roughly in the ratio 3:1).

Public transport into and within the Peak District

Railways

Five lines serve the area of the Park:

(1) The Inter-City line from Stoke to Manchester, which runs outside the western boundary of the Park, with stations at Macclesfield, Prestbury, Adlington and Poynton.

(2) The Inter-City line from Manchester to Sheffield which runs through the northern area of the Park with stations at New Mills,

Chinley, Edale, Hope, Bamford, Hathersage, Grindleford and Dore & Totley.

(3) A branch line from Manchester and Stockport to Buxton with stations at Middlewood, Disley, Newtown (New Mills), Furness Vale, Whaley Bridge, Chapel-en-le-Frith, Dove Holes and Buxton.

(4) A branch line from Derby to Matlock with stations at Ambergate, Whatstandwell, Cromford, Matlock Bath and Matlock.

(5) A branch line from Manchester to Glossop with stations at Broadbottom, Dinting, Hadfield and Glossop.

Information Offices for rail services are at Manchester: (061) 832 8353; Sheffield: (0742) 726411; Buxton: (0298) 7101; and Derby: (0332) 32051.

Buses

Several express coach services cross the area of the Peak District from Blackburn, Blackpool, Derby, Hull, London, Manchester, Norwich, Nottingham, North Wales and Sheffield. There are connecting services to these.

An excellent booklet, *Peak District Public Transport Timetable*, is published by Derbyshire County Council with amendments at suitable intervals. This timetable has been compiled by Derbyshire County Council in co-operation with the transport operators to include all bus services operating in High Peak and West Derbyshire (excluding the area south of the A515); services in the adjoining areas of the Peak Park in Cheshire, Staffordshire and South Yorkshire are also included. The booklet includes information on hospitals, early closing and market days, Tourist Information Centres, timetables of Express Coach Services, timetables of rail services and town maps.

Up-to-the-minute information on all bus and coach services in Derbyshire can be obtained from Busline: Derby (0332) 372078; Buxton (0298) 3098.

Accommodation

Camping barns

Camping barns provide simple overnight shelter similar to camping, hence their name. Each has a wooden sleeping platform, an eating area with table and benches, a cooking space and toilet facilities. Campers must provide their own personal equipment such as sleeping bags and cooking stove, in addition to food. All accommodation is unisex.

The barns are available for use to anyone over the age of five, although young people under eighteen must be with an adult. Advance bookings and further information can be obtained from the Peak National Park Study Centre, Losehill Hall.

Campsites

The Peak Park Joint Planning Board publishes a booklet, *Camping and Caravanning in and around the Peak District*, which lists sites recognised by the appropriate local authorities. A similar list, *Accommodation Guide to the Derbyshire Dales – Caravan and Camp Sites*, is published by the Derbyshire Dales District Council.

The Board and the Derbyshire Dales District Council also operate a 24-hour advisory service which is available on Bakewell (062 981) 4341 from Easter to mid-September. The service cannot reserve places but will give advice on which are the busiest sites and where a pitch is likely to be found.

A number of campsites have been established by the Board:

Hagg Farm, Ashopton, near Bamford (see below)
Fieldhead, Edale
North Lees, Hathersage
Hayfield*
Crowden*
Losehill, near Castleton*
Blackshaw Moor, Upper Hulme, Leek*
Eric Byne Memorial Campsite, Birchen Edge, Baslow, near Bakewell

Those marked with an asterisk are owned by the Board but managed on its behalf by the Caravan Club.

Finally, it should be noted that the National Park is in the main privately owned; campers therefore have no right to pitch their tents without the permission of the landowners concerned. This applies equally to areas where access has been allowed under an Access Agreement. Some farmers do allow camping on their land, but their prior permission for this must always be obtained.

Caravans
There are a large number of sites within and around the Park which provide caravans for hire, temporary sites for touring vans and permanent sites for static vans; trailer tents and motor caravans are accepted on some sites. The majority of sites are open from March to October only, but a few remain open all year. See the entry for campsites above.

The Countrywide Holidays Association Guest Houses
The Countrywide Holidays Association, Birch Heys, Cromwell Range, Manchester, M14 6HU, telephone: 061-225 1000, runs a guest house, Moorgate, near to the village of Hope. Guest houses are open to all and provide comfortable accommodation: single or shared bedrooms, full meals and evening entertainment. Normally walking excursions are available, but these are optional and the centres may be used simply for accommodation.

Hagg Farm Hostel and Campsite (110-162888)
The hostel is situated on the north side of the A57, Sheffield to Glossop road, near the western end of the Ladybower Reservoir. It is managed by the Peak Park Joint Planning Board and is open to all as a self-catering hostel. Hagg Farm Hostel, Snake Road, Bamford, Sheffield, S30 2BJ; telephone: Hope Valley (0433) 51594.

Hotels, guest houses and self-catering establishments
As this region is one of the main holiday areas in the British Isles, there is an abundance of private accommodation in the villages and the country. These will be heavily booked in the main tourist months of July and August and at those times advance booking is advised; there should be no problem at other times. An

accommodation booking service is available to visitors calling at the Bakewell Information Centre.

The Ramblers' Yearbook, published annually by the Ramblers' Association, lists hundred of addresses throughout the United Kingdom. The Peak Park Joint Planning Board publishes a booklet, *Accommodation and Catering*, which gives information on hotels, guest houses and self-catering establishments. The Derbyshire Dales District Council produces two accommodation guides to the Derbyshire Dales covering *Hotels* and *Self-catering*.

Youth hostels

Currently there are sixteen youth hostels within the area of the National Park and four others just outside the boundary. Many of these hostels have family rooms with four to six beds.

Maps for the walker

The following cover the area of the Peak District National Park:
Ordnance Survey *1:25 000 Outdoor Leisure Maps* (2 sheets)
  The Dark Peak
  The White Peak
Note that a substantial area to the east and smaller areas to the north, south and west of the National Park are not covered by these two maps. The White Peak map is given in two parts: East Sheet and West Sheet.

Ordnance Survey *1:50 000 Landranger Maps* (4 sheets)
  109 Manchester
  110 Sheffield & Huddersfield
  118 Stoke-on-Trent & Macclesfield
  119 Buxton, Matlock & Dovedale

Ordnance Survey *1:63 360 Tourist Map* (1 sheet)
  The 'Peak District' map covers the entire area of the Park.

The face of the Peak District

The Dark Peak

The Dark Peak has the general shape of a horseshoe with the central area and the open end to the south occupied by the limestone area of the White Peak; altogether it takes up about three-quarters of the total area of the Park. No walker who has had first-hand experience of this region will have any doubt whatsoever as to the origin of its name or its appropriateness, for most of the year there is little colour to relieve the monotonous greys, browns and blacks which are characteristic of it. (The one exception to this is in the autumn when heather moors – which form part of the Dark Peak – are ablaze with purple.) The alternative name of High Peak is not so appropriate as the region is neither particularly high – the highest point is a mere 2088 ft (636 m) – nor is it a 'peak' in the normally accepted meaning of the word. (The name Peak itself is derived from the Old English word *peac* which means hill. The district at various times has been called Pecsaetna, Peaclond, Pec and Pech.)

Erosion of the great upward fold – the anticline – of the Peak District rocks stripped away much of the lower central region to reveal the older and deeper limestone. Down the western and eastern edges and over a great area of the north, however, the rocks of the Millstone Grit series – consisting of shales and hard-wearing grits – were left intact. Along each side the thick layers of grit were exposed forming the steep and impressive 'edges' which nowadays give such superb walks and magnificent climbs. Backed by flat moorland plateaux and overlooking the deep river valleys these edges run for considerable distances – Stanage is the longest continuous stretch at over 3 miles (5 km) in length.

An examination of pollen grains trapped in the peat beds of the moors has indicated that the now bare moorlands had originally a thick tree cover of birch, oak and pine which developed in a warmer period after the Ice Age. As in the White Peak this began to disappear from about 3000 BC, largely as a result of systematic clearance. Other factors (for example, sheep grazing which has prevented the regeneration of the woodlands by destruction of seedlings) have certainly played a part, however. Even today on the high moors the remains of trees which grew many centuries ago can still be found in the peat banks and on the sides of groughs. Only in a few places now, such as on the rocky sides of hillside cloughs and below the edges, do remnants of this forest still linger on and even here they are in slow retreat. The thick beds of peat on the moor tops were formed – from about 6000 BC – from the gradual accumulation of the remains of sphagnum moss – mainly of now extinct types – which had developed in bogs formed in the water-logged hollows of the plateaux.

The Millstone Grit moorlands with their very acid soil or peat cover, generally low temperatures and high rainfall form an environment in which relatively few plants can grow. On the flat ground on the plateaux the conditions are at their worst and heather and cotton grass are the main plants with mat grass and the cloudberry in some locations. With the disappearance of the sphagnum moss the peat surface has become broken and the high rainfall has begun to scour channels in the surface of the moor; in some cases these channels – called groughs – can be as much as 10–12 ft (3–4 m) in depth. In extreme cases, such as around Kinder Low, the cover of vegetation has disappeared altogether and only black peat remains. Overgrazed, trampled on each year by thousands of visitors and with a spatter of 'acid rain' thrown in for good measure it is scarcely surprising that on some parts of the plateaux Mother Nature seems to have decided to call it a day. On moorland slopes the conditions, though still harsh, relax to some extent and bilberry, bracken and flowering plants such as the tormentil and heath bedstraw are to be found. In boggy areas on the lower lying reaches of moor the presence of rushes and bright green sphagnum moss indicate to the knowledgeable walker the parts to be avoided.

As with the plant life the animals and birds of the gritstone

The Dark Peak – the River Kinder near the edge of the Kinder Scout plateau just above the Downfall.

moorlands are relatively few in number. Probably the best known is the red grouse for it advertises its presence by rising up close to the walker and beating away low over the moor with a rapid whirring of the wings and a loud cry of 'go-back, go-back, go-back'. Most walkers, however, would probably express a personal preference for the curlew, whose haunting liquid call is the very breath of early spring days on the moors. The largest wild mammal found on the gritstone uplands is the blue (or mountain) hare, so called because of its blue-grey fur which turns white in winter-time.

The White Peak

The White Peak is an irregularly shaped region in the southern part of the National Park, roughly 20 miles (32 km) long from north to south and 5–12 miles (8–19 km) wide, approximately one quarter of the total area of the Park. It owes its name to the colour of the predominant rock, limestone, which is much in evidence along the dalesides and in the long lines of drystone walls. It is also sometimes called the Low Peak, but this is altogether a less satisfactory name for the region is by no means low, generally attaining a height of over 1000 ft (304 m).

As a limestone area it has much in common with the southern region of the Yorkshire Dales although there the landscape is much harsher and the rock even more obvious in the form of great scars, screes and pavement areas than it is in the White Peak. These differences are the direct result of the conditions prevailing in the two areas during the Ice Age which ended some 8000 years ago. There is a popular misconception that the Ice Age was a single uninterrupted period of intense cold with widespread glaciation; in fact, it consisted of several cold spells separated by 'interglacial periods' in which the climate became considerably warmer. In the first and second of these spells glaciers reached the area of the Peak District to produce an ice sheet over the entire region, whilst in the third spell the conditions were tundra-like with large snowfields rather than glaciers. Although some modification of the landscape took place during these glaciations this was limited as the ice, nearing the end of its range, was slow-moving with little eroding power. Similar glaciation took place in the Yorkshire Dales, but there the ice was altogether more active and the effect on the landscape therefore much greater. Faulting also played a major role in the formation of the enormous scars, such as those near Malham and Giggleswick, which are such striking features of the Yorkshire Dales.

In the Peak District therefore we have an absence of those dramatic landscape features usually associated with districts which have been subjected to the effects of glaciation. The landscape remained largely unchanged, but covered with a deposit of boulder clay left behind as the glaciers retreated. During the final period of the Ice Age cold winds, sweeping across the open plateau, brought dust particles with them which collected on the limestone as a thick deposit called loess. It is these deposits – absent from the Yorkshire Dales – which have made the plateau so suitable for agricultural purposes and have led to its widespread use as pasture land.

The first men coming into the area would have found it extensively covered with deciduous woodland which had come in since the end of the Ice Age. The present landscape is the result of a systematic clearance of this woodland over a period of some 5000 years, partly to provide the open spaces needed for the growing of crops or for the grazing of domestic animals and partly for fuel to be used for cooking and warmth or the smelting of lead. By the end of the sixteenth century most of it had probably gone. What woodland there is nowadays on the plateau is usually the product of deliberate planting to provide windbreaks around the farms. With the removal of the tree cover the drainage of the plateau was much improved so that lime was readily leached out from the soil, with the production of extensive areas of acid heathland. This has now largely been destroyed by improved farming techniques to produce the uniform grasslands of the plateau – it also explains why it is necessary to add lime to the fields even though the base rock is limestone. The building of numerous drystone walls has also changed the appearance of the plateau to a considerable extent.

The melting of the glaciers and snowfields produced vast quantities of water. It was this which produced the river system of the area and the numerous dry dales which today have no active streams in them – some dales have rivers which only flow during periods of heavy rainfall. Rich in lime and nutrients and with remarkable clarity the rivers of the dales support a large number of insects, such as the mayfly and the stonefly, which provide food for trout and grayling. Rivers such as the Dove and Lathkill have therefore become famous for fly fishing, and with this in mind have been improved by the construction of weirs to provide both still pools and the turbulence necessary for water creatures to survive. In contrast to the plateau the steep sides of the dales are often well covered with shrubs and trees, and support a wide variety of flowering plants.

The geology of the Peak District

The rocks of the Peak District were mainly formed by the accumulation of sediments during the Carboniferous period between 280 and 345 million years ago. Throughout that period much of the area that is now northern England was covered by a warm shallow tropical sea (Britain was much nearer to the equator at that time than it is at present). This was by no means a static situation, however, but one of constant change, so that the conditions in a relatively small area such as the Peak District could move comparatively rapidly – and repeatedly – from, for example, marine to deltaic to swamp and back again.

The first deposits which collected on the bed of the Carboniferous seas were largely formed from the shells and calcareous skeletons of marine organisms. The remains of crinoids (sea lilies) growing up to 10 ft (3 m) in height, shell animals such as brachiopods, corals and trilobites (a common unassuming creature which had inhabited the sea floor since the early Cambrian over 200 million years earlier) were some of the life-forms from which this primeval sludge was composed. In the deeper basins the deposits would contain an appreciable amount of mud and be dark in colour, while on very shallow shelves a purer, cleaner and paler product would result. It is likely too that reefs formed – in the same way as they do today in tropical seas – either as isolated mounds or as fringes along the edges of lagoons. With the passage of long periods of time all of these deposits compacted to form hard limestones, basically of the same chemical composition, but with their colour and properties reflecting to some extent the different conditions under which they were formed.

It is likely that as the Carboniferous period progressed the land around this limestone-forming sea was elevated and later deposits were formed therefore not in the sea itself but in the rapidly changing conditions of a continental coastline. The limestone deposits were covered by dark-coloured muds which later hardened into dark grey shales. These in turn were hidden by deposits of sharp irregular angular grains brought down from a wide area by a great river or river system, coming in from the north or north-east. The rocks produced by these later deposits are very coarsely grained and renowned for their hard-wearing properties, a fact which led to their use in the grinding of flour – hence their name, Millstone Grit. Finally, in the late Carboniferous, the region lay above sea-level, at least for a sufficient time to allow vegetation to develop, with the subsequent formation of peat and then coal.

In post-Carboniferous times the rocks were subjected to moderate folding which raised the centre part of the Peak District in an arc with the rock strata dipping away to both east and west. As usually occurs in these cases, the upper parts of the fold were eroded away exposing some of the rocks lower in the sequence.

As a result of this erosion, the lower layer of limestone is now exposed over the central region of the Park from Castleton in the north to near Ashbourne in the south. Almost surrounding this, in a thin irregular pattern, are the shales. The Millstone Grit then forms a belt around this, except to the south where all the Carboniferous rocks dip below rock strata formed later during Triassic times. The Millstone Grit therefore lies exposed in a horseshoe-shaped area with its greatest extent to the north over Kinder Scout, Bleaklow and Black Hill. These are regions of barren, wild, peat-covered, acid moorlands, cut into by groughs, their edges defined characteristically by long thin lines of crag. The limestone further to the south forms a flattish plateau, deeply cut in places by narrow river valleys of outstanding beauty. The reefs, formed from limestone which has been more resistant to erosion, stand out as well-defined hills; examples of this are Thorpe Cloud and Bunster Hill which flank Dovedale. The division between the gritstone and limestone areas has in many cases been accentuated by wide valleys such as Edale which have been produced along the easily eroded shales. When exposed to the weather these shales rapidly disintegrate back to their original state as soft black mud, a characteristic which is responsible for the numerous landslips within the Park, such as at Mam Tor and Alport Castles. The Coal Measures are largely absent from the Park except for small areas to the east and west. Finally, some volcanic activity took place during the deposition of the limestone with lava flow and ash fall and the products of these can be found within the limestone areas.

The development of gritstone climbing

It is impossible to overestimate the importance of the gritstone edges and outcrops of the Pennines – and particularly those of the Peak District – in the development of British rock climbing. This importance arose partly as a result of the locality of the outcrops and partly from the unique properties of gritstone as a climbing rock. The crags are, first of all, within easy reach of the great conurbations around Manchester, Derby and Sheffield. Hours of climbing can therefore be enjoyed at weekends and on the long evenings of summer without excessive travel – there are even tales of one leading climber who was able in his younger days to take in several climbs on his way to school! Secondly, the rock faces are relatively short in height – the vast majority of the routes are less than 100 ft (30 m) in length – so that the protection of a top rope can be used to provide that feeling of security which is so helpful in the early formative days and then later, when skill has developed, to give a safe environment in which moves can be practised and techniques improved. The unusual roughness of gritstone also adds

Rock climbing on Curbar Edge.

considerably to that feeling of security. Finally, the faces are steep with a marked lack of sharp in-cut holds which helps to develop a sound and balanced style of climbing.

The credit for the discovery of gritstone as a climbing rock is usually given to James William Puttrell, a Sheffield silversmith, who began exploring Wharncliffe Crags in 1888. Other developments were taking place in rock climbing around that time (for example, in the Lake District at Wasdale Head), but it seems that Puttrell had no association with them (although he did later). After a period of solo climbing he was joined by W. J. Watson and the pair extended their explorations to other crags, such as Rivelin Edge and Stanage. In 1900 with E. A. Baker and a number of others he founded the Kyndwr Club which included rock climbing amongst its activities and was in fact the first club to be formed which was based upon gritstone. In 1903, Baker – who was a very prolific author – wrote a book, *Moors, Crags and Caves of the High Peak and the neighbourhood*, which described those early climbs.

The gritstone edges were gradually opened up during the period between the World Wars and with greater vigour afterwards. Even today, after about a century of exploration, new routes are still being discovered. Stanage alone has about 500 climbs upon it and a figure of more than 10,000 has been suggested for the Peak District as a whole. Looking at the whole period from Puttrell to the present day, it is striking how many of the best British climbers began their careers upon gritstone. Siegfried Herford, the brilliant cragsman who conquered Central Buttress on Scafell with G. S. Sansom and who so tragically lost his life during the First World War, began his climbing there. Jack Longland, who was on Everest in 1933, made a name for himself on the Black Rocks at Cromford; and after the Second World War the formidable trio of Peter Harding, Joe Brown and Don Whillans, who with a number of others ushered in a new era of climbing, were first of all gritstone men. Even among the modern stars the formative influence of gritstone is very apparent.

The limestone cliffs of the Peak were neglected until after the Second World War, mainly on account of the reputation of the rock for lack of soundness. Even when climbing started the use of a multitude of pitons was considered essential. This attitude has now changed considerably, however, and the methods employed today are generally similar to those on gritstone.

The struggle for access

Present-day walkers, who enjoy almost total freedom of access to Kinder or Bleaklow, may find it difficult to imagine the situation that their fathers or grandfathers knew at the turn of the century. At that time most of the moorland areas of the Peak District were private property from which the general public were firmly excluded.

In the main the refusal to allow access to those areas came from two groups. The first was the grouse-shooting fraternity, on the grounds that ramblers would disturb the birds in their breeding season – as well as the privacy of their own parties – and constitute a hazard at shooting time. The second group was made up of local water authorities who were anxious to maintain the purity of their water supplies. (To be quite fair, water was at that time purified by natural filtration and the current thinking therefore was that the gathering grounds had to be protected against contamination.)

In enforcing their privacy the landowners were in a strong position. On the moors themselves they employed gamekeepers – usually fit strong stocky men who would not hesitate to use force if the situation demanded it (it should be remembered that at a time of high unemployment and living in tied cottages the gamekeepers themselves were under strong pressure to produce results). Away from the moors the landowners could usually count on the sympathetic understanding of local magistrates to grant injunctions which would then be enforced by the constabulary.

Faced with this problem of lack of access, two different approaches were tried by ramblers: negotiation and outright defiance. As far as negotiation was concerned, the main hopes of the inter-war years were based upon the Access to Mountains Bill which was presented to Parliament as a private member's motion by Arthur Creech Jones in 1938. Similar bills had been presented on numerous occasions previously but without any success. Although this became law in 1939, it was extensively modified during its parliamentary passage and finally emerged in a form which was widely condemned – even by its earlier supporters – as making things worse rather than better. An application for access under the Act involved a costly and lengthy procedure and in practice the provisions of the Act were never applied. The demands of the Second World War effectively stopped any further legislation during its duration (this was also a factor in the failure to operate the 1938 Act), but important preparatory work was carried out by the Scott Committee early in the war and by the Dower Committee in 1945.

Outright defiance was represented by deliberate trespassing upon the forbidden lands both by individuals and by organised groups. Although some deliberate trespasses by groups had occurred much earlier and outside the Peak District in the nineteenth century, the most famous took place in 1932 over Kinder and to the east of the Derwent Valley. The great Mass Trespass of 24 April (see page 150) on to Kinder Scout was followed by one on the Duke of Norfolk's Road at Abbey Brook on 18 September. Over fifty years later controversy still rages on the effectiveness of these Mass Trespasses – they produced, for example, some lively letters in *Rucksack*, the Ramblers' Association Magazine (now *Rambler*), around the time of the fiftieth anniversary in 1982.

The National Parks and Access to the Countryside Act of 1949 was an important milestone in the fight for access. This Act did not automatically concede as a right freedom of access to all uncultivated land – which had long been the demand of many ramblers; what it did claim to do was to provide a workable procedure for achieving access. It was under this Act that the National Parks Commission (later the Countryside Commission) was established and subsequently the designation of the ten National Parks.

One of the most important provisions of the Act was the power given to National Park Authorities for the negotiation of Access

Plaque in the quarry on the Kinder Road near Hayfield which commemorates the mass trespass of 1932.

THE MASS TRESPASS ONTO
KINDER SCOUT STARTED FROM
THIS QUARRY 24TH APRIL 1932

Agreements. An Access Agreement is made between a National Park Authority and a landowner whereby access is allowed for walkers and rock climbers (but not horse riders). In return the landowner or tenant receives a payment for allowing access and also to cover the costs of any damage that may be caused. The area may be closed for up to twelve days each year for grouse shooting. The Peak Park Joint Planning Board has been by far the most successful of the National Park Authorities in negotiating such agreements; at present they cover an area of 76 sq miles (19 760 ha) of moorland.

Although much has certainly been achieved, the old walkers' aim of unrestricted access over all areas of uncultivated land has not (a *statutory* right of access probably exists over less than one tenth of all mountain and moorland areas of Britain). With the present rapid increase in the popularity of walking and climbing the pressure for this is likely to build up in the future rather than go into reverse. In which case it is clear that further chapters in the story of the fight for access have still to be written.

Well dressing

Well dressing – i.e. the art of decorating wells or springs – is now almost exclusively a Derbyshire custom, although records indicate that it was once much more widely practised. Some clootie-wells can still be found in Scotland, for example in the Inverness area, where 'clooties', which are short lengths of cloth, are hung on trees around the wells by people who believe that by so doing they can rid themselves of their problems. Several wells at Bisley in Gloucestershire are decorated with flowers and garlands by the village children on Ascension Day each year, as they have been since 1863, and Endon in Staffordshire has also a long-standing tradition along similar lines. These few cases should be compared to the situation in Derbyshire, however, where at present about thirty villages regularly practise the custom, some of them decorating several wells each year.

Well dressing at Stoney Middleton in 1986.

GOLDEN
JUBILEE

FOLLOW ME

STONEY
1936 MIDDLETON 1986

The practice varies in detail from village to village, but the general approach is much the same. Each display is mounted on a stout wooden frame made up from several sections. These are first immersed in a local stream or pond until thoroughly soaked – this extends the life of the exhibit – and then covered in a layer of clay, 'puddled' to a smooth consistency with water and salt, about half an inch (13 mm) thick. Hundreds of nails, protruding from the boards, help to hold the clay in place. Full-sized drawings of the final picture are then laid over the clay so that the outlines of its design can be pricked through with a sharp tool. After the drawings have been removed the lines are then made clearer by pushing small alder cones or berries into the clay. The spaces between the lines are filled in, first with long-lasting materials such as moss and bark and then with less durable materials such as flower petals or heads. Each fragment is carefully placed into position and fixed into the clay, the work proceeding from the bottom to the top to produce an overlap which helps to reduce the damaging effect of heavy rain (in the same way as the tiles of a roof). Finally the frames are erected, usually – but not always – at the site of an existing well.

The life of a picture is relatively short, usually about one week, but this is dependent upon the weather. As would be expected, the first few days are the best time to see a display before deterioration begins to be obvious. Other events are often held in the village around the same time, such as fairs, processions, carnivals and commonly religious ceremonies as at Cutthorpe and Eyam.

The origins of the custom are now obscure and little is known about it before the present century. It is likely, however, that it had its origin in early pre-Christian superstitions. Wells and springs which provided fresh, clean water would always be highly prized. Villages and farmsteads would be built by them and would have to be abandoned if the supply failed, as could so easily happen on the limestone of the White Peak. It is scarcely surprising that our pagan ancestors, living in an age when so little was understood and when superstitions about every aspect of life abounded, should have attributed a failure of their supply to the actions of malevolent spirits. Doubtless, it would also have been considered a prudent move to dedicate a particularly good well to some favoured god or goddess. Such customs would not, of course, have been well regarded by the early Christian Church and it is known that some attempts were made to ban them. An alternative approach used by the Church was to absorb these practices and beliefs into Christian doctrine and it is likely that this in the end was the more profitable course. Wells were blessed, their malignant spirits banished, and the water in them thereafter declared holy. It is noticeable that religious themes predominate in the displays and that a 'blessing of the wells' by a local clergyman frequently forms part of religious ceremonies. Finally, it is surely significant that most of the villages involved lie on limestone.

Safety

The terrain of the Peak District National Park is relatively low-lying compared, for example, with the Lake District or Snowdonia. The highest point is a mere 2088 ft (636 m) in height. Newcomers to the Park, however, should not fall into the error of thinking that the walking will be a little on the soft side. This may be true for most of the White Peak – although this should not be underestimated, particularly in bad weather – but the Dark Peak moors are an altogether different proposition. Kinder, Bleaklow and Black Hill offer walking which is at least as demanding as any to be found elsewhere. It should not be underestimated. In thick mist the featureless terrain can challenge the route-finding ability of the most experienced; on bad days a combination of rain, heavy winds and peat-bog can sap the strength of the hardiest. If any doubt exists about your ability to cope with the terrain and its problems then it is far better to turn back or not to start at all; at the end of the day the fells will still be there.

The routes described in this guide vary considerably in length and difficulty. Some of the easy walks should, with reasonable care, be safe at any time of the year and under almost any weather conditions; some of the more difficult walks, however, cross very wild country and are only suitable, even on good summer days, for fit walkers who have the correct clothing and equipment and know what they are doing.

It must be emphasised that conditions can change very quickly in mountain areas, not only during the day but from one part of a mountain to another or as you climb to higher ground. You must bear this in mind when choosing your clothing and equipment before a walk. The challenge of a walk will also generally be greater (perhaps much greater) in the winter, when snow and ice are lying on the moors, than in the summer months.

So, please, for your own safety in mountain and moorland areas:

DO: Carry suitable clothing and equipment, which should be in good condition.

Carry sufficient food for the day, plus more for emergencies.

Carry a map and compass and know how to use them.
Plan your route carefully before you start.
Leave a note of your planned route with a responsible person (and stick to it unless changed circumstances make it dangerous to do so).
Report your return as soon as possible.
If you are going to be seriously delayed then inform your base, or the police, as soon as possible.
Keep warm (but not too hot) at all times.
Eat nourishing foods and rest at regular intervals.
Avoid becoming over-tired.
Know some First Aid and the correct procedure in case of accidents or illness.
If you are leading a party always go at the pace of the slowest member, and never separate (except possibly in the event of a serious accident in order to obtain help).
Obtain a weather forecast before you start and take this into consideration as you proceed. A written forecast is put up daily at each Information Centre within the Park area.

DO NOT: Go on to the fells by yourself unless you are very experienced; three is a good number.
Attempt routes which are beyond your skill and experience.

In the eighteenth and nineteenth centuries the White Peak was the centre of a thriving lead-mining industry and numerous remains of it in the form of open shafts and levels are to be found around this region. They can constitute a source of danger. To avoid accidents the Peak Park Joint Planning Board in co-operation with Derbyshire County Council has prepared a leaflet, *Mind that Mine*. It contains information on mines and draws up a Code of Conduct Near Mines:

DO walk with caution and constant care, especially when with children.
DO keep to well-used paths – shafts are often quite near.
DO look out for hummocky ground.
DON'T go near mining areas in fog, snow, dark, or stormy weather.

DON'T go near shafts, climb on shaft walls, or throw rocks down shafts.
DON'T go in the depressions of collapsed shafts or open rakes.
DON'T attempt to explore shafts or levels unless in a properly equipped party with experienced leaders.

Finally, do not damage remains in any way or collect samples of minerals or fossils in the vicinity of workings (or elsewhere).

Weather forecasts for the Peak District may be obtained from Edale (0433) 70207 (northern part) or Bakewell (062 981) 3227 (southern part).

How to give a grid reference

A grid reference is a useful method of pin-pointing a position on an Ordnance Survey Map. The grid lines on OS 1:25 000 and 1:50 000 maps are the thin blue lines going vertically and horizontally across the map, covering it with a network of small squares.

The method of determining a grid reference is as follows. Figure 3 shows a section of an Ordnance Survey Landranger map (1:50 000) with the position of a youth hostel marked.

Step 1: Write down the number of the 'vertical' grid line to the left (or west) of the hostel. This is 72.

FIGURE 3

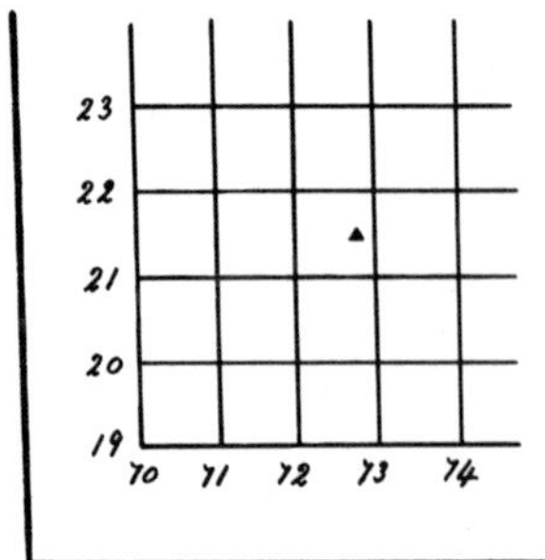

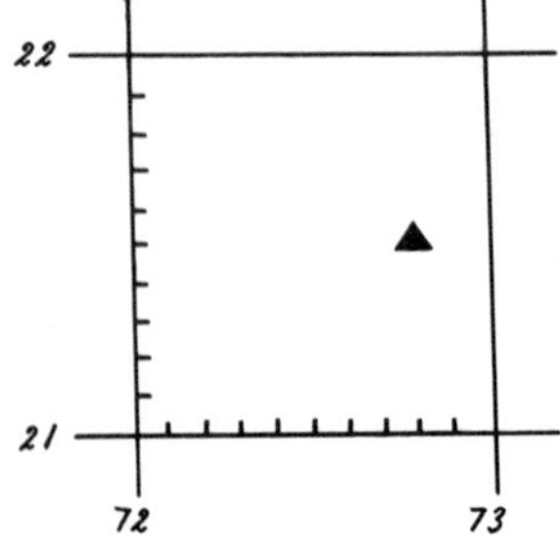

Step 2: Now imagine that the space between this grid line and the next one to its right is divided into tenths. Estimate the number of tenths that the hostel lies to the right of the first grid line. This is eight. Add this to the number in Step 1, making 728.

Step 3: Add on the number of the grid line below the hostel (i.e. to the south). This is 21; so the number becomes 72821.

Step 4: Now repeat Step 2 for the space between the grid lines below and above the hostel. The hostel is five tenths above the bottom line. Add this to the number, making 728215. This figure is called a six-figure grid reference. Coupled with the number of the appropriate Landranger or Outdoor Leisure sheet, it will enable any point to be identified.

Step 5: The numbers of the grid lines repeat after 100. There will therefore be many other places in the United Kingdom with exactly the same six-figure grid reference. To overcome this problem, the maps are also divided up into large squares with sides made up from 100 of the small squares, each of which is designated by two letters; on the Landranger sheets these are given on the small diagram which shows the adjoining sheets. In the example above, if the large square is designated by SP, then the full grid reference is SP 728215. There is only one place in the United Kingdom with this grid number.

The Countryside Access Charter

The Countryside Access Charter was prepared by the Countryside Commission for practical guidance in England and Wales only. Fuller advice is given in a free booklet *Out in the country* available from the Countryside Commission.

Your rights of way are:

Public footpaths – on foot only. Sometimes waymarked in yellow.

Bridleways – on foot, horseback and pedal cycle. Sometimes waymarked in blue.

Byways (usually old roads), most 'Roads Used as Public Paths' and, of course, public roads – all traffic.

Use maps, signs and waymarks. Ordnance Survey Pathfinder and Landranger maps show most public rights of way.

On rights of way you can:
Take a pram, pushchair or wheelchair if practicable.
Take a dog (on a lead or under close control).
Take a short route round an illegal obstruction or remove it sufficiently to get past.

You have a right to go for recreation to:
Public parks and open spaces – on foot.
Most commons near older towns and cities – on foot and sometimes on horseback.
Private land where the owner has a formal agreement with the local authority.

In addition you can use by local or established custom or consent, but ask for advice if you're unsure:
Many areas of open country like moorland, fell and coastal areas, especially those of the National Trust, and some commons.
Some woods and forests, especially those owned by the Forestry Commission.
Country Parks and picnic sites.
Most beaches.
Canal towpaths.
Some private paths and tracks.
Consent sometimes extends to riding horses and pedal cycles.

For your information:
County councils and London boroughs maintain and record rights of way, and register commons.
Obstructions, dangerous animals, harassment and misleading signs on rights of way are illegal and you should report them to the county council.
Paths across fields can be ploughed, but must normally be reinstated within two weeks.

Landowners can require you to leave land to which you have no right of access.
Motor vehicles are normally permitted only on roads, byways and some 'Roads Used as Public Paths'.
Follow any local bylaws.

And, wherever you go, follow the Country Code:
Enjoy the countryside and respect its life and work.
Guard against all risk of fire.
Fasten all gates.
Keep your dogs under close control.
Keep to public paths across farmland.
Use gates and stiles to cross fences, hedges and walls.
Leave livestock, crops and machinery alone.
Take your litter home.
Help to keep all water clean.
Protect wildlife, plants and trees.
Take special care on country roads.
Make no unnecessary noise.

Notes on the route descriptions and maps

Difficulty

The routes were selected to give a wide range of walks from the point of view of both length and difficulty. This was done to make the book attractive and useful to as many as possible. It does make it essential, however, to give a clear indication of the difficulty of each route.

A number of factors play a part in determining the time necessary to complete a walk. The most important of these are distance and the amount of climbing involved, and the effect of these can be assessed by Naismith's Rule (see below). Roughness of terrain or difficulties of route-finding can also, of course, play a part, but usually these are restricted in their effects to a small proportion of the total distance involved.

The method used in this book to obtain a measure of difficulty involved three stages: (1) a calculation of the time required for each route on the basis of Naismith's Rule; (2) listing the routes on the basis of the time needed to complete them; (3) a review of the list after surveying each route. The difficulty of each route can therefore be assessed in three ways: (1) the total distance and the amount of climbing involved, which are given at the head of each route description. Difficulties of a special nature are pointed out in the introduction to the route; (2) its position in the list – Route No 1 is the easiest, No 32 the hardest; and (3) its grading.

As far as this last is concerned, all the walks have been divided into four categories – easy, moderate, more strenuous and very strenuous. As a guide, a 'typical' walk within each category would be:

Easy. A short walk (say, up to 5 miles, 8 km) over good paths, with no problems of route-finding. Some climbing may be involved, but mostly over fairly gradual slopes with only short sections of difficult ground.

Moderate. A longer walk (up to 10 miles, 16 km) mostly over good paths but with some more indefinite sections where route-finding

will be difficult. Mountain summits may be reached, necessitating climbing over steeper and rougher ground.
More strenuous. A fairly long walk (10–20 miles, 16–32 km) with prolonged spells of climbing. Some rough ground calling for good route-finding ability, perhaps with prolonged stretches of scrambling.
Very strenuous. For very good walkers only. Over 20 miles (32 km) with much climbing and stretches of very difficult ground calling for good route-finding ability.

As far as the last two categories in particular are concerned it is usually possible to break a route down into two or more sections which may be walked a day at a time. The main problem here, of course, will be arranging transport to the start and from the finish.

Distance
These are 'map miles' which take no account of the amount of climbing involved. They are given in miles and kilometres, since both are in common usage.

Ascent
This is also given in both feet and metres.

Naismith's Rule
An estimate of the time required to complete each route is not given in the book, as this will vary so much from one walker to another. But the usual method of estimating time is by Naismith's Rule, which is:

> 'For ordinary walking allow one hour for every 3 miles (5 km) and add one hour for every 2000 ft (600 m) of ascent; for backpacking with a heavy load allow one hour for every 2½ miles (4 km) and one hour for every 1500 ft (450 m) of ascent.'

For most walkers this tends to underestimate the time required, and each walker should try to form an assessment of his or her own performance over one or two walks. The Rule also makes no allowance for stops, for the roughness of the ground, or for the influence of weather conditions.

Car-parks

Almost all the walks described start at a car-park or parking place. This is indicated on the first map of each route and in the information given on the starting point.

Route descriptions

The letters 'L' and 'R' indicate left and right respectively, and for changes of direction imply a turn of about 90° when facing in the direction of the walk. 'Half L' and 'half R' indicate turns of approximately 45°, while 'back half L' and 'back half R' indicate turns of about 135°. All bearings given are magnetic bearings. It should be assumed that all stiles and gates mentioned in the description are crossed, unless there is a statement to the contrary. PFS stands for 'Public Footpath Sign', PBS for 'Public Bridleway Sign', OS for 'Ordnance Survey' and PW for 'Pennine Way Sign'.

The maps

The maps take the same numbers as the routes; where there is more than one map for a route then they are given the suffixes A, B, C, etc. Thus, Route No 32 has five maps: 32A, 32B, 32C, 32D and 32E to be used in that order.

Unless otherwise stated the maps are drawn to a scale of 2 ins to one mile (1:31 680). Place-names were mainly taken from the appropriate Bartholomew's map of the Peak District and are generally the same as on Ordnance Survey maps. The maps have been drawn, with some exceptions, so that the route goes from the bottom to the top of a page. This will enable the walker to 'line-up' a map, i.e. hold it in the same direction as his route, while still holding the book in the normal reading position. The arrow on each map points to grid north.

It should be emphasised that the maps show only the approximate line of paths and are not meant to be a replacement for Ordnance Survey maps, particularly where mountain and moorland areas are

This map shows the starting points for Routes 1 to 32, in relation to the principal towns and villages of the National Park (see Figure 1 on page 17).

FIGURE 4

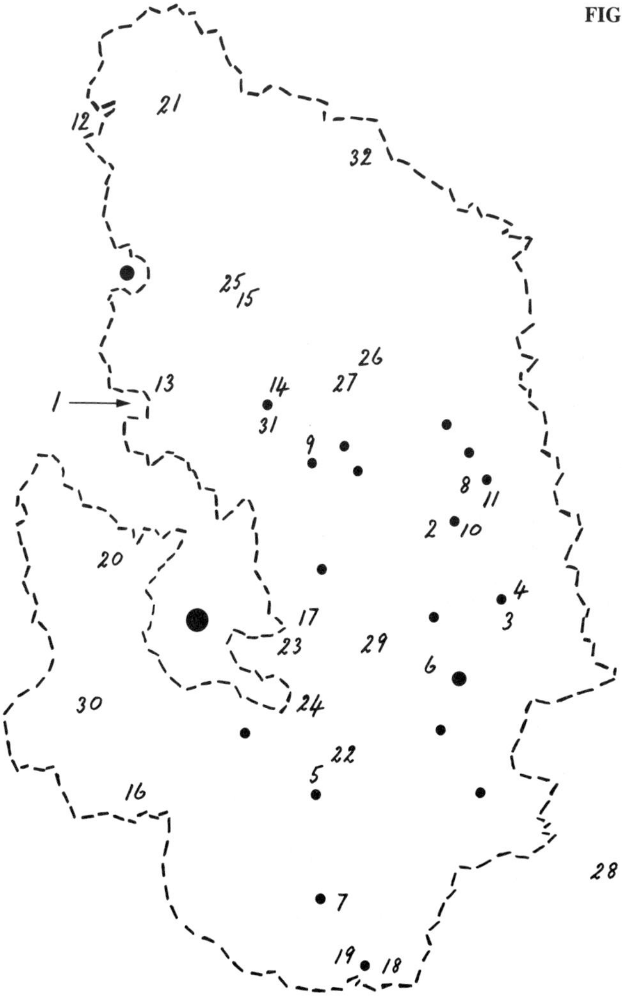

concerned. In these areas of country, walkers should always carry Landranger or Outdoor Leisure Ordnance Survey maps in addition to this guide; these should be used, for example, where difficulty of route-finding arises, if the route is lost, or where bearings have to be taken.

Features of interest

Some information on features of interest along the way is given with each route description. The best position for seeing these features is indicated both in the route description and on the accompanying map.

The location of each feature of interest is indicated, by the number of the appropriate Landranger (1:50 000) sheet with a six-figure grid reference. Thus, 119-174711 gives the location of Fin Cop, i.e. in position 174711 on Landranger sheet no 119.

Access

As far as is known the routes described (a) use public rights of way, (b) cross areas over which there is a current access agreement, (c) use a concessionary path, (d) cross land which is privately owned but which has been opened to the general pubiic, or (e) cross land which is privately owned but which has been walked over for a considerable time. In no case therefore is it expected that any difficulties will be encountered. Nevertheless, it must be emphasised that walkers have an obligation to behave properly when using footpaths or crossing areas of wild country so that no damage is caused nor any nuisance given to other people. It should also be pointed out that the position on an area of land may change with time. In particular, official diversions, for example to allow a badly eroded path to recover, should always be followed.

A special note is necessary with regard to those routes which cross access areas. During the grouse-shooting season, from 12 August to 10 December, landowners suspend public access for safety reasons (this does not apply to public rights of way which go through such areas). Details of the shooting dates are published at

Key to the signs used on the route maps.

FIGURE 5

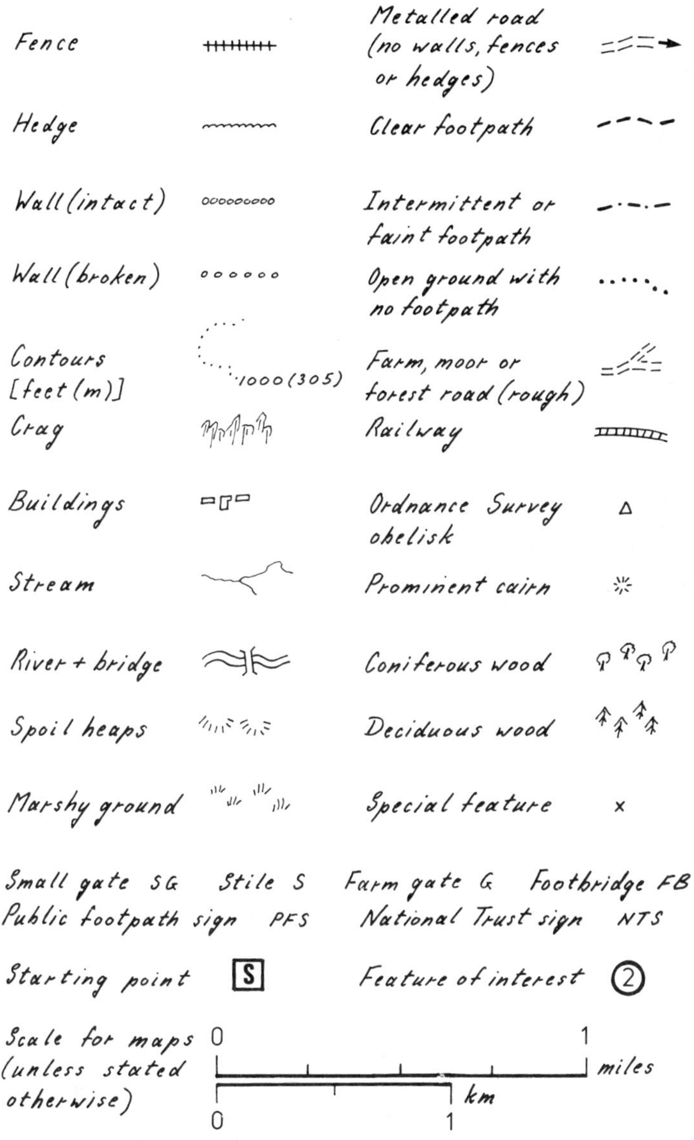

Fence		Metalled road (no walls, fences or hedges)	
Hedge		Clear footpath	
Wall (intact)		Intermittent or faint footpath	
Wall (broken)		Open ground with no footpath	
Contours [feet (m)]	1000 (305)	Farm, moor or forest road (rough)	
Crag		Railway	
Buildings		Ordnance Survey obelisk	
Stream		Prominent cairn	
River + bridge		Coniferous wood	
Spoil heaps		Deciduous wood	
Marshy ground		Special feature	×

Small gate SG Stile S Farm gate G Footbridge FB

Public footpath sign PFS National Trust sign NTS

Starting point **S** Feature of interest ②

Scale for maps (unless stated otherwise) 0 1 miles

0 1 km

many villages and railway stations in the Peak District and can also be obtained from Information Centres. Those routes where this applies are shown in the appropriate sections. On those dates when grouse shooting is in progress the routes indicated should *not* be used. Maps showing the extent of the access areas can be obtained from the Peak Park Joint Planning Board.

The best walks

Easy Routes

Route 1 The Sett Valley Trail

Undoubtedly one of the most attractive features of the Peak District are the trails which have been laid out along the lines of old and now disused railways. Altogether there are five of these, of which the Sett Valley Trail is by far the shortest. Running along the valley of the Sett, it passes through an area of the Dark Peak which has an industrial past, unlike the others which traverse the predominantly pastoral countryside of the White Peak. Although there are attractive and interesting places at each end and some points along the way which give good views it must be admitted that on the whole this trail lacks much of the attractiveness of the others. As a pleasant family walk with frequent stops for refreshments or for a quiet undemanding stroll in the cool of the evening it has, however, some considerable merit. To those unfamiliar with the railway trails, it will moreover serve as an excellent introduction which should whet their appetites for the bigger challenges down in the south.

Length: 2½ miles (4 km).

Ascent: Virtually none, except for some rises up flights of steps in one or two places.

Starting point: Hayfield (110-036869). There is an Information Centre and a large car-park at the start, which are sign-posted in the village.Bicycles may be hired at the Centre for use on the Trail.

Finishing point: New Mills (110-000855). Torr Top car-park is at the end of the Trail and the bus station is only about 100 yds (90 m) away. There is a regular bus service between the start and finish – ask for information on this from the Information Centre at Hayfield before you start.

Maps: Landranger 110; Outdoor Leisure The Dark Peak.

MAP 1

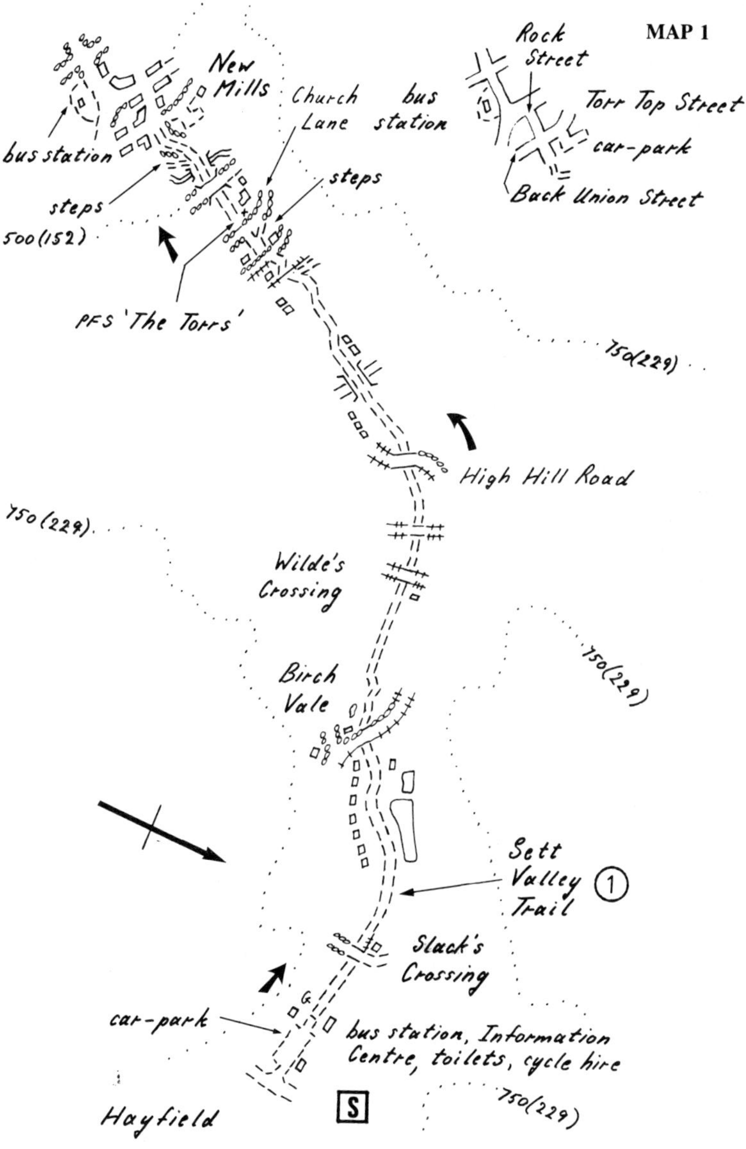

New Mills

bus station

steps

500(152)

Church Lane

bus station

steps

PFS 'The Torrs'

Rock Street

Torr Top Street

car-park

Back Union Street

750(229)

High Hill Road

750(229)

Wilde's Crossing

Birch Vale

750(229)

Sett Valley Trail

1

Slack's Crossing

car-park

bus station, Information Centre, toilets, cycle hire

G

Hayfield

S

750(229)

Route description (Map 1)
A route description is unnecessary except possibly towards the end. For this reason the main features only are described; all distances given are from the car-park at Hayfield. Before starting see (1) The Sett Valley Trail.

0 miles, 0 km: Leave the car-park through a gate at the far end and start to walk along the track. 650 yds, 600 m: Slack's Crossing.

1 mile, 1.6 km: Reach the road at Birch Vale. Cross and go through the small gate directly opposite and continue to follow the path.

1⅓ miles, 2 km: Wilde's Crossing. Notice the old paving on the streets on both sides of the crossing.

1⅔ miles, 2.5 km: High Hill Road. Again cross the road and go through the small gate opposite.

2⅓ miles, 3.7 km: Cross the third road and down some steps. Go through a small gate and up to the next road, Church Lane. Cross and take the footpath ahead, signed 'The Torrs'. At the end go under a bridge and up the steps ahead to reach a cobbled street. Turn R up the street soon crossing a street coming across. The Torr Top car-park is on the R. At the top reach a T-junction and turn to the L, the bus station is directly ahead across the road.

(1) *The Sett Valley Trail.*
The railway to Hayfield was a branch line which connected with other lines at New Mills. It was built for the Midland and Great Central Joint Railway Company and opened for passenger traffic in 1868 and goods some four years later. Apart from the station at Hayfield there was another at Birch Vale. Like so many lines, it was closed down in 1970. Fortunately it was acquired by Derbyshire County Council in 1973 who converted it into a walking/cycling/horseriding trail.

Route 2 The Plague Village

There is no other town or village in the Peak District which can start to compare with Eyam (pronounced 'Eem', not 'Ee-am') for sustained interest. With its beautiful church and lovely old buildings it would be worth visiting on its own account, but its main claim to fame undoubtedly lies in the events of 1664–6 when the Great Plague struck the village. The villagers, led by their parson William Mompesson, decided to isolate themselves from the outside world in order to prevent the disease spreading; 267 out of 350 villagers died from it. Their story is one of courage and fortitude. This walk visits most of the main buildings, graves and other features around Eyam which are associated with the events of those years. It is relatively short but, taken in a leisurely manner as it should be, can fill most of a day. It is possible, however, to take several short-cuts to lessen the distance further and, in particular, to avoid the main climb out of the village to Mompesson's Well (this is indicated in the route description).

Length: 4¾ miles (8 km).

Ascent: 725 ft (225 m).

Starting and finishing point: The car-park on Hawkhill Road, Eyam (119-216767).

Maps: Landranger 119; Outdoor Leisure The White Peak (East Sheet).

Route description (Map 2)
(Before starting read the general account of the incident which has made this village famous – see (1) Plague).

From the car-park turn L in the road and go down to a T-junction passing some interesting stone troughs to the R – see (2) Early water supplies in Eyam. At the junction turn L and walk down the street (Main Street) keeping on the L-hand side. Just after a road comes in from the R pass a lovely old hall – see (3) Eyam Hall – and then some more stone troughs by a metal roasting jack. Immediately beyond are a group of three cottages. The centre one is particularly famous – see (4) The Plague Cottage. Just beyond, reach Eyam Church.

Turn L at the first entrance into the churchyard and go to the

MAP 2

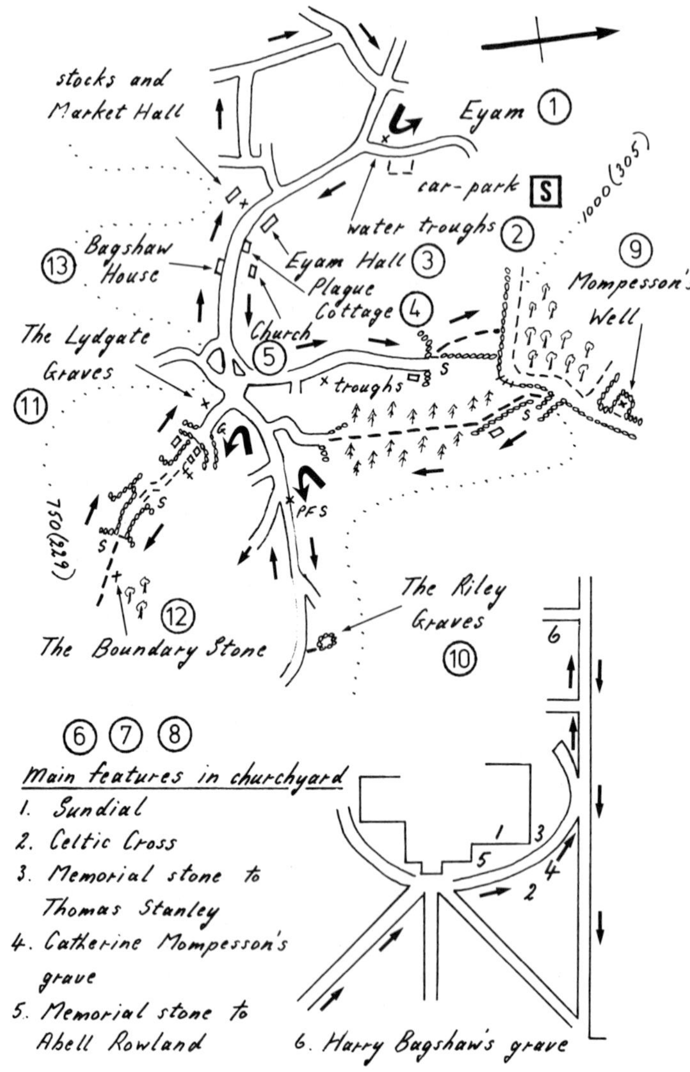

stocks and Market Hall
Eyam 1
car-park
S
water troughs 2
1000 (305)
Eyam Hall 3
Plague Cottage 4
9
Mompesson's Well
13 Bagshaw House
Church 5
The Lydgate Graves
11
troughs
S
S
S
PFS
750 (229)
S
12
The Boundary Stone
The Riley Graves
10
6 7 8
Main features in churchyard
1. Sundial
2. Celtic Cross
3. Memorial stone to Thomas Stanley
4. Catherine Mompesson's grave
5. Memorial stone to Abell Rowland
6. Harry Bagshaw's grave
6
1
3
5
4
2

church door. This church is open during the day and should not be missed – see (5) The Church of St Lawrence. After the visit turn L from the door (i.e. to continue in the same direction as before) and go by the church wall. A number of features will be found near to the first corner on the L. Immediately to the L as you go round the corner is the gravestone of Abell Rowland, who died of the plague on 15 January 1665; above the priest's door also on the L is a most remarkable sundial; on the R is a superb cross; just beyond is the grave of Catherine Mompesson, the wife of the Rev. William Mompesson who was Rector during the plague – see (6); and finally against the wall at the next corner is a memorial to Thomas Stanley – see (7). The path curves to the L beyond the church; follow this along the R-hand side of the churchyard. Just before the second path goes away on the L look for a black headstone to Harry Bagshaw – see (8) A Cricketer's Grave. Then go down the path on the east side of the churchyard to return to the street.

Turn L and continue to The Square where several roads meet. Take the first street to the L (Water Lane). Before going up Water Lane find a small black plate with a finger hole in the road just in front of the corner shop; the plate can be lifted to reveal an old metal ring – see plaque. (NOTE: At this point you may omit visits to Mompesson's Well and the Riley Graves if you wish. To avoid the former continue ahead along the Grindleford/Hathersage road; to avoid both go to the R across the Square to Lydgate.)

Now go up Water Lane passing the Miner's Arms and later some more troughs – see (2); where the lane ends turn L over a stile and follow a path which soon climbs half R away from the wall. Go up the hillside to a road, there turn R. Soon the road bends to the L and slowly rises; at a junction keep ahead along the Grindleford road. A small enclosure will be found down on the L after about 100 yds (90 m) – see (9) Mompesson's Well.

Return down the road past the junction and go through a stile immediately after a lane on the L. This leads to a delightful path which descends the hillside through a coniferous wood to reach a metalled road in Eyam (Riley Back Lane). Lower down where this meets a main road turn L. Where this road curves R go straight ahead along a minor road (PFS 'Riley Graves'). Go up and at the top keep R at a fork. Continue to reach a small walled enclosure in a field on the L – see (10) The Riley Graves.

Return the way you came to the junction of Riley Back Lane and then past it to The Square. There go L up a narrow lane (Lydgate). After a short distance you will pass another walled enclosure on the R – see (11) The Lydgate Graves. Where the lane swings L go ahead through a gate (PFS 'Stoney Middleton') and down a farm road. Where this goes through a gateway leave it over a stile into a narrow walled lane. At the end go over a further stile and across a field; after about 200 yds (180 m) reach a large boulder with several holes in the top – see (12) The Boundary Stone.

Retrace your steps back to The Square. There turn L and return along the road leading to the church, i.e. the R-hand of the two main roads. Keep on the L-hand side of the road, past the church, noting the house opposite – see (13) Bagshaw (or Bagshawe) House. Where the road bends pass the village stocks and the Market Hall. Turn L at the junction immediately afterwards and L again after a few yards. Follow this quiet metalled road as it goes around the south and east sides of the village. Later where it joins Tideswell Lane turn R to reach the main road, there turn R again (it is now better to cross and walk along the L-hand side of the main road).

Shortly, reach the bottom of Hawkhill Road where you started and turn L up to the car-park.

(1) *Plague*

Plague, which is caused by the bacillus *Yersinia pestis* carried by the rat flea, is primarily a disease of rodents. It can be found in a few animals at any time, but on occasions under the right environmental conditions can spread rapidly and can then affect large numbers. This causes a large number of rodents to die – and hence a drastic and rapid reduction in the number available to give hospitality to the flea, which therefore quite naturally transfers its attention to nearby humans. To say the least, the results of this attention have from time to time been devastating.

According to Bede, in 664, 'a sudden pestilence depopulated the southern coasts of Britain and afterwards extending into the province of Northumbria ravaged the country far and near and destroyed great multitudes of men.' Far far worse than that was to come, however. Arising in China in 1333 and carried along the great trade routes from the East the scythe of the bacillus cut a broad swathe of death over India, the Mediterranean countries and Europe. Arriving at Melcombe Regis in Dorset in June 1348 it had by the following year spread to all parts of Britain. Perhaps a third of the population were dead by the end of it. Further outbreaks took place at intervals throughout the following three centuries, although at a lower level. The Great Plague of 1664–6, however, although the last of these outbreaks, was undoubtedly the worst since that some 300 years earlier.

In London it is probable that the Great Plague made its appearance 'in the middle of the Christmas Holy-Days' of 1664, although an unusually cold winter kept it largely at bay until the following Easter. Over the next fifteen months or so, it is estimated from official records that nearly 70,000 died of it, although this figure is almost certainly too low as official records were inaccurate and sometimes apparently deliberately falsified. (It should be remembered that the total population of London at that time was probably less than a half million.) The victims were mainly from the poorer groups, for by and large the richer inhabitants of the city – King, courtiers, Members of Parliament, clergy, doctors and merchants – rapidly deserted them. By about February 1666 the plague was largely spent, for reasons which even today remain obscure. It was certainly not due to advances in medical knowledge or, as is often supposed, to the Great Fire later that same year.

In Eyam the first victim died on 7 September 1665 – see (4) The Plague Cottage – rapidly followed by several others over the next two weeks or so. As the plague had been raging in London for some five months by that time, it is likely that the symptoms were quickly recognised for what they were; twenty-three deaths in the following month of October alone provided final proof that a major epidemic had reached Eyam.

As in London the rich made a rapid exit from the scene; although perhaps one should not be too critical of them. It is quite likely in fact that more of the villagers would have left had it not been for the example and the persuasion of the Rector, the Rev. William Mompesson. In any event the villagers collectively made the decision to stay within the boundaries of their parish until all danger had passed in order to stop the disease spreading to neighbouring areas. They paid a heavy price for it. Between September 1665 and October 1666 – when the last deaths occurred – some 267 out of 350 villagers died.

The disease may take three clinical forms. Bubonic is the most common; many sufferers do recover from this, however, and it is not directly infectious. Pneumonic plague has the symptoms of bronchopneumonia with death occurring in three to four days while the third variety, septicaemic plague, leads to prostration and brain damage, death occurring within twenty-four hours. Pneumonic plague is highly infectious.

Thanks to streptomycin, tetracycline and the sulphonamides, suitable vaccines and improvements in sanitation, plague is no longer the menace to us that it once was; the cottage plaques and walled grave enclosures of Eyam reminding us of the debt that we owe to medical science and practice. There may also be another reminder in the words of that ever-popular children's song 'Ring-a-ring o'roses' which could be a comment on the Great Plague of 1664.

Ring-a-ring o'roses,
A pocket full of posies;
Atishoo, atishoo, we all fall down.

'Ring o'roses' were marks upon the skin caused by the plague, the sneezing was a typical symptom of pneumonic plague followed by a fall down due to death. It was a common practice to carry a posy of flowers in a vain attempt to ward off any disease.

(2) *Early water supplies in Eyam*

Most of us in this country have become so accustomed to having a supply of clean water that we usually take it for granted. It is a sad fact, however, that this is very far from true for a large proportion of the world's population.

Even in England some 50,000 people died of cholera in 1831 and as recently as fifty years ago many small places in the country lacked piped water and had to collect their supplies locally from springs, wells or rivers. Old household books always gave instructions as to the type of water to be used for various purposes – spring water for cooking, well water for ale-making and rain water for washing. Such supplies, however, could become contaminated (ensuring that people kept a supply clean was usually more difficult than finding or supplying the water in the first place) and in dry summers disappear altogether.

At least ten series of troughs were provided in Eyam in 1588 for domestic and agricultural use; this must have been one of the first public water supplies in this country. One of these series, the Hall Hill Troughs, is situated on Hawkhill Road near the car-park. A further series is passed on the appropriately named Water Lane later in the walk; in this case the main troughs supplied hard water for drinking and the trough round the corner to the right gave soft water for washing clothes.

(3) *Eyam Hall*

The large and very fine building on the left, just before the church and the Plague Cottage, is Eyam Hall. It was built in the late sixteenth or early seventeenth century, although the south front, i.e. the one facing the road, was added later, probably in 1676. It was owned by the Bradshaw family until 1735 when that branch became extinct. In the late seventeenth century it was purchased by the Wright family who have lived there ever since.

(4) *The Plague Cottage*

The first victim of the plague, George Viccars, died in the centre cottage of the group of three. Viccars was thought to have been a travelling tailor lodging at the cottage which was occupied by a widowed lady, Mrs Cooper, and her two sons. Cloth, sent in a box from London to the tailor, was found to be damp on arrival and was placed before an open fire to dry. It is supposed that the cloth contained the plague bacillus which was inhaled by Viccars. In any event he became ill and died a few days later on 7 September 1665 after displaying symptoms which were at that time strange to Eyam but which were unfortunately all too familiar in London where the plague had been raging for some months. One of the sons, Edward

Cooper, died two weeks later on 22 September and a neighbour, Peter Halksworth, who lived in the cottage to the right, the following day. The second son, Jonathan, also became a victim on 2 October. Mrs Cooper survived the plague and later remarried.

Two other victims of the plague died in the cottage on the left, Rose Cottage. These were Thomas Thorpe, who died on 26 September 1665, and Mary Thorpe, who died four days later.

(5) *The Church of St Lawrence*

It is possible that there was a church at Eyam in Saxon times and that part of the present building rests on its foundations. Apart, however, from the Celtic cross, the font in the north aisle is the only fragment which can now be positively dated to that period. The oldest parts of the church itself – some pillars on the north side of the nave – were probably erected in the first half of the twelfth century. The most interesting features are a series of wall paintings (late sixteenth to early seventeenth century) representing the twelve tribes of Israel, the Creed and the Lord's Prayer; a cupboard made it is said from the box which carried the plague to Eyam in 1665 – see (4) above; a Jacobean pulpit from which Mompesson preached; and a beautiful oak chair carved in 1656 and used by him in his study.

(6) *The grave of Catherine Mompesson*

Perhaps the saddest of all the plague memorials at Eyam is the grave (a table tomb) of the Rector's wife, Catherine (or Katherine), situated near to the cross. Born in Durham, she married Mompesson in 1661 and had two children, George and Elizabeth, before the family came to Eyam in 1664, only eighteen months or so before the plague broke out. The two children were sent away to the safety of Yorkshire, but Catherine herself refused to leave the side of her husband. She died of the plague on 25 August 1666, the 220th victim. Although some bodies were buried in the churchyard during the plague this is the only one still marked with a headstone (Abell Rowland was not buried where the present headstone rests.) Note the correction made by the stonesmith to the spelling of her name.

Eyam Hall.

(7) *Thomas Stanley*
Although credit is usually given to William Mompesson for leading the villagers at Eyam during the plague years, there seems little doubt that he received strong support from one of his predecessors, Thomas Stanley. Stanley had been appointed to the living at Eyam in 1644 when the Rev. Shorland Adams was deprived of it because of his support for the royalist cause during the Civil War. At the Restoration in 1660, however, the positions were reversed when Shorland Adams was reinstated. After possibly serving as a curate in Eyam for two years, Stanley left the established Church in 1662. He was, however, still living in the village when the plague began some four years later. It is unlikely now that we shall ever know the relative importance of the roles played by Mompesson and Stanley during those troubled times but there is no doubt that both men played a part. The memorial stone at the south-east corner of the church does not mark the position of Stanley's grave, although he was certainly buried within the churchyard.
(8) *A Cricketer's Grave*
In the churchyard, a short distance to the north-east of the church, is a tall black pointed headstone. This was erected to the memory of Harry Bagshaw. At the top is the raised finger used in cricket to indicate that a batsman is out, and underneath a wicket shattered by a cricket ball.

Henry Bagshaw – usually known as 'Harry' Bagshaw – was born at Foolow, Tideswell on 1 September 1859. He was a professional cricketer with his native county from 1888 until 1902 playing in 123 first-class matches (his appearances were limited as Derbyshire lost first-class status in the period 1887–93). A free-hitting left-hand batsman, usually going in at number two or three, he scored 5456 runs (average 26.10) in his career, which included seven centuries; his highest was 127 not out against Yorkshire in 1895. He was also a useful right-arm medium pace bowler taking a total of 73 wickets for 29.09 runs each. An old photograph of the Derbyshire team of 1901

The Celtic Cross in the churchyard at Eyam. This was probably an eighth-century wayside preaching cross originally erected away from the village and used for communal worship before the present church was built.

taken towards the end of his playing career shows him as a short stocky man with a slight moustache.

After his retirement as a player be became a first-class umpire and served until 1924. He died at Crowden in Cheshire on 31 January 1927 and was buried at Eyam. He was buried in his umpire's coat with a cricket ball in his hand.

(9) *Mompesson's Well*

The well is situated on the left a short distance along the Grindleford road after the junction. As with the Boundary Stone, provisions for the village were left there during the plague by people from the outlying area.

(10) *The Riley Graves*

The small walled enclosure, now owned by the National Trust, contains a tomb and grave headstones for several members of the Hancocke family who lived at the nearby Riley Farm. The table tomb covers the grave of John Hancocke.

The six headstones were removed from the actual grave sites and re-erected within the enclosure. All seven members of the family died between 3 August and 10 August 1666, the only survivor being the mother who, not surprisingly, later left the village to live elsewhere.

(11) *The Lydgate Graves*

The name Lydgate (or Lidgate) is derived from the Old English word *hlidgeat* which meant swing-gate. This was erected across the lane, leading to Stoney Middleton, which was once the main way into the village. The gate was guarded throughout the night by a watchman, a post held in turn by the male inhabitants of the village, who had the duty of stopping and questioning any travellers arriving there. This system was known as 'Watch and Ward'.

A small walled enclosure on the right a short distance up Lydgate contains the graves of George Darby, who died on 4 July 1666, and his daughter, Mary, who died on the fourth day of the following September.

(12) *The Boundary Stone*

The large boulder, with several holes cut into the top surface,

The Riley Graves, poignant reminders of the tragedy of the plague years.

marked the original boundary of the parish. Although the village would probably have been fairly self-sufficient at the time of the plague some provisions would have had to be brought in. It is said that these were left by the Boundary Stone; money to pay for these goods was left in the small holes on the top which were filled with vinegar in an attempt to stop the infection spreading to the recipient.

(13) *Bagshaw (or Bagshawe) House*

Just across from the church and the Plague Cottage is this house in which six members of the Sydall family died of the plague. Sarah died on 30 September 1665 – one of the first victims – followed by four others the following month. Emmot was the last to die on 29 April 1666.

Route 3 Chatsworth Park

Chatsworth Park was the creation of that fine landscape gardener Capability Brown during the eighteenth century – and what a good job he made of it! With a total area of 1100 acres (445 ha), most of it open to the public, it is big enough to contain a decent walk in its own right. The route described here has about half of its total distance within the park, visiting some of the finest parts and most interesting features of the estate. The great house of Chatsworth – which can be visited – is seen from two points on the route; together they show it at its best.

Length: 5½ miles (9 km).

Ascent: 450 ft (140 m).

Starting and finishing point: Car-park at Nether End, Baslow (toilets). The village is approximately 7 miles (11 km) west of Chesterfield on the A 619 Bakewell road (119-257721).

Maps: Landranger 119; Outdoor Leisure the White Peak (East Sheet).

MAP 3

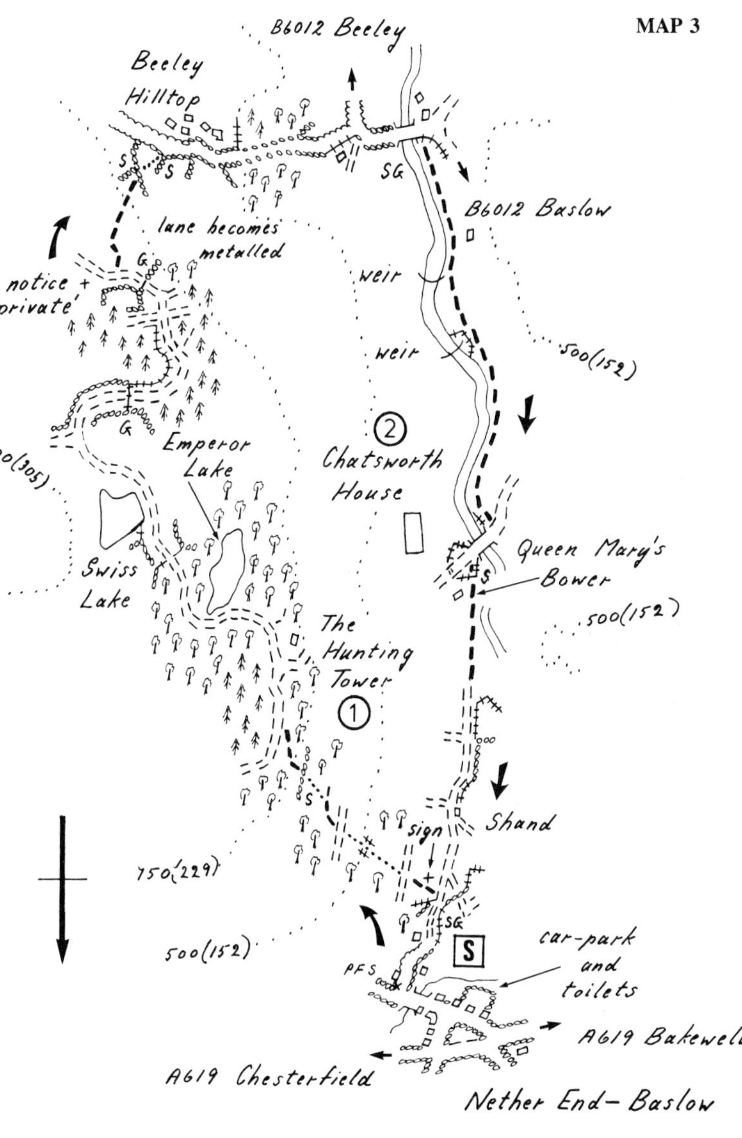

B6012 Beeley
Beeley Hilltop
S
S
SG
B6012 Baslow
lane becomes metalled
G
notice 'private'
weir
weir
500(152)
G
2
Chatsworth House
Emperor Lake
00(305)
Swiss Lake
Queen Mary's Bower
S
500(152)
The Hunting Tower
1
S
Shand
sign
750(229)
SG
500(152)
S
car-park and toilets
PFS
A619 Bakewell
A619 Chesterfield
Nether End–Baslow

Route description (Map 3)

Leave the car-park into the minor road and turn R. At the fork do not bend to the L towards the main road, but go ahead over a small bridge. Immediately after the bridge turn R (PFS 'Chatsworth 1¼') and follow the path. After 350 yds (320 m) go through a gate into Chatsworth Park and turn half L (sign 'Concessionary Footpath Stand Tower 1. Concessionary Footpath Beeley 3½') to leave the main path. Where the side path ends after a few yards keep in the same direction going up towards a wood on the hillside.

Soon cross a metalled drive, then between two shorts lengths of fence with seats and finally to the L of a stile and a seat (there are white arrows to indicate the route on trees at intervals). Enter the wood over a stile in a wall and follow the path up through the wood until it reaches a forest road. Turn R. After a short distance go L at a T-junction. A tall and unusual tower will be seen on the R after a few yards – see (1) The Hunting Tower. Follow the forest road as it goes past Emperor Lake and then Swiss Lake ignoring any side paths. About ¾ mile (1.2 km) after the second lake reach a crossroads and go directly across. This path bends L to a gate where it leaves the woods.

150 yds (140 m) further at several yellow arrows leave the moor road and take a footpath going down to the R. This drops down across the moor and ends at a stile and a small gate near to a wall corner. Cross and head across a field towards a farm, entering a lane just in front of it. Turn R and follow the lane for ½ mile (800 m) to the main road. There turn R and follow the road to a bridge over the river.

Immediately on the opposite side go R through a small gate. Follow the path by the river for 1 mile (1.6 km) gradually approaching Chatsworth House. Cross a bridge in front of the building – see (2) Chatsworth – and immediately turn L to a stile. Keep in the same direction along the estate road for about 1 mile (1.6 km), ignoring any others to L or R, to reach the gate where you entered the park. Continue along the path beyond back to the car-park.

(1) *The Hunting Tower (119-265706)*
The tall square building, with rounded corner-towers and guarded by three cannon, is a hunting tower erected about 1582 by the then owners of Chatsworth, Bess of Hardwick and her fourth husband, the Earl of Shrewsbury. It offers a superb view over the Derwent valley with Chatsworth House immediately below.

(2) *Chatsworth (119-261702)*
Undoubtedly the outstanding feature of this route is the great house of Chatsworth. Chatsworth is the end product of over 450 years of development and is now not merely the largest country house within the National Park – although there are relatively few of these – but one of the largest in Britain. It also houses a priceless collection of paintings, sculptures, books and furniture.

The original house at Chatsworth was built in the mid-sixteenth century by Bess of Hardwick and her second husband, William Cavendish, on the site of the present building. Mary, Queen of Scots, was imprisoned at Chatsworth on several occasions between 1569 and 1584, in the custody of Bess's fourth (and last) husband, the 6th Earl of Shrewsbury; some rooms at Chatsworth are still referred to as the Queen of Scots' Apartments. Bess – who was obviously a very durable and enterprising lady – died at the age of about eighty-one having outlived all her husbands.

The house stayed substantially unaltered until the end of the seventeenth century when a major period of rebuilding took place under the 4th Earl of Devonshire – later the 1st Duke of Devonshire. This lasted from 1686 until 1707, when the Duke died, and left the main block of Chatsworth looking much the same as it is today. Formal gardens in the Grand French style of the day were laid out by George London and Henry Wise, famous garden designers and suppliers who founded the Brompton Park nursery in Kensington. Although most of the work of this period at Chatsworth was swept away later, the Cascade, the Sea Horse Fountain and the canal pond still remain.

The present park was created largely by the 4th Duke, who also had the distinction of being Prime Minister for six months from November 1756 to May 1757. Under the direction of Lancelot Brown, the outstanding garden designer and architect of his time who earned the nickname of 'Capability Brown' from his habit of assuring potential customers that their estates had capability for improvement, the old formal gardens were largely swept away. In their place came the open, natural-looking landscape which we see today. One casualty was the old village of Edensor: the 4th Duke pulled down that part of the village visible from the house, leaving the remainder intact; the 6th Duke in the nineteenth century demolished the remainder and with Paxton built a new model village. This was and still is used for housing estate workers. New stables were constructed – the square block to the north-east of the house – and a bridge built across the River Derwent to carry a new road from the west; both of these were the work of the architect James Paine.

Another man who made his mark on Chatsworth was Joseph Paxton. Appointed head gardener by the 6th Duke, he was responsible for the Emperor Fountain in the canal pond which throws water to a height of 280 ft (85 m) in the best conditions. He also built a Great Conservatory covering three-quarters of an acre (3035 sq m) – now unfortunately gone – and a long wall conservatory for the cultivation of fruit, which is still there. Rare plants were collected and brought to the gardens from all over the world.

Following the sudden and early death of the 10th Duke, heavy death duties forced the sale of many assets, the Derbyshire estates – and some elsewhere – passing into the care of the Trustees of the Chatsworth Settlement. The house itself is now run by the Chatsworth House Trust, a charitable foundation.

Route 4 Birchen Edge

Birchen Edge is, to all intents and purposes, the end of that superb line of long gritstone crags which run down the eastern side of the National Park. As might be expected, therefore, the main feature of this route is the walk along the edge, but the approach below Gardom's Edge and across the valley of Bar Brook is extremely pleasant. Two interesting monuments are passed on the way, dedicated to those two great heroes Wellington and Nelson, which appropriately face each other across the valley.

MAP 4

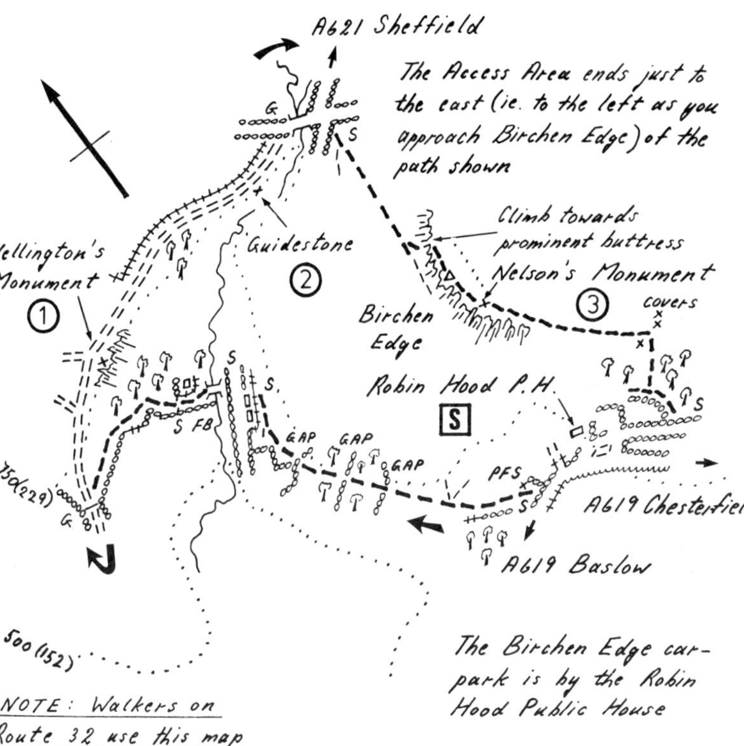

NOTE: Walkers on Route 32 use this map from Wellington's Monument to the finish.

Length: 4¼ miles (7 km).

Ascent: 750 ft (225 m).

Starting and finishing point: Birchen Edge car-park by the Robin Hood Inn on the B6050 just off the A619, Chesterfield-Bakewell road, about 1¾ miles (3 km) from Baslow.

Maps: Landranger 119; Outdoor Leisure The White Peak (West Sheet).

Route description (Map 4)
Leave the car-park and turn R down the minor road passing the Robin Hood Inn. At the main road keep in the same direction, i.e. to the R. After 200 yds (180 m) go R over a stile in the wall (PFS). Follow the clear path beyond which soon goes to the R of a wall. Keep on the path in the same direction to a gap in a wall. After the gap the path continues in the same direction to a wood and a further gap. 150 yds (140 m) further it leaves the wood and bends to the R to a third gap at a wall corner. Continue to descend until you approach a road where a cross-path is met. Turn R to reach the road by a water trough.

Cross the road and the stile opposite and follow the path through the wood, soon crossing a bridge. Do not go through the gate ahead, but bend L with the path to pass a house and garden on the L. At the end of the garden go over a stile to re-enter access land. Keep following the clear path as it slowly rises through the trees keeping to the R of a wall. Where the walls bends L the path goes half L to meet it again higher up the hill. The path now runs level with a wall/fence to the L and a steep slope to the R, eventually meeting a wide track near to a gate. Do not go through the gate but turn back half R and follow the rough track as it climbs. After 325 yds (300 m) near to the hilltop the track forks; take the R fork towards an obvious monument – see (1) Wellington's Monument.

Pass the monument and keep on the broad track for about ¾ mile

Wellington's Monument.

The Chesterfeild Roade Guidestone.

Rock climbing on Birchen Edge.

(1.2 km) to reach a road. Along the way, notice the tall monolith which used to mark the line of an old turnpike – see (2) The Chesterfeild Roade Guidestone. Turn R to a crossroads and then take the road opposite. Immediately go R over a ladder stile and 75 yds (70 m) later L at a path junction. Follow the path as it slowly rises up the moor. When you notice a prominent rock buttress on the edge to the L take a path which climbs up towards it. At the top turn R along a path. This soon curves to the L along the edge to reach a second monument – see (3) Nelson's Monument.

Keep in the same direction beyond Nelson's Monument, slowly descending the ridge. Eventually after about ½ mile (800 m) at some metal covers the path goes to the R and descends more steeply. Lower down reach a broad crossing path and turn L. Cross a ladder stile into the road (B 6050) and turn R back to the car-park.

(1) *Wellington's Monument (119-263737)*
The plain cross constructed of stone blocks and standing on a rocky promontory overlooking the valley of Bar Brook is called Wellington's Monument. On one side is Wellington's name and his dates: Born 1769, Died 1852. Below are the words 'Erected 1866 by E. M. Wrench, late 34 Regt.'
(2) *The Chesterfeild Roade Guidestone (119-275740)*
An Act of Parliament in 1702 laid down that for the convenience of travellers in the country a stone or post should be erected where two highways crossed with an inscription in large letters of the next market town to which the highways led. In the Peak District many of these 'guideposts' still remain in their original position, one example being passed soon after leaving Wellington's Monument. It was erected on the packhorse way which came up from Baslow past the monument, just before it met the way from Curbar Gap to Chesterfield.
(3) *Nelson's Monument (119-279729)*
This monument stands on Birchen Edge opposite Wellington's Monument. A simple obelisk made from gritstone, it is frequently used by climbers as a belay point. It was erected in 1810. On the

Victory, Defiance and Royal Soverin situated on the moor behind Nelson's Monument.

moor behind are three large blocks of weathered gritstone, carved respectively from left to right with the names 'Victory, Defiance, Royal Soverin'. Knowledgeable walkers who are students of the Battle of Trafalgar will remember that at that battle the British ships advanced in two columns led respectively by Collingwood in *Royal Sovereign* and Nelson in *Victory*.

Moderate Routes

Route 5 Biggin, Wolfscote and Beresford Dales

This is a lovely route which takes the walker through three beautiful dales: Biggin, which is a dry valley, and then Wolfscote and Beresford which form part of the Dove valley. The old packhorse way over from Hartington to Biggin Dale, which forms the first section of the route, is also an inspiring walk. Undoubtedly, however, the main attraction – particularly for keen rodsmen – will be the close association between this part of the Dove and that great angler, Izaak Walton, and his friend, Charles Cotton, who lived nearby at Beresford Hall. The walk is fairly short, the amount of climbing small, the footpaths well marked, the beauty of the area through which the route passes considerable. Only good companions and a fine day are needed to make it memorable.

Length: 6½ miles (11 km).

Ascent: 500 ft (150 m).

Starting and finishing point: Hartington (119-18604). Cars may be parked around the centre of the village.

Maps: Landranger 119; Outdoor Leisure The White Peak (West Sheet).

Route description (Map 5)
From the centre of the village go along the road (i.e. the road to Newhaven, B5054) directly opposite the Charles Cotton Hotel – see (1). After a few yards you will pass an interesting old building with pillars at the front (on your L) which is now the village store – note the figure at the top holding a pair of scales – and reach a crossroads. A short diversion can be made up the road to the L to visit the church – see (2) St Giles' Church. Otherwise, turn R at the crossroads and follow the road which soon bends L up a hill. After 400 yds (375 m) pass a beautiful old building on the L which is set

MAP 5

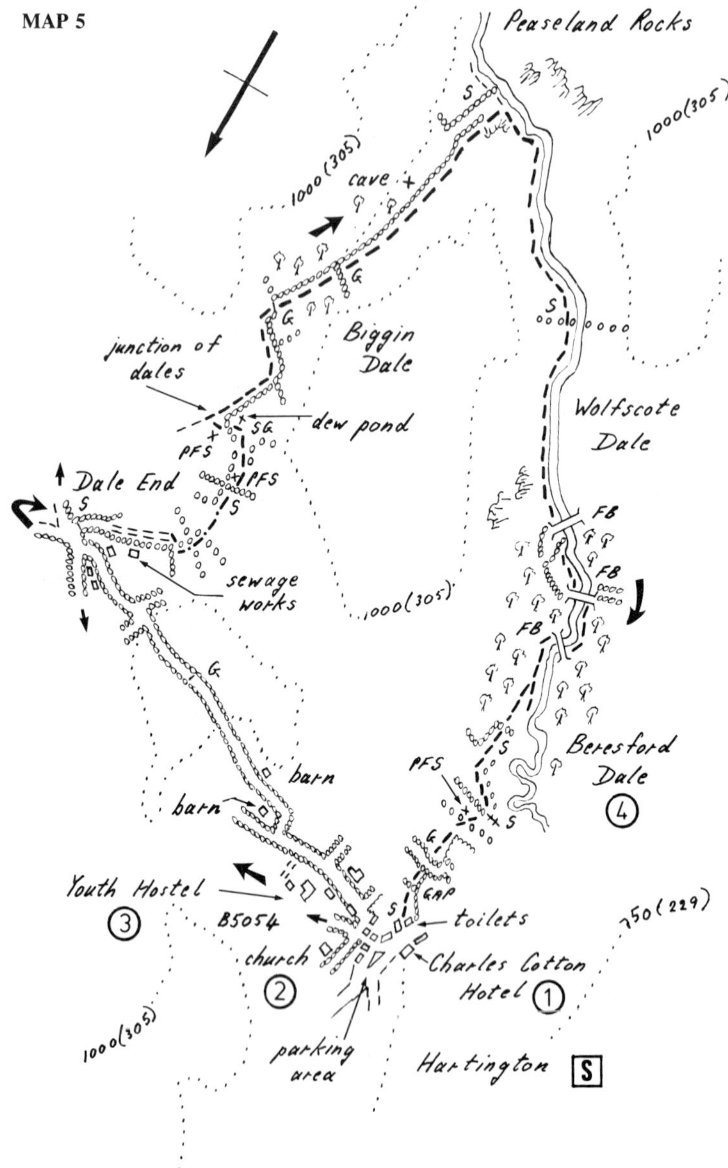

Peaseland Rocks
1000(305)
1000(305)
cave
S
G
G
Biggin Dale
junction of dales
dew pond
SG
PFS
PFS
S
Dale End
S
sewage works
1000(305)
Wolfscote Dale
S
FB
FB
FB
G
barn
barn
Beresford Dale
4
PFS
S
S
G
GAP
Youth Hostel
3
B5054
S
toilets
750(229)
church
2
Charles Cotton Hotel
1
1000(305)
parking area
Hartington
S

back from the road – see (3) Hartington Hall. About 250 yds (225 m) after the hall and just before a small barn turn R along a rough walled lane. This lovely lane, which rises slowly for about a half mile (800 m) before descending towards the road at the end of Biggin Dale, was once a packhorse route to Wirksworth.

Keep on the lane until you reach the road by some cottages. There turn R. After 100 yds (90 m), just before a junction, go R over a stile by a gate (PFS). Follow a farm road past a small sewage works. After the works keep in the same general direction along the bottom of a dry valley to a stile in a wall. Beyond continue along the valley past a PFS to reach a wall corner by a dew pond at the junction of three dales. Go through a small gate and immediately at a PFS turn R (Biggin Dale). Follow the path which goes to the L of a wall to a gate where you enter National Trust property. Beyond, the path keeps to the R of the wall soon entering a wood. Leave the wood at a second gate and continue down the dale to reach the valley of the Dove.

Turn R and follow the path to the R of the river for 1¼ miles (2 km) to a footbridge. Do not cross, but keep on the same side across the large field ahead. At the end cross the river at a second footbridge and immediately turn R along a wide path to the L of the river. Soon cross the river at another footbridge and continue now on the R-hand bank. To the L on this stretch is the site of Beresford Hall and Charles Cotton's Fishing House – see (4) *The Compleat Angler*. Later the path moves to the R away from the river and leaves the wood at a stile. Soon a broken wall begins on the L; where this bends half L go with it to a stile and a gate in a corner. Cross the next field half R to a gate leading into a lane. Cross and follow the path in the next two fields to the R of a wall. Eventually go through a stile in a corner by a barn. This leads to a road (by some toilets) where you turn R back to the centre of Hartington.

(1) *The Charles Cotton Hotel (119-128604)*
Named, of course, after Izaak Walton's friend, the hotel was originally the Sleigh Arms, the name change occurring around the turn of the century. The Sleighs were an old Hartington family who had been associated with the village for several centuries.

(2) *St Giles' Church (119-130605)*
Most churches today are the end-product of centuries of modification, addition and rebuilding. St Giles' Church at Hartington is no exception. The foundations were laid in the early thirteenth century, although there may well have been an earlier church of which all traces have now disappeared. Further building took place at intervals, however, until Tudor times, some 300 years later, and in the mid-nineteenth century major repair work was carried out.

In the churchyard, to the right of the path as you go along it, is the gravestone of Elizabeth Barker of Newhaven which is heavily covered with fossils of crinoids and by the south wall of the chancel there is a very old tomb containing bones which can be glimpsed if the sun shines through a crack below the lid. Inside the church, there are memorials to Thomas Brindley who owned the cheese factory in Hartington, to Augustus Wirgman, a mid-nineteenth-century vicar who provided a new school for the village, to Thomas Mellor who lived to the age of 103, to Richard Edensor who gave a sum of money in 1764 for bread 'to be distributed . . . to the deserving poor of Hartington' and to Thomas Bateman who also contributed so that they could have clothing.

(3) *Hartington Hall (119–132604)*
The present hall was built in 1611 by Thomas Bateman, a yeoman farmer of Hartington, on the site of an earlier hall said to have been built in 1350. It is a fine stone building which has been owned by the YHA since 1934.

(4) *The Compleat Angler*
No name is more closely associated with Dovedale than that of Izaak Walton. Walton was born in 1593 in Stafford where his father kept a tavern. He began as an apprentice in London to a relative who was an ironmonger, but at the age of thirty-one set up his own business and in due course became a successful tradesman in his own right. A part-time writer, he wrote biographies of several contemporaries which were published between 1640 and 1678. His most famous work however was *The Compleat Angler, or the*

Gargoyle by the south porch of Hartington Church.

Contemplative Man's Recreation. Being a Discourse of Fish and Fishing, not unworthy of the perusal of most Anglers, first published in 1653. This was a treatise on angling written in the form of a dialogue. Three men – an angler (Piscator), a huntsman (Venator) and a fowler (Auceps) – each describe their own interest; then Venator is instructed in the art of fishing by Piscator before they angle together on the Lea, a river which rises in Hertfordshire and runs into the Thames. The book was an immediate success and ran quickly to several editions.

The fifth edition of *The Compleat Angler*, published in 1676, was enlarged with an additional contribution from Izaak Walton's friend, Charles Cotton. Cotton, the son of a wealthy landowner, was born at Beresford Hall on the Staffordshire side of the Dove valley. After travelling to France and Italy in his youth he spent most of his life at the Hall. Some literary successes – translations, poetry and burlesques – provided only limited income and his style of hard living gradually eroded into his resources. He was forced bit by bit to dispose of his holdings, until even the Hall itself had to go in 1681. Cotton's addition to *The Compleat Angler* was also in the form of a dialogue and dealt with the techniques of fly-fishing which had not been covered by Walton.

The Dove is still very much an angler's river, with fly-fishermen much in evidence. Beresford Hall was reduced to ruins over a hundred years ago, although there are other reminders along the river of Walton and Cotton: Pike Pool, marked on the Outdoor Leisure Map, was named by Cotton because of the imposing pike of rock which rises from it, and Viator's Bridge because Viator, crossing it with Piscator, left us a striking description (see page 182). The most poignant reminder of all however is given by a glimpse – it is on private property – of the small Fishing Temple built by Cotton in 1674 at the northern end of Beresford Dale near where the path leaves the river and heads northwards towards Hartington.

Wolfscote Dale.

Route 6 Monsal Dale

In an area of river valleys justifiably famous for their beauty, Monsal Dale is generally considered to be one of the finest. Even the presence of the famous railway viaduct at Monsal Head – whose construction in the middle of the last century was so deplored by Ruskin – seems nowadays to add to its beauty rather than to detract from it. From Ashford in the Water this circular walk packs an enormous amount of variety into a fairly short distance: the Wye valley, Great Shacklow Wood and a typical section of the limestone plateau. Clear paths are used over most of the walk and route-finding should not present any problems.

Length: 6½ miles (11 km).

Ascent: 700 ft (220 m).

Starting and finishing point: A small car-park in Ashford in the Water (toilets). This will be found up Court Lane which runs alongside and around the back of the church (119-195698).

Maps: Landranger 119; Outdoor Leisure The White Peak (East Sheet).

Route description (Map 6)
For general information about Ashford in the Water see (1).

Leave the car-park and go down the street opposite. At the end turn R and go up Vicarage Lane; after 75 yds (70 m) cross the road and up a foothpath (PFS 'Monsal Dale 2'). After a few yards the path turns R and passes a few houses to a stile leading into a field. Keep in the same direction up the field to a stile in the far R-hand corner which leads into a walled lane. In the lane go L, i.e. keeping in the same general direction. After ⅔ mile (1.1 km) the lane ends at a gate; go through this and turn L. Keep by the wall. At the end

The viaduct at Monsal Head.

MAP 6

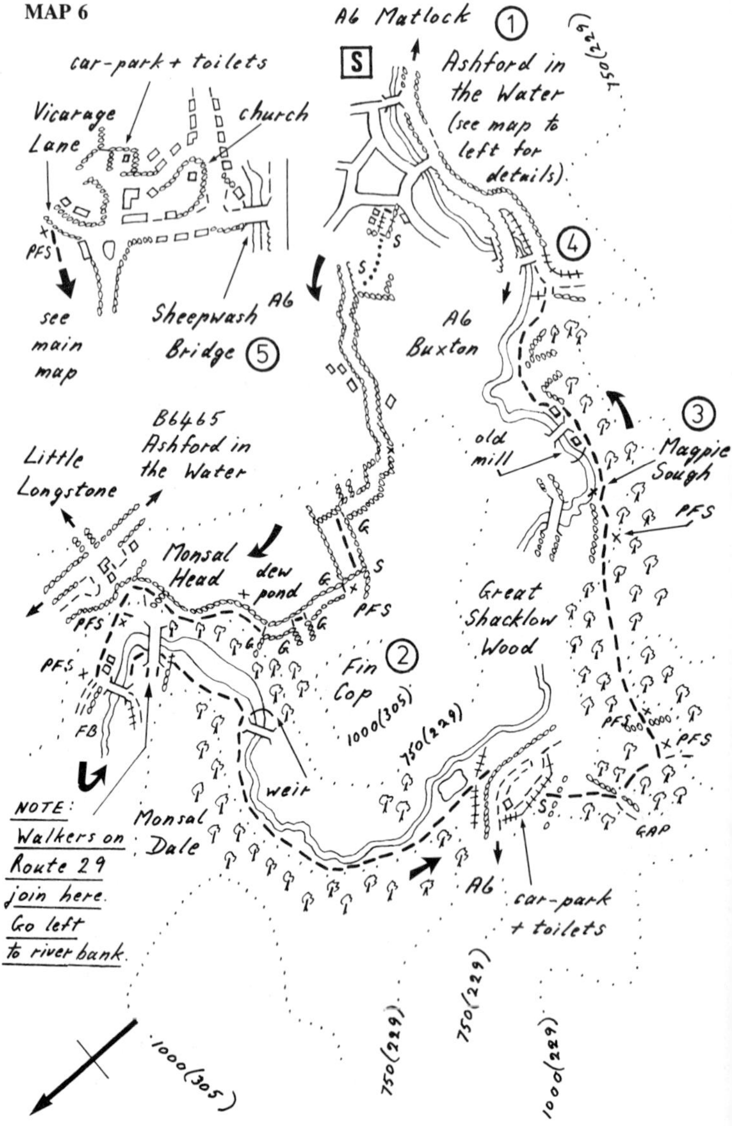

A6 Matlock
1
S
Ashford in the Water (see map to left for details)
750(229)
car-park + toilets
Vicarage Lane
church
PFS
see main map
Sheepwash Bridge 5
A6
S
S
4
A6 Buxton
3
old mill
Magpie Sough
PFS
B6465 Ashford in the Water
Little Longstone
Monsal Head
dew pond
G
S
G
PFS
G
G
G
PFS
PFS
Great Shacklow Wood
Fin Cop
2
1000(305)
750(229)
FB
weir
PFS
PFS
S
GAP
NOTE: Walkers on Route 29 join here. Go left to river bank.
Monsal Dale
A6
car-park + toilets
750(229)
750(229)
1000(229)
1000(305)

of the field go over a stile and turn R to the beginning of another stretch of lane.

After 300 yds (275 m) the lane ends at a gate, but resumes again a short distance further along at another gate. 170 yds (155 m) further the lane finally ends at a gate overlooking Monsal Dale. Follow the wall beyond as it curves to the R, enjoying the superb views down to the L. After 600 yds (550 m) reach the road and car-park at Monsal Head. The Head is probably the finest viewpoint in the Peak District, offering unrivalled views down Monsal Dale to the south-west and along Upperdale to the north-west.

From the café, etc., return to the gap where you reached the road. Go through and turn R descending steeply. Ignore the path to the L after a few yards and keep descending in the same direction to a farm. Immediately after a barn turn L and go down to a footbridge. On the opposite bank turn L and follow the wide path which soon goes under the viaduct. Keep on the path to the R of the river through Monsal Dale to reach the Buxton-Bakewell road (A6) after 1¼ miles (2 km). The prominent hill to the L across the river during this section is the site of a hill-fort – see (2) Fin Cop.

Cross the road and go up to the car-park (there are toilets to the R at the far end). Go half L up to a stile. Follow the footpath beyond for 300 yds (275 m) to reach a wall. After a few yards by the wall turn L through a gap and 225 yds (210 m) later at a PFS 'Footpath to Ashford and Sheldon' turn L, climbing into the wood (Great Shacklow Wood). Shortly cross a wall (PFS) and continue ahead through the wood. The path soon levels out and later starts to descend. Keep on this clear path, ignoring paths off to L or R, for ⅔ mile (1.1 km) to reach the bank of the River Wye. A few yards after reaching the bank note the stream emerging into the river just to the L of the path; this is a drainage channel from underground mine workings – see (3) The Magpie Mine.

Keep on the clear path by or near to the river until it meets a road. On the way you will pass an old mill with waterwheel. Walk along the road in the same direction to reach the A6. The bridge passed to the L led to some famous granite works – see (4) The Ashford black marble mines. Turn R along the main road, turning L over an old bridge – see (5) Sheepwash Bridge – after 300 yds (275 m). In the road beyond the bridge turn R. Immediately after the church turn L down a narrow lane (Court Lane) back to the car-park.

(1) *Ashford in the Water*
This village was called Aisseford in Domesday Book and Asford in the Book of Fees of 1242, 'in the Water' being added comparatively recently. The original meaning in Anglo-Saxon times was 'The ford of the ash tree'.

It was a highly appropriate name at that time for an important highway, the Old Portway, crossed the River Wye at that point. Of prehistoric origin it was called 'old' to distinguish it from other 'through-ways' or 'portways' created by the Anglo-Saxons. By medieval times the section of the Old Portway through Ashford was known as Castlegate, probably acquiring this name from a castle situated to the north of the present church, but which is now no longer extant. By the seventeenth century this was still used as an important highway for the movement of packhorse trains, as was a second route which ran from the ford to Great Longstone and on to Eyam. The 1810 turnpike from Buxton along the Wye valley (substantially the line of the present A6) also ended at Ashford where it joined a further turnpike to Edensor.

(2) *Fin Cop (119-174711)*
The hilltop over to the left as you come down Monsal Dale is Fin Cop, the site of a late Iron Age hill-fort probably of the first century BC. The hilltop is in the form of a right-angled promontory with very steep slopes down to the north and west; as these would in themselves provide sufficient defence, a rampart and ditch were erected on the south and east sides only to enclose an area of 4 hectares. At the northern end the rampart is double and there was an entrance on the east side.

(3) *The Magpie Mine*
A profusion of rakes and scrins (i.e. veins of lead ore), running in a south-east to north-west direction, cross the limestone upland around the small village of Sheldon. Their names have a romantic ring about them – the Ditchfurling, the Fieldgrove, the Trueblue and the Dirty Redsoil. As in other parts of the Peak District these

veins have been exploited for profit and the remains of several old mines can be found in the area.

Of these, the most famous was undoubtedly the Magpie Mine which is situated about a half mile (800 m) almost due south of Sheldon. Mining began in the seventeenth century and was well established by midway through the next. It continued intermittently under a number of different owners until 1958 when it was finally closed.

The mine itself is not passed on this route, but the tail of a sough coming down from the mine will be seen on the left a few yards after meeting the river bank following the descent from Great Shacklow Wood. A sough is a tunnel cut from a mine level to a neighbouring valley in order to lower the water table and hence enable mining operations to be carried out at a greater depth.

The Magpie Sough was commenced in 1873 and completed in 1881, the owner at that time being John Fairburn of Sheffield. It came into the mine at a depth of about 579 ft (176 m) and was about 2 miles (3.5 km) long. A very expensive venture, it was not a success and Fairburn was forced to close the mine in 1883; working after that time under other owners was only on a very small scale.

(4) *The Ashford black marble mines (119-191694)*

In the church at Ashford in the Water there is a memorial tablet to Henry Watson of Bakewell who in 1748 established the black marble industry near the village.

The material used for this purpose was a very dark, fine-grained limestone, quite different to the usual form from which it was produced by heat (a rock produced in this way is called a metamorphic rock). It was extracted by mining and quarrying in the Arrock Quarry – this is to the right of the Sheldon Road just before it reaches the A6 – and was worked at a mill nearby, i.e. over the bridge to the left just before the quarry. Some marble was also obtained from the Rookery Mine on the opposite side of the A6. The black marble formed the base material for articles, but was inlaid with shaped stones of other colours to form patterns. A superb example – a marble table – can be seen in the village church. The industry was in production until 1905, its most flourishing period being in Victorian times.

(5) *Sheepwash Bridge (119-194696)*
The beautiful old bridge of three arches which crosses the River Wye at the south-west corner of Ashford in the Water is called Sheepwash Bridge. It was originally a packhorse bridge built near the ford where the Old Portway crossed the river. The name originated from the annual practice of washing sheep there prior to shearing. The ewes, with halters around their necks, were made to swim the river to their lambs who were on the opposite side. The enclosure at the end of the bridge nearest to the A6 was used for holding sheep during the operation.

Route 7 Wolfscote Dale and Narrowdale

This route continues the exploration of the Dove valley which was begun on Route 5, linking up with it at the entrance to Biggin Dale. Sturdy walkers, fancying a bit of exercise, can therefore join the two routes together to make a superb figure-of-eight walk. It is even possible to add Route 18 on to these, but for the vast majority of walkers this will probably be taking things too far. It is much better to take each of the three routes in turn: separately and at leisure, savouring to the full the changing beauty of the Dove.

Length: 7½ miles (12 km).

Ascent: 500 ft (150 m).

Starting and finishing point: Alstonefield (119-131556). There is a small car-park (with toilets) near the centre of the village.

Maps: Landranger 119; Outdoor Leisure The White Peak (West Sheet).

Route description (Map 7)
The church and a number of interesting old houses will be passed as you leave the village; read (1) Alstonefield before you start out.

Sheepwash Bridge, Ashford in the Water.

MAP 7

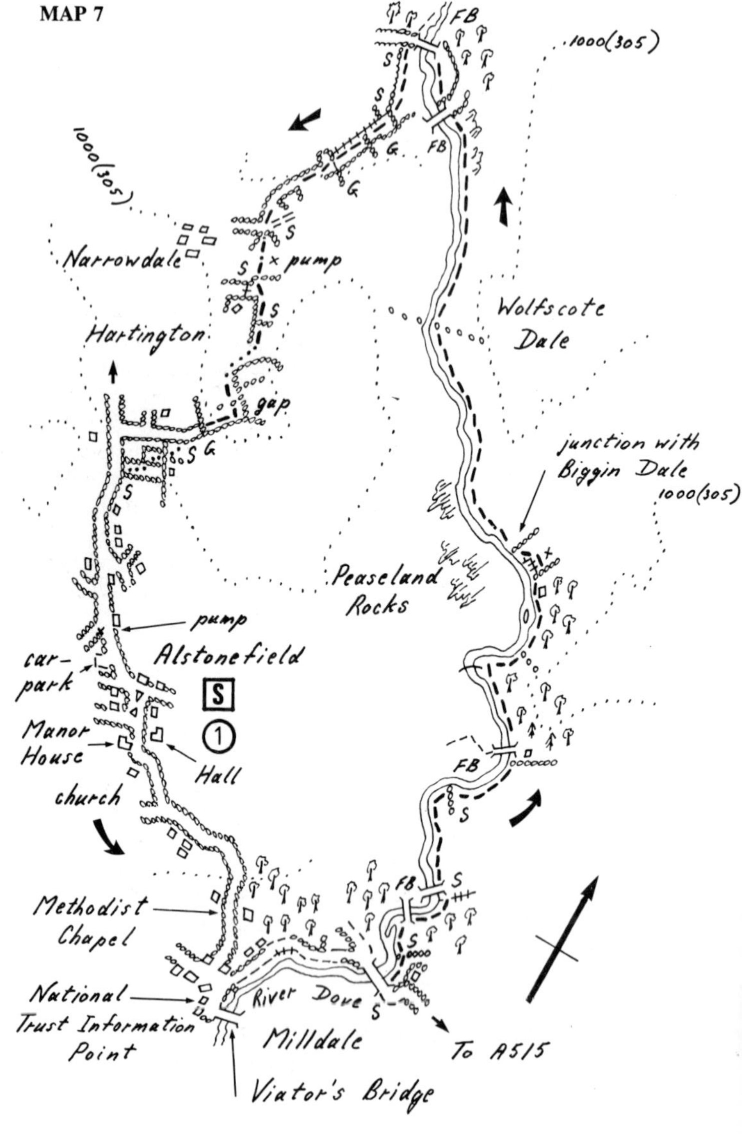

FB
1000(305)
1000(305)
S
S
G
FB
G
S
Narrowdale
S
× pump
S
Wolfscote
Dale
Hartington
gap
S
G
junction with
Biggin Dale
1000(305)
S
Peaseland
Rocks
pump
car-
park
Alstonefield
S
1
Manor
House
Hall
FB
church
S
Methodist
Chapel
FB
S
S
National
Trust Information
Point
River Dove
S
Milldale
To A515
Viator's Bridge

Leave the car-park into the road and turn to the R. After a few yards the road bends to the L. After the bend take the first turn on the R by a fenced green, going to the L of a second green after a few yards. Go down the road straight ahead, soon bending L by the church. Follow this delightful lane – partly metalled – as it descends into Milldale. At the road in the village of Milldale turn L.

Follow the road by the River Dove for just over a half mile (800 m) to a bridge over the river. Cross and immediately turn L over a stile on to the river bank. After about 1 mile (1.6 km) a dale comes in from the R and there is a footbridge over the river. Keep in the same direction along the main valley. After a further ¾ mile (1.2 km) there is a second dale, Biggin Dale, also coming in on the R.

Keep in the same direction by the river for another 1¼ miles (2 km) to a further footbridge. Do not cross, but keep on the same side across the large field ahead. At the end cross the river at a second footbridge and go up the lane ahead, i.e. leaving the river. After 90 yds (80 m) go L over a stile by a gate. Keep to the L of a hedge – later a wall – soon bending R to a stile in a corner. Continue in the same direction on a grassy path going through two gates and along a farm road. Where this farm road swings R to a farm (Narrowdale) go ahead over a stile and down the narrow valley beyond soon passing a pump.

At the end of the valley cross a stile and cross to a wall corner a short distance ahead. Keep in the same direction with a wall to the R soon crossing a further stile. Where the wall ends go half R to another wall corner and start to climb, this time with a wall to your L. At the top, at a crossing wall, turn R to a gate which leads into a lane. After 120 yds (110 m) the lane bends half R; 100 yds (90 m) further along go L over a stile and head across the field half R to the L-hand corner of a small wood. Cross the next field diagonally to the far corner and again in the third field. Enter the road over a stile and turn L. Follow the road for ½ mile (800 m) back to Alstonefield.

(1) *Alstonefield (119-131556)*
This beautiful village with its delightful greens lies on the limestone plateau to the west of the Dove valley. It seems likely that a small

church existed here about the end of the ninth century for there is a record of a visit by St Oswald, Archbishop of York, to dedicate a church in 892. The present church – built much later – contains a font, a stone coffin and the remains of several crosses which are Saxon in origin. After Hastings the lands and village were granted to William de Malbanc. In 1130 his successor, Hugh de Malbanc, founded a Cistercian abbey at Combermere in Cheshire with Alstonefield as part of its endowment. Granges were established in the area into which tithes were gathered – Hanson Grange (to the south-east), Wolfscote Grange (to the north) and Gateham Grange (to the north-west) were three of these which still exist today as farmsteads.

Following the granting of a charter in 1308 markets were held regularly at Alstonefield during the Middle Ages up to about 1500, the goods coming into the village along a number of packhorse ways which radiated out to neighbouring areas.

The Manor House and the Hall lie opposite each other just before the church is reached when coming from the centre of the village, the former being on the right. The centre part of the Manor House was constructed in 1750 although the two ends are more recent. The Hall was built in 1587 by the owner, John Harpur.

The present church was probably built around 1100, but very extensive alterations and additions have taken place since. The entrance is now by the north porch built in the eighteenth century, but the old entrance used for some four or five hundred years was the south porch on the opposite side. At the end of the north aisle is the Cotton family pew, made for the father of Charles Cotton, friend of Izaak Walton (see page 92). Next to it is a magnificent 'two decker' pulpit. Outside, in the churchyard, are two interesting headstones: the first to Anne Green who died on 3 April 1518 and the second to Margery Badaly who died in 1731, aged 107. These can be found near the wall directly opposite the south porch.

Millway Lane, an old packhorse way from Alstonefield to Milldale.

Route 8 The Burbage Valley

The hilltops of Carl Wark and Higger Tor are prominent features in the upper reaches of the Burbage valley, shapely rocky summits that should be irresistible to any walker worth his salt. Although a convenient approach can be made from Hathersage to the west, it is far better to come from Grindleford in the south up the lovely wooded reach of Padley Gorge, returning by Burbage Edge and the Longshaw estate to the east. Apart from the superb walking, the main attractions are the magnificent views from both sides of the upper Burbage, Padley Chapel (slightly off-route), Padley Gorge and the Longshaw estate.

Length: 7 miles (11 km).

Ascent: 700 ft (220 m).

Starting and finishing point: A parking area by the café at Grindleford station on the B6521 about ¾ mile (1.2 km) north-east of Grindleford (119-251788).

Maps: Landranger 119 and 110; Outdoor Leisure The White Peak (East Sheet) – part only.

Route description (Map 8)
From the café cross the railway bridge. After some cottages at a junction turn R and go uphill. (A diversion can be made at this point by continuing ahead for 325 yds (300 m) to view an unusual chapel – see (1) Padley Chapel. Afterwards return to the junction and turn L.) Go up to a gate at the top. Beyond follow the path which leads into National Trust woodland (Padley Gorge). After ⅔ mile (1.1 km) the path leaves the wood and continues in the same direction by the stream. Cross the stream over the second footbridge on the R – 325 yds (300 m) after a small building and a weir – and go up the hillside to a road. Turn L.

Immediately after the bend and bridge turn R up to a stile. (The unusual rock on the R just after the bridge is called the Toad's

MAP 8

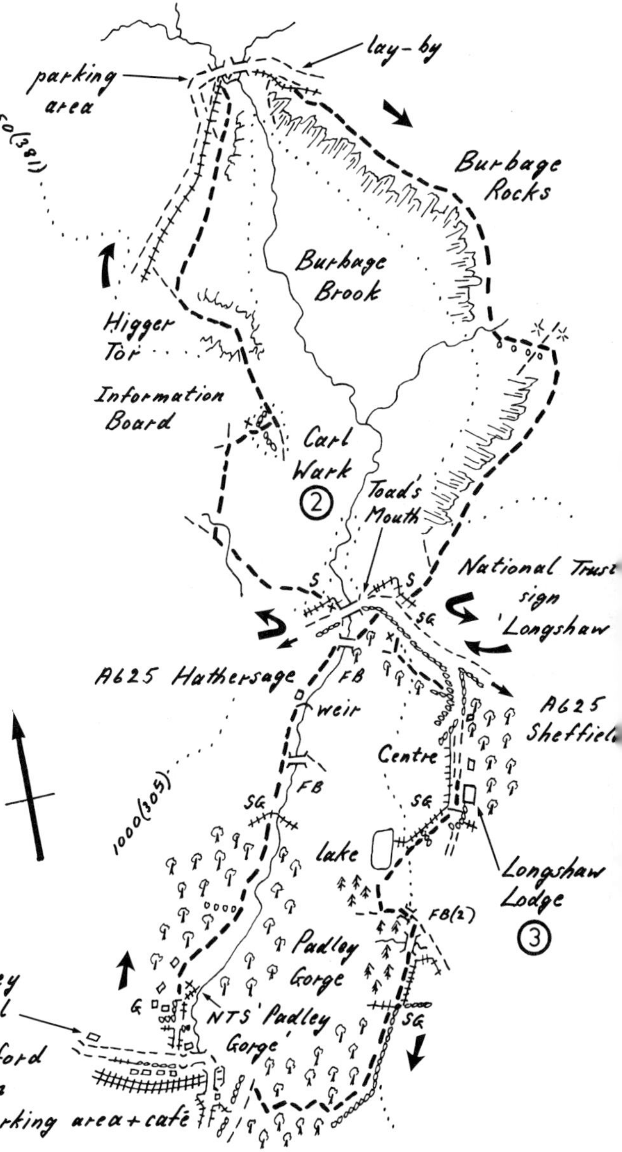

lay-by
parking area
1250(381)
Burbage Rocks
Burbage Brook
Higger Tor
Information Board
Carl Wark
②
Toad's Mouth
National Trus
sign
'Longshaw
S
S
SG
A625 Hathersage
FB
weir
A625 Sheffiel
Centre
FB
SG
1000(305)
SG
lake
Longshaw Lodge
FB(2)
③
①
Padley Chapel
Padley Gorge
G
NTS 'Padley Gorge'
SG
Grindleford Station
parking area + café
S

Mouth. It is not entirely natural, however, and some additional work has been carried out to create the effect.) Take the clear grassy path heading across the moor towards a prominent rocky hill. After a mile (1.6 km) at a cross-track turn R and climb up to the highest point of the hill. This is the site of a hill-fort built about 2000–2500 years ago – see (2) Carl Wark.

At the summit a crossing path comes in along the edge to the R; turn L and follow it down and then up to a second rocky hill. This is Higger Tor. Cross over the top to the opposite side and then half L along the edge to the end. Here at a path junction go R to keep roughly parallel with the moor edge. After ⅔ mile (1.1 km) reach a road and turn R along it, soon crossing two bridges.

Immediately after the second bridge turn R through an opening at the far end of the small parking area. Follow the path which keeps above the crag and enjoy the superb views R towards Higger Tor and Carl Wark. Where the cliff on the R fades away the path bends L and rises to the start of a second line of rocks; there it resumes its original line along the edge. Eventually at the end of the rocks follow the path down to a road.

Cross the road and go through a small gate on to a path. After a few yards the path bends L to run parallel with the road. Shortly rejoin the road and cross half R to a drive entrance. About 125 yds (115 m) down the drive you will reach the National Trust Visitor Centre just before a large house – see (3) Longshaw Lodge; take the path to the R opposite the Centre which runs alongside a fence past the house. After the house go through a small gate, turn R and follow a path down to a small lake. On reaching the lake immediately leave it again keeping in the same direction as before along the edge of a group of tall coniferous trees. After 125 yds (115 m) the path bends half L through bracken. At a wide cross-track turn L. After 160 yds (145 m) cross a small bridge and then at a fork go R (i.e. not straight ahead between the two posts). Soon the path goes by a fence to a small gate. Continue on this beautiful path through bracken with wonderful views to the R down to Grindleford station and Padley Gorge. Directly above the station

The Toad's Mouth.

the path bends R and descends steeply, soon reaching a road. Cross and turn L for a few yards before going back half R down a path to the café.

(1) *Padley Chapel (119-256790)*
The fine building, a short distance from Grindleford station, is Padley Chapel, the only surviving part of a large house which dates from the fourteenth century. The remains of other parts of the house can be seen behind the chapel. It is worth visiting on its own account, but also for its association with the Padley Martyrs.

In 1588, during the reign of Elizabeth I, the house was owned by Sir Thomas FitzHerbert, a devout Roman Catholic. As a centre of Catholicism it had already been the subject of several raids and in a further one on Thursday, 12 July two priests, Nicholas Garlick and Robert Ludlam, were found hiding there. They were brought to trial and then hanged, drawn and quartered a few days later at Derby; afterwards the dismembered bodies were impaled on spikes. Sir Thomas did not share their immediate fate, but he did die in the Tower of London in 1591.

It is very important to view this incident in the general context of that time. The early years of Elizabeth's reign were marked in fact by a considerable degree of religious tolerance – in stark contrast to the final three years of the reign of the previous Queen, Mary, who in her desire to establish the Catholic faith in England had burned nearly 300 Protestants at the stake. From 1568, however, the situation began to change dramatically. Jesuit priests – young and well-trained propagandists – began to slip across the Channel; by 1580 it is estimated that there were over a hundred actively working in England and more on their way. A number of plots – usually centred around Mary, Queen of Scots, who was deeply Catholic – were directed against Elizabeth; there was, for example, a rebellion in the north in 1569. There was also a Papal Bull of 1570 which excommunicated Elizabeth and called upon Catholics everywhere to repudiate and overthrow her authority. Finally, it should be remembered that 1588, the year of the incident described, was also

Padley Chapel.

the year of the Armada, raised as a direct consequence of that Papal Bull.

It was undoubtedly a time for firm and decisive action on the part of Elizabeth and her government, and they did not shrink from it. In 1581 it became treasonable to convert anyone or to be converted to Catholicism, in 1584 all priests ordained abroad were declared outlaws and in 1585 all Catholic priests were ordered to leave the country within forty days or be automatically guilty of treason. It was under these laws that the two priests were condemned.

Later Padley Chapel gradually fell into ruin, even being used as a cattleshed towards the end of the last century. Fortunately, restoration work was commenced in 1933 and the chapel was re-opened. Each year on the Thursday nearest to 12 July a pilgrimage takes place to the chapel where a service is held. A further service takes place on the following Sunday.

(2) *Carl Wark (110-259816)*

The rocky summit of Carl Wark on Hathersage Moor overlooking the valley of Burbage Brook is the site of a small hill-fort which occupied an area of about 2 acres (0.8 ha). Its age is uncertain but it was probably constructed during the late Iron Age, about the first century BC; although it may also have been re-used at the end of or after the Roman occupation.

The fort is basically rectangular in shape, protected on the east side by a steep slope. On the west side, where attack would be easiest, there is an earth rampart 20 ft (6 m) wide at the base, faced by a stone wall some 9 ft (2.7 m) high; the latter has now inclined back to some extent; walls of Millstone Grit boulders were used on the remaining two sides to the north and south. The main entrance was at the south-west corner where the walls turn inwards and there was a further one on the eastern side.

(3) *Longshaw Lodge (119-264799)*

Longshaw Lodge was built about 1830 by a Duke of Rutland, although it was considerably extended later. The Duke of Wellington and George V were two famous visitors. The estate of about 11,500 acres (4650 ha) was put up for sale by the 9th Duke in

Higger Tor from Carl Wark.

1927. Fortunately the Lodge and an area of the estate around the Lodge were bought by the Council for the Preservation of Rural England and the Sheffield Council of Social Service following an appeal; the property was handed over to the National Trust in 1931. Further additions since then have brought the total local holding of the Trust to over 1600 acres (650 ha). The Lodge was used as a guest house until 1961 when it was converted into private flats; the immediate area around is a country park with a National Trust Visitor Centre and restaurant.

Route 9 The Great Ridge

The imposing ridge which defines the northern side of the Hope valley offers one of the finest walks in the Peak District. An obvious line, it was used extensively by packhorse trains which came along it or crossed it at strategic points. Although Edale to the north is an obvious starting point for a traverse of the ridge, Castleton on the opposite side is very much superior giving an impressive approach past the ravine of Winnats and the great crumbling face of Mam Tor. A number of show caves can also be visited, but a visit will take 1–2 hours each. With the exception of The Plague Village (see Route 2) no other walk in this book offers more concentrated or more continuous interest.

Length: 6¼ miles (10 km).

Ascent: 1350 ft (410 m).

Starting and finishing point: The car-park in Castleton (110-149830).

Maps: Landranger 110; Outdoor Leisure The Dark Peak.

Route description (Map 9)
Leave the car-park into the main road and cross half R to go down the street between the Three Roofs Café and The Island. At the end of the street continue along a footpath which goes by a stream up to a higher road, there turn R. Cross a bridge and start to climb

MAP 9

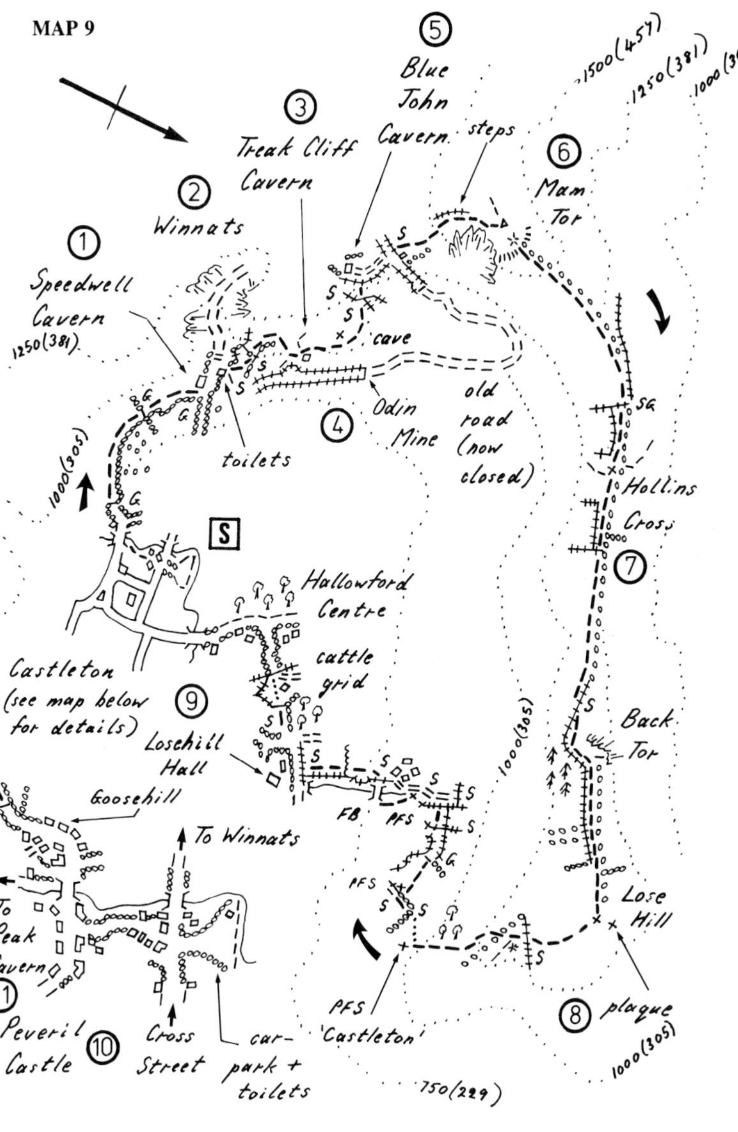

5
Blue John Cavern
1500(457)
1250(381)
1000(305)
3
Treak Cliff Cavern
steps
6
Mam Tor
2
Winnats
1
Speedwell Cavern
1250(381)
cave
toilets
Odin Mine
4
old road (now closed)
Hollins Cross
7
1000(305)
S
Hallowford Centre
cattle grid
Castleton (see map below for details)
9
Losehill Hall
Back Tor
1000(305)
Goosehill
To Winnats
FB
PFS
To Peak Cavern
11
Lose Hill
PFS 'Castleton'
8
plaque
Peveril Castle
10
Cross Street
car-park + toilets
750(229)
1000(305)

(Goosehill). Soon the road becomes rough and goes between walls to a gate. Beyond the gate follow the clear path to the L of the wall across two fields to eventually reach a road. Turn L and go up the road as far as the show cave – see (1) Speedwell Cavern. Directly ahead is a spectacular ravine – see (2) Winnats.

Directly opposite Speedwell Cavern go over a stile to the L of the toilets. Beyond go straight ahead following a path to a stile in the field corner, then keep to the L of a wall to reach a concrete path coming down from Treak Cliff Cavern. Turn L up to the cavern – see (3) The Treak Cliff Cavern. There go up some concrete steps to the L, turning R at the top to pass the cavern building on their L. The path climbs slowly up the hillside, later curving to the L to reach an extremely wide stile. During the climb look down and across the road to the R where some evidence of mining activities can be seen – see (4) The Odin Mine. Continue in the same direction to a further stile by a third show cave – see (5) The Blue John Cavern.

Leave the cavern to the R to reach a road. Walk along the road to the R for a short distance for a superb view of the steep east face of Mam Tor and to see the destruction wrought upon the A625 – see (6) Mam Tor – the Shivering Mountain. Afterwards return to the end of the rough road to the Blue John Cavern. Directly opposite this turn R over a stile by a small building and follow the path which climbs steeply up to the L of the great cliff. Eventually reach the OS obelisk on the summit of Mam Tor.

At the summit turn R and follow a path which goes to the R of a broken wall. Follow this superb path for about 2 miles (3 km) keeping on or near to the crest of the ridge. Along the way pass the direction indicator on Hollins Cross – see (7), and magnificent viewpoints there and on Back Tor. Finally, reach a further viewpoint at Lose Hill; from the summit walk a few yards to the north to find a small memorial plaque – see (8) Ward's Piece.

Leave the summit half R to your approach route and descend along a path to reach a stile; beyond keep in the same direction to a large cairn. At this point do not be tempted to continue down the clear path which descends the ridge; instead go to the R over a broken wall. On the opposite side the path bends half L roughly parallel to the wall for a short distance, but soon leaves it down the slope to the R. After a few trees, at a PFS 'Castleton', turn R down to a ladder stile. Keep to the L of a wall to reach a stile on the R after about 80 yds (70 m) (PFS). Turn R over it and cross the field directly ahead to a further stile by a gate leading into a farm road. Where the farm road bends sharply to the L go over the stile ahead keeping in the same direction. After the next stile at the end of the field turn L into a further farm road. At a broad area (just before a farm) leave the farm road over a stile to the L by a PFS.

Continue now in the same direction as before keeping to the R of the field as you bypass the farm. At the end after the farm cross a small footbridge and stile. Turn L, keeping now to the L-hand side of two fields, to reach a road in front of a large house – see (9) Losehill Hall. Go R along the road until it bends sharply L; there go ahead over a stile. Keep to the R side of the first field and then to the L of a barn in the second to reach a farm road. Go along this farm road past Hallowford Centre to a T-junction, there turn L and continue along the road back to the centre of Castleton.

Although the natural inclination – particularly on a hot summer's day – will be to go immediately into one of the numerous tea-shops to be found in Castleton, time should certainly be spared for exploring Peveril Castle whose presence dominates the town – see (10) – and Peak Cavern – see (11).

(1) *Speedwell Cavern (110-139828)*

The Speedwell Cavern is unique among the caverns of the Castleton area which are open to the public in that most of the way is by boat propelled along a narrow canal. From the entrance at the foot of the Winnats Pass a flight of steps leads down to a landing stage below the road. From there a narrow boat transports up to twenty passengers at a time along a passage about 7 ft (2 m) wide for some 500 yds (450 m) to a second landing stage from which a cavern, called the Bottomless Pit Cavern, can be reached. This marks the limit of the journey and it is only necessary to repeat the passage of the canal back to the entrance.

It appears that the canal was cut deliberately into the hillside to connect up with workings at the Bottomless Pit Cavern and the

Stream Caverns further along which had been entered previously from the surface. It was the intention to remove ore directly along the canal, a system which had already been used successfully in coal mines near Manchester and for limestone near Dudley. The cutting of the canal probably took about ten years from 1771 to 1781. Although the method itself was sound, the quantity of lead in the mine did not justify the expense involved and the mine closed down at about the end of the century, although there was a brief resumption later. The use of the mine for the tourist trade began about the time the mine first closed.

(2) *Winnats (110-136826)*

The Hope valley ends abruptly a short distance to the west of Castleton where it meets the imposing face of Mam Tor, flanked on its southern side by Long Cliff and to the north by the Great Ridge. Although it is possible to outflank this obstacle from further back in the dale, once within it the only promising breach occurs at the south-west corner where the steep and savage ravine of Winnats, cutting through the cliff, carries a road to the higher ground beyond.

Although the gradient of the Winnats road is impressively steep it has nevertheless provided a valuable through-route to and from the west for many centuries. Packhorse trains used it frequently for the transport of a variety of goods, one of the most valuable of which was salt taken from the brine pits in Cheshire to the population of Sheffield. It was also the route taken by a new turnpike, part of the link between Manchester and Sheffield, constructed in 1758. Fifty-five years later, however, this was superseded by a new road constructed by the Manchester and Sheffield Turnpike Company which bypassed the Winnats by means of a hair-pin bend up the lower slopes of Mam Tor below the sheer east face. Due to the very unstable nature of this ground, which was formed from land-slip debris, this was not a wise decision and major roadworks have had to be carried out on five occasions during this century. Finally, in 1976, following exceptional weather serious cracks began to appear in the surface of the road and it had to be closed two years later apart from limited traffic to a local farm. This foiled a scheme of traffic control in the Winnats whereby the road there was closed during summer weekends to allow visitors to walk up the pass free from the disturbing influence of motor vehicles.

The name Winnats probably originated as 'Gate for the Wind'; walkers coming up the pass on a rough and boisterous day will think it singularly appropriate.

(3) *The Treak Cliff Cavern (110-136832)*

Treak Cliff is the steep and rocky northern slope of the Winnats Pass which curves round to face east down the Hope valley. Records for the middle of the eighteenth century indicate that some kind of quarrying or mining activity was taking place there at that time; it is also known that in 1762 Blue John of a variety now to be found only in parts of the Treak Cliff Cavern was used by Robert Adam in the construction of a chimneypiece at Kedleston Hall, near Derby. From that time extraction of the Blue John continued into and throughout the nineteenth century. During the First World War production actually increased due to the use of Blue John as a flux in blast furnaces and by the chemical industry and some small quarries were opened up on the hillside above. The caverns worked at that time are those which are now known as the Old Series.

In 1926, blasting opened up a further series of natural caverns which greatly extended the system. These additional caverns are now referred to as the New Series. As these were totally free of Blue John they were left substantially in their original state. In any case mining activity was reduced considerably later that year.

At Easter 1935 the caverns were opened to the public. At the present time they are open through the year and parties may visit the combined series. The Old Series contains substantial quantities of Blue John and the New Series some fine stalagmites and stalactites.

(4) *The Odin Mine (110-135835)*

The Odin Mine is situated a short distance up the road from the Treak Cliff Cavern and can be reached by a short diversion from the route. As you ascend, Odin Gorge will be seen on the left. This marks the line of the vein from which the ore was removed and is not therefore a natural feature; although the gorge leads into the main level the original entrance – now closed – was actually on the right-hand side of the road near to the crushing circle. The crushing circle was added in 1823 and is a remarkable feature with an iron track about 18 ft (5.5 m) in diameter on which ran a round gritstone with an iron band tyre. The stone was carried around the track by a horse using a beam pivoted on a centre post. The purpose of this, of course, was to crush lead ore prior to separation and smelting.

(5) *The Blue John Cavern (110-132832)*

It was discovered and developed some three centuries ago by miners, who used to enter the system through a vertical shaft; the present entrance was produced by the widening of a natural fissure very much later when the system was being developed as a show cave. The main attractions nowadays are the Crystallised Cavern with its coloured minerals and rocks; Lord Mulgrave's Dining Room – so called because Lord Mulgrave is said to have given a dinner there to a group of miners; and the Variegated Cavern, 200 ft (60 m) high, which marks the end of the section open to visitors. There are also a few relics of the old mining days with veins and nodules of Blue John. Blue John is a type of fluorspar which is characterised by a series of bands, the colours of which vary considerably: blue-black, light blue, purple, white and yellow. It is used for the production of ornaments and jewellery.

(6) *Mam Tor – the Shivering Mountain (110-128836)*

The sheer and bare eastern face of Mam Tor provides a superb glimpse of the underlying rock strata around the Hope and Edale valleys. The base of the cliff is made up of Edale Shales – dark, soft and crumbly rocks which were originally formed from mudbanks in an estuary some 300 million years ago; when wet these rapidly lose their coherence and bearing strength as they revert back to their original form. Above this is a succession of layers of sandstones, gritstones and shales which make up the Millstone Grit series; the individual layers stand out clearly from each other because of their colour and their different resistance to weathering processes. This exposure owes its existence to a massive land-slip which occurred in comparatively recent times (geologically speaking, that is). As with Alport Castles (see page 237), this was due to undermining on the harder layers by removal through weathering of the softer supporting shales.

The crushing circle at the Odin Mine.

The debris of the landslide covers an area 1000 yds (900 m) long and 600 yds (550 m) wide i.e. about 35 ha, across the two arms of the A625 which form a hairpin bend; the area of the slip is clearly indicated by the uneven nature of the ground lying away from the foot of the great cliff. Although the main land-slip occurred some considerable time ago, the process of destruction still goes on as weathering of the softer bands continues. This is shown by the constant fall of rocks down the face and the cracks which have appeared in the tarmacadam surface of the A625. It is for this reason that this road section has had to be closed, forcing traffic up the steep incline of the Winnats. It is also for this reason that Mam Tor has long been known as the Shivering Mountain.

The summit of Mam Tor contains a hill-fort of about 16 acres (6.5 ha) which makes it the largest hill-fort in Derbyshire.

(7) *Hollins Cross (110-136845)*

The direction indicator (or orientation table) on Hollins Cross is inscribed 'In memory of Tom Hyett of Long Eaton'.

(8) *Ward's Piece (110-153854)*

A few yards to the north of the direction indicator on Lose Hill is a metal plaque attached to a short face of rock. It is inscribed in memory of a famous walker and fighter for walkers' rights.

G. H. B. Ward was born in Sheffield on 12 June 1876, the son of working-class parents. After school he worked as an engineer at a local steel works until the First World War when he was recruited by the Ministry of Labour. Between the wars he served as Chief Officer in the Conciliation Department of the Ministry, responsible for north-east England, finally retiring in 1941.

It is, however, for his achievements and for his great contribution to the cause of rambling that he will be most remembered. In 1900 he established the Sheffield Clarion Ramblers (one of the earliest rambling clubs in Britain), in 1912 the Hallamshire Footpaths

Previous pages

Left: Mam Tor – the Shivering Mountain.

Right: Cracks in the surface of the A625 caused by movement of the unstable land-slip debris on which the road was constructed. Because of this the road had eventually to be closed.

Preservation Society and in 1926 the Sheffield and District Federation of the Ramblers' Association. He was the first Chairperson of the National Standing Council of Ramblers' Federation (later called the Ramblers' Association) which was formed in 1931.

In addition to his considerable ability as an organiser and leader he had a reputation as a formidable walker until well into old age; he was also a fine orator and a productive writer as his many articles in the *Sheffield Clarion Ramblers' Handbook* testify. He played an important part in many of the early struggles for access in the High Peak and elsewhere. It was fitting that he was elected a Fellow of the Royal Geographical Society in 1922 and received the honorary degree of Master of Arts of Sheffield University in 1957.

Ward's Piece around the summit of Lose Hill at the end of the Great Ridge was presented to him in the presence of 2000 ramblers on 8 April 1945, to be passed into the safe-keeping of the National Trust. He died twelve years later, in October 1957. Ward's slogan, 'A rambler made is a man improved', was used for many years on the front cover of the *Sheffield Clarion Ramblers' Handbook*.

(9) *Losehill Hall (110-153838)*

The large and impressive house passed during the descent is Losehill Hall, the National Park Study Centre. It was built originally in 1882 as a private residence and opened as a centre ninety years later in 1972, the first residential centre established by a National Park Authority in Britain. It has accommodation for sixty persons, in single and double bedrooms, who may use the facilities of the centre; these include a well-equipped lecture theatre, a slide library, a dark room and a book library.

(10) *Peveril Castle (110-149827)*

The hillside to the south of the present-day village of Castleton – formerly owned by two Saxons, Gernebern and Hundine – was given as a gift by William the Conqueror to one of his knights, William Peverel. It is uncertain if this gift also included a castle, but one certainly existed there by 1086 for there is an entry about it in Domesday Book. It was probably built to control the valuable lead-mining area to the west.

The castle is situated in a superb natural defensive position with cliffs to the south, east and west. It is likely that the first wall was built on the northern side overlooking Castleton, but curtain walls on the other sides to totally enclose the courtyard were added later. The square keep – built in the south-west corner to guard the main gateway – was added in 1176; building work was completed by early in the following century. Ownership of the castle changed several times during the centuries, some of the more well-known owners being Eleanor of Castile, Simon de Montfort and John of Gaunt.

By late in the fourteenth century, however, the castle had ceased to be a place of any importance and by the seventeenth had become ruinous. In 1932 it was taken into the care of the Office of Works.

(11) *Peak Cavern (110-149826)*

Peak Cavern can be easily reached from the main car-park in Castleton by a lovely path which follows Peakshole Water. Its most memorable feature is undoubtedly its size for the entrance hall is the largest natural cave entrance in Britain with an opening some 33ft (10 m) high and 100 ft (30 m) wide. The floor of this hall is cut into a number of terraces which were used for the manufacture of hemp rope until fairly recently (1974) and once contained a row of cottages which were lived in up to the middle of last century.

From the far end of the hall a passage, called Lumbago Walk, leads on to the Great Cave which is 50 ft (15 m) high, there was originally an opening from this cave into Cave Dale, but this is now blocked. Further along is a chamber known as Roger Hain's House where there is a waterfall and a balcony from which choirs once entertained groups of visitors. The final section of the show cave is about 500 ft (150 m) long and is by a small stream – the River Styx.

Mam Tor and the head of the Hope Valley from Peveril Castle.

Route 10 Eyam Moor and Eyam Edge

A lovely walk up the steep edge and the great moorland area to the north of Eyam. The walking throughout is excellent, but it is the descent from the moor into Abney Clough along a fine curving grassy shelf that will be most remembered.

Length: 7 miles (11 km).

Ascent: 1250 ft (380 m).

Starting and finishing point: The car-park on Hawkhill Road, Eyam (119-216767).

Maps: Landranger 119; Outdoor Leisure The White Peak (East Sheet).

Route description (Map 10)
Although Eyam is the most interesting village in the Peak District it is best to ignore that fact here. Sufficient of its interest will become apparent, however, within the first five minutes of this walk to guarantee a speedy return.

Leave the car-park into the road and turn L. At a T-junction turn L again and go along the main street of Eyam as far as the church. Take a path to the L (PFS) which goes up the R-hand side of the churchyard. Leave the churchyard at its far end through a small gate and go up the wide sunken track half L. This soon goes between a fence and a wall to a stile. Keep in the same direction going up the R-hand side of the field beyond to reach a stile in a corner. Cross and continue to climb, but now on the L-hand side of the field, to a small gate at the top which leads into a road.

Cross half L to a stile. Follow the path which leads up through a wood until a wall is reached after about 300 yds (275 m). There turn L and follow the wall to a stile. Keep in the same direction along the edge of the hillside with a wall and a wood to your L to a further stile, then half R to a third stile in a corner. Cross the next field diagonally, heading towards a prominent mast, to a stile which leads

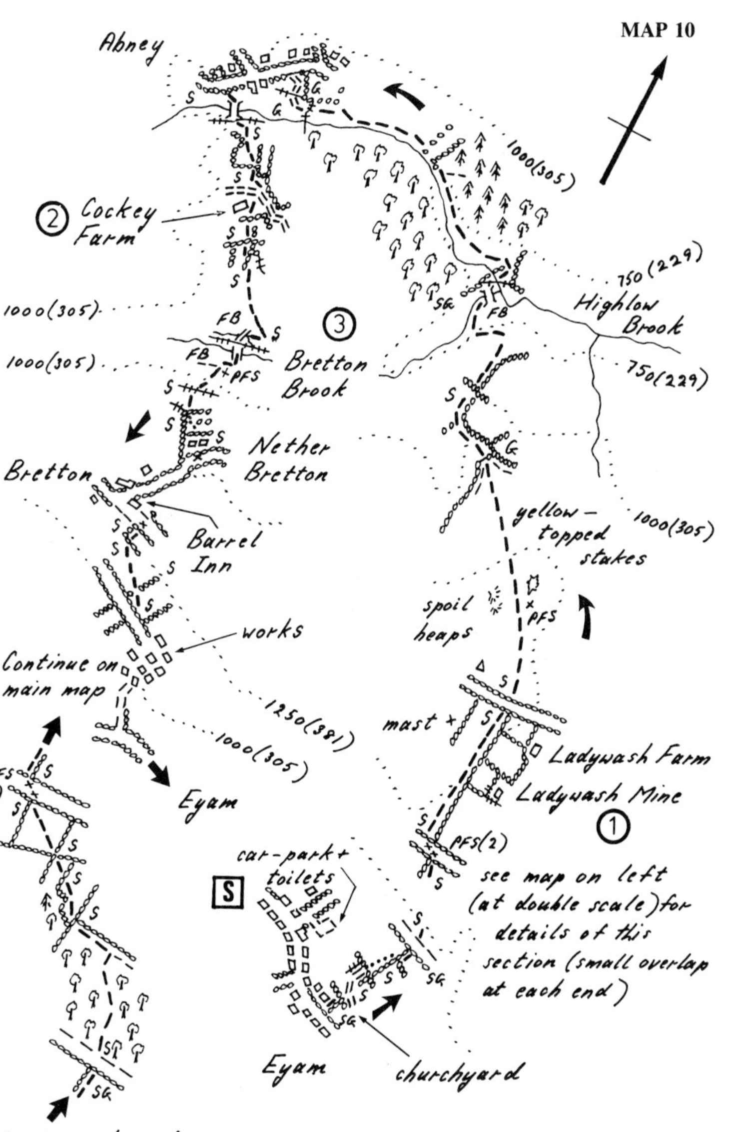

MAP 10
Abney
1000(305)
2 Cockey Farm
750(229)
Highlow Brook
750(229)
1000(305)
FB
3
1000(305)
FB
PFS
Bretton Brook
Nether Bretton
Bretton
Barrel Inn
yellow-topped stakes
1000(305)
spoil heaps
PFS
works
Continue on main map
1250(381)
mast
1000(305)
Ladywash Farm
Ladywash Mine
Eyam
1
PFS(2)
PFS
car-park + toilets
see map on left (at double scale) for details of this section (small overlap at each end)
Eyam
churchyard
Continue here from main map

into a road. Turn L in the road for 35 yds (30 m), then R over a stile. Beyond keep to the L of the wall for about 700 yds (650 m) to a ladder stile which leads into a rough lane; there is a prominent mast to the L and a mine building to the R during this section – see (1) The Ladywash Mine.

Cross to the ladder stile on the opposite side of the lane and then follow the lovely footpath which rises slowly up the heather-covered moor beyond. The highest point, marked by some small spoil heaps, is soon reached; from there the path descends steadily, its way marked at short intervals by wooden posts, for about ½ mile (800 m). At the end reach a stile in a corner formed by converging walls. The track beyond, which curves to the R along a hillside shelf with bracken-covered slopes falling steeply away to the L, can only be described as superb. Keep by the wall as you descend, soon crossing a ladder stile. Lower down, the path leaves the wall, finally going through zigzags to a small footbridge. Go through the small gate nearby and then turn R to a second small gate. Do not go through this gate; instead turn L and follow a prominent footpath into a wood.

Follow the path through the wood keeping to the R of a stream. After about ½ mile (800 m) leave the wood and continue in the same direction still keeping to the R of the stream. After a further 750 yds (700 m) go over a stile by a gate. Keep in the same direction to the road through Abney. Turn L through the village.

After about 250 yds (225 m), where the road bends to the R, go L over a stile (PFS 'Nether Bretton'). Drop down to a footbridge and then up half L to a ladder stile. Turn L, soon bending R to follow a small stream. At the first section of wall (i.e. an irregular section jutting out) head half L across the field to a stile in the far corner. Cross, turn to the L around a wall corner and head towards a farmhouse a short distance away – see (2) Cockey Farm.

Go down the farm road to the L of the farm building, but leaving almost immediately afterwards slightly R towards a prominent ladder stile. In the next field keep to the L-hand side to a gateway.

The descent from Eyam Moor. The valley to the left is Bretton Clough and the wooded valley beyond is Abney Clough.

Ahead is a small valley descending towards a large clough. Go down the valley for about 100 yds (90 m), then L over a stile by a trough. Beyond, the path descends across the side of the clough to reach two footbridges – see (3) The Bretton Clough Footbridge. Cross these and follow the path up the opposite side of the clough to a stile at the top.

From the stile keep straight ahead to a corner formed by a fence and a wall. Keep on the R-hand side of the next field to a gateway, then at a PFS half L towards a farmhouse. Cross a stile between the farmhouse and a barn which leads to a drive, there go half L to a road. Turn R and follow the road for about ¼ mile (400 m) to a T-junction by the Barrel Inn. Turn L. After 125 yds (115 m) turn R over a stile (PFS) and follow a path along the R-hand side of a field to a second stile. Beyond, the path goes half L descending steeply across the hillside. Lower down cross a wall at a stile and keeping in the same direction reach a walled lane. Enter the lane at a stile and turn L, soon entering a large works area. Opposite the first building on the L turn to the R between large buildings and go down to the weighbridge and into the works road. Continue along this to the main road. Turn L and walk along the road for ⅔ mile (1.1 km) back to Eyam.

(1) *The Ladywash Mine (119-218776)*
This old lead mine, with a name which would not have been out of place in the 1845 Klondyke gold rush, lies just to the right as you go up the fields between Eyam Edge and Sir William Hill. The ore-containing veins, which lie in limestone, become progressively deeper as they traverse the area from the direction of Great Hucklow, roughly parallel with the road above Eyam Edge. As a result of this the shafts had to be sunk to a depth of nearly 800 ft (240 m) – the New Engine Mine just to the east of the Ladywash went even deeper and reached 1092 ft (333 m), making it the deepest in Derbyshire.

(2) *Cockey Farm (119-199793)*
The name of this farm was probably derived from Thomas De Cockeye who lived there in the fourteenth century. It was the birthplace on 25 November 1750 of William Newton who later

became known as the 'Ministrel of the Peak'. After a fairly limited education he followed, as they say, in his father's footsteps and became a carpenter, eventually gaining employment at the cotton mill at Cressbrook. After a disastrous fire at the mill in 1788, however, Newton and his wife were left destitute. Through the help of Anna Seward – a local poet known as the 'Swan of Lichfield' – and one of his godmothers he was able to obtain a partnership in another mill at Monsal Dale where he became reasonably prosperous. After retirement he lived at Tideswell where he died on 3 November 1830. He is buried in the churchyard of Tideswell Church. His poetry earned him both the respect of his contemporaries and the title by which he is still known.
(3) *The Bretton Clough Footbridge (119-202788)*
The second footbridge in Bretton Clough 'was built in memory of Ken Holloway (1915–1980) who walked these hills'. Surely no more fitting memorial has ever been erected to the memory of a walker.

Route 11 Froggatt, Curbar and Baslow Edges

One of the finest edge walks in the Peak District with magnificent views over the Derwent valley. The path is very clear and route finding quite straightforward. If you want solitude, however, it is best to go during the week or away from the summer months as these edges are extremely popular, not just with walkers but also with rock climbers, hang gliding enthusiasts and even with the flyers of radio-controlled model aircraft. The general public – as distinct from walkers – also make their way there, coming up from the car-parks by the Grouse Inn and at Curbar Gap. The only problem is how to connect the two ends of the edges without returning along the same route; this is solved here by a lovely walk through the valley which includes a long river stretch.

Length: 8½ miles (15 km).

Ascent: 950 ft (290 m).

MAP 11

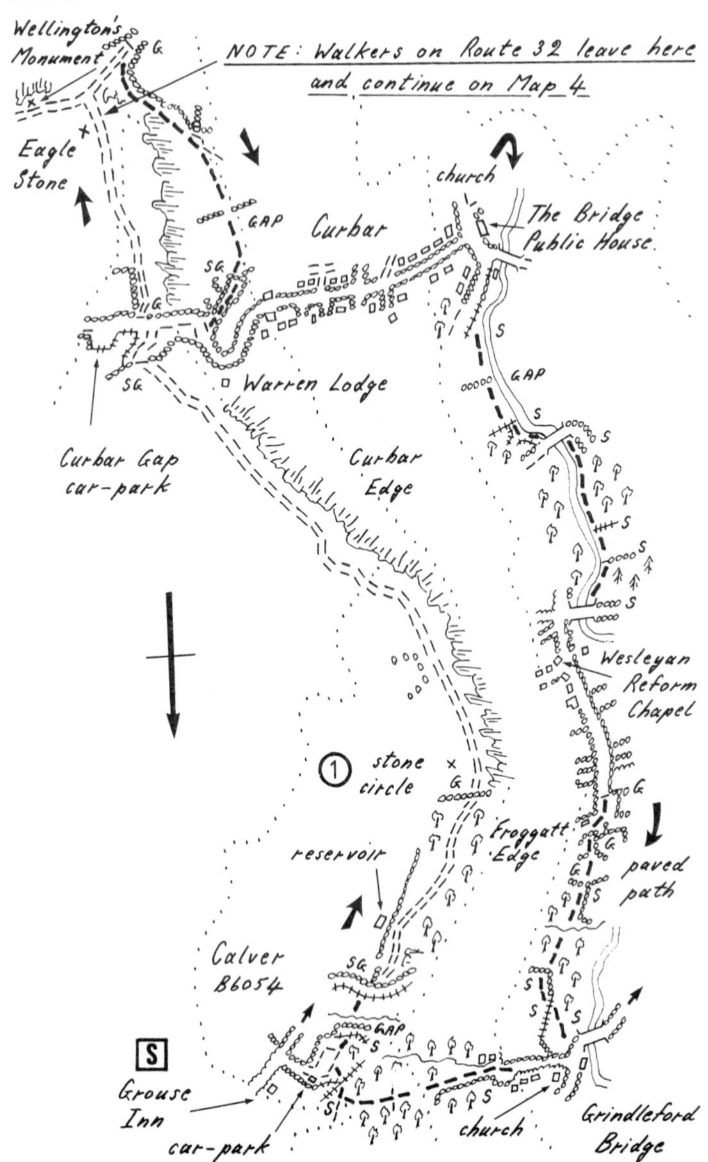

Wellington's Monument
G
NOTE: Walkers on Route 32 leave here and continue on Map 4
Eagle Stone
church
The Bridge Public House
GAP
Curbar
SG
G
SG
Warren Lodge
S
GAP
S
Curbar Gap car-park
Curbar Edge
S
S
S
S
Wesleyan Reform Chapel
1
stone circle
G
G
Froggatt Edge
reservoir
G
G
paved path
S
Calver B6054
SG
S
S
S
GAP
S
S
Grouse Inn
car-park
S
church
Grindleford Bridge

Starting and finishing point: A car-park at the northern end of Froggatt Edge on the Calver-Dronfield road (B6054) about 2½ miles (4 km) from Calver. Approaching from that direction the entrance is on the L a short distance before the Grouse Inn (119-256777).

Maps: Landranger 119, Outdoor Leisure The White Peak (East Sheet).

Route description (Map 11)
Leave the car-park at the far end and take a path which goes half R to a stile. Descend to a wall and stream and then up to a road. Turn R. After 65 yds (60 m), before the road bends, cross and go through a small gate by a large gate. The path beyond is superb – wide and level with a beautiful walking surface, winding its way through trees with glorious views over the valley to the R. There is a stone circle to the L of the path a short distance after starting – see (1) The stone circle below.

Continue for 2¼ miles (3.5 km) along the top of Froggatt and Curbar Edges to reach the road at Curbar Gap. Cross the road and go up the wide path opposite continuing in the same direction over the moor. After ⅔ mile (1.1 km) reach a T-junction on the edge of a steep slope. Turn L for a short distance to a monument (Wellington's Monument) on the edge of the cliff to the R of the path, then retrace your steps back to the T-junction – see page 84. Keep in the same direction (i.e. to the R from your original direction) soon starting to descend. In 200 yds (180 m) the track reaches a gate in a corner formed by converging walls; about 85 yds (80 m) before the gate turn back half R along a rough track keeping to the R of a wall. After a wall corner the path bends half L. Later meet the wall again and shortly afterwards go R at a path fork to go across the hillside (the L branch descends). Eventually go through a gap, then a small gate and finally up to a road. Turn L and follow the road down through two sharp bends.

Keep in the same direction following the road down for over a half mile (800 m) to a T-junction opposite the The Bridge public house. Turn back half R up Froggatt Road and after 200 yds (180

m) go L over a stile on to the river bank. Go along the path on the R bank of the river; at a bridge cross and continue in the same direction but now on the L bank. Cross the river again at the next bridge and go L at the T-junction just beyond. Keep ahead passing a road to the R. Where the road bends R by the Wesleyan Reform Chapel keep in the same direction down a lane (PFS 'Grindleford Bridge'); this is metalled at first then partly paved. At the end, at a gate, keep in the same direction bending half R at a wall corner after 70 yds (65 m) to a gate opposite a barn. Keep by the wall to a second gate and then across a field on a paved path to a stile. Follow the lovely path beyond though a wood and across several small streams to a stile at a wall corner. The path then follows the wall to a stile to the L then across a field to the road near Grindleford Bridge.

Turn R in the road and then almost immediately R again up a lane just before the church. At the end the lane bends R; do not enter the farmyard but turn L up a footpath to the L of the farm buildings. Keep to the R of a wall as you climb slowly through a wood. When the wall bends to the L keep climbing in the same direction. Go over a crossing path 300 yds (275 m) after the corner and the same distance later at a second crossing path go to the R. Cross a stile in a fence and turn L up to the car-park.

(1) *The stone circle (119-249768).*
Shortly after passing through the gate or stile on Froggatt Edge a stone circle will be found on the L a few yards from the path. It consists of two concentric rings of stones with a bank between them, the overall diameter being about 36 ft (11 m). There are entrances on both the north and south sides. It was probably built between 2200 and 1400 BC.

The Derwent Valley from Froggatt Edge.

Route 12 Saddleworth Moor

A mere glance at the The Dark Peak sheet of the Outdoor Leisure series, which covers the north-western extremity of the Peak District National Park, will reveal the great walking potential of the Saddleworth Moor area and its immediate surroundings. To the experienced eye the signs of it are unmistakable, and the first visit will immediately confirm the soundness of that preliminary judgement. The route described here is the best that the area can offer, giving a combination of superb walking, features of interest and magnificent scenery that should delight anyone. The first part of the route is through the valley by the Dove Stone, Yeoman Hey and Greenfield Reservoirs. A climb up to Birchen Clough is then followed by the best part of the walk: the traverse of the long edge over to Chew Reservoir. The final part takes the road down the right-hand side of Chew Brook back to the car-park at Dove Stone Reservoir. The ascent of Birchen Clough involves some scrambling for a short distance. (This crosses an access area – see page 54.)

Length: 8 miles (13 km).

Ascent: 1200 ft (370 m).

Starting and finishing point: The car-park (toilets) by the dam of Dove Stone Reservoir, a short distance off the A635, Mossley-Holmfirth road (110-013035).

Maps: Landranger 110; Outdoor Leisure The Dark Peak.

Route description (Map 12)
Leave the car-park and turn L going up a minor road which curves to the L to the end of the reservoir dam. At the end turn L and go along the clear path which runs along the top of the dam. At the far end go directly ahead up some steps. Follow the path which bends

Approaching Grindleford Bridge in the Derwent Valley below Froggatt Edge. This beautiful path is partly paved.

MAP 12

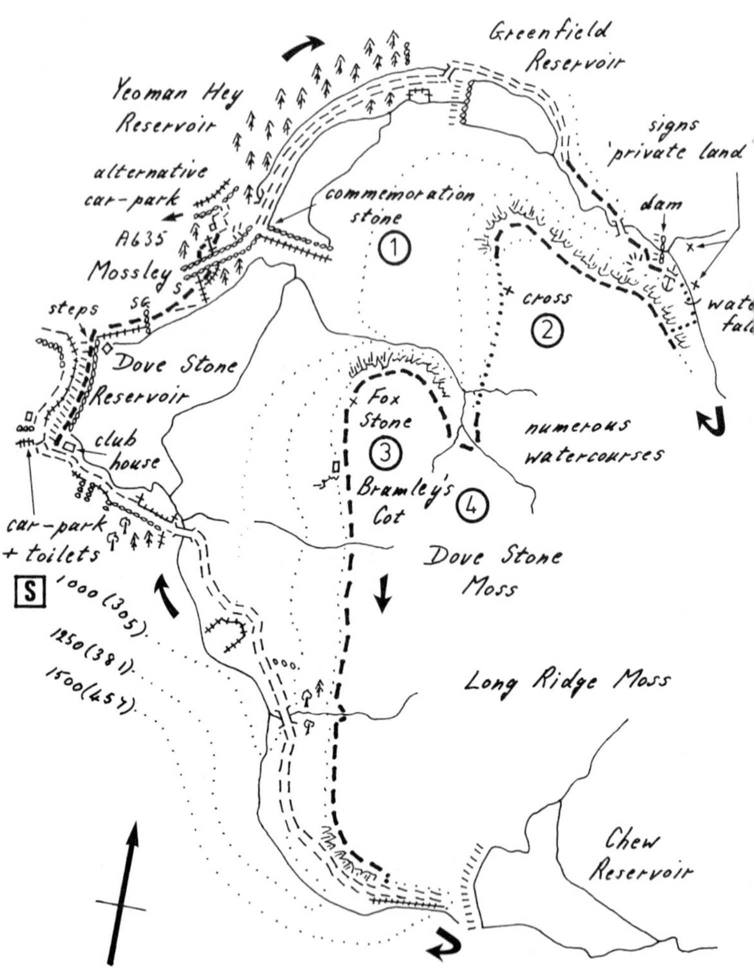
Greenfield
Reservoir
Yeoman Hey
Reservoir
signs
'private land'
alternative
car-park
commemoration
stone
dam
A635
Mossley
1
cross
2
wate
fal
steps
SG
Dove Stone
Reservoir
Fox
Stone
numerous
watercourses
club
house
3
Bramley's
Cot
4
car-park
+ toilets
Dove Stone
Moss
S
1000 (305)
1250 (381)
1500 (457)
Long Ridge Moss
Chew
Reservoir

to the R and goes by a fence parallel to the reservoir. After a small gate go to the L at a junction and continue along crossing a stile until you reach a reservoir road. There turn R.

Follow this reservoir road for 1½ miles (2.5 km) past the three reservoirs of the valley – Dove Stone, Yeoman Hey and Greenfield – keeping always to their L. On the dam of Yeoman Hey Reservoir there is a small stone plaque (facing you as you reach it) – see (1) The King of Tonga.

At the end of the final reservoir continue on the clear path to the L of the stream which comes into the reservoir at that point. Shortly after a spoil heap on the R you will reach a deep stone-lined water course with a large tunnel entrance to the R (this point is at the junction of two streams). Cross this water course by means of a small bridge to the L and follow a path to the R of the R-hand stream – Birchen Clough.

Your aim at this point is to ascend the steep slope to the R of the stream; with care this can be done at a number of places, but probably the best plan is to go up the stream for a short distance keeping either on the R-hand side or up the boulders of the stream bed until a reasonable way presents itself. (As will be obvious from the notice on the boulder on the L-hand side of the stream this is the limit of the access area.) When possible, therefore, climb up the hillside to the R to reach a path running along the edge at the top.

Turn to the R and follow the edge path. Rocks soon appear on the edge to the R. After about ⅔ mile (1.1 km) the edge bends sharply to the L – soon afterwards there is an unusual rock to the R with three small summits. Shortly after the corner the edge goes directly south and then bends to the east. (In mist there may be a tendency, if you are not careful, to drop down the moor from this bend towards the reservoirs. Resist this and regain the higher ground over to the L.) Aim for a cross on the skyline. This cross was erected as a memorial to a local Member of Parliament – see (2).

Continue along the edge beyond the cross soon crossing an area of bare peat until you reach a stream. Cross and rise up on the opposite side following a path to the R. Soon the edge bends to the L and after a further short distance to the L again. Shortly after the second bend you will reach a cairn on the top of a rock (Fox Stone)

– notice the plaque on the rock face as you reach it – see (3). About 300 yds (275 m) later reach the remains of a small stone building below some rocks slightly down to the R from the edge; this is Bramley's Cot – see (4). From the ruin continue to follow the edge for about a mile (1.6 km) until you overlook the road coming up by Chew Brook; you should also see the dam of Chew Reservoir over to the L. Drop down to the road.

Turn R and follow the road down for 1½ miles (2.5 km) to Dove Stone Reservoir in the valley. By the reservoir pass the club house of the Dove Stone Sailing Club and continue for a few more yards back to the car-park.

(1) *The King of Tonga (110-020046)*
The small plaque on the dam wall of Yeoman Hey Reservoir is inscribed 'This stone was laid by H.M. The King of Tonga 1981'. Tonga Islands – also called the Friendly Islands – lie between Fiji and Samoa in the central Pacific. The King, Taufa'ahau Tupou IV, who was in London for the royal wedding in that year, was invited to the North-west by the managing director of a firm of contractors who were working on the reservoirs at that time and who had also built a wharf in Tonga some fifteen years earlier. The King travelled up from London by train and – after being entertained by the Mayor of Oldham – toured the reservoirs before laying the stone and returning the same day.

(2) *Memorial cross (110-030045)*
The ornate stone cross, supported at the front and back by metal rods and set in a commanding position on the edge overlooking the valley, is inscribed 'Here by the accidental discharge of a gun James Platt MP for Oldham lost his life 27 August 1857.' James Platt was born at Oldham in 1823, the son of Henry and Sarah Platt. A partner in the firm of Platt Brothers & Co., engineers and machinists of Oldham, he married Lucy Mary in 1847 and became a Liberal Member of Parliament in April 1857. He was a supporter of universal suffrage, the ballot and shorter parliaments, but strongly opposed to any legislation on factory labour. His career in

Bramley's Cot.

Parliament was very short-lived, however, as he died in that tragic manner a mere four months after election.

(3) *Memorial plaque on Fox Stone (110-025037)*

The small metal plaque on the rock face below the cairn is 'In memory of Brian Toase 17.8.1949–18.8.1972 and Tom Morton 16.10.1950–18.8.1972 who lost their lives whilst descending the second Sella Tower Italian Dolomites'.

(4) *Bramley's Cot (110-027035)*

Although now in a fairly ruined condition and offering comparatively little shelter, the small stone building just below the edge a short distance beyond Fox Stone is worth a visit, if only to appreciate the considerable effort that must have gone into its construction. It consists of two walls of dressed stones built across a corner cut out of the gritstone edge. Grooves which used to support the roof timbers can be seen on both of the rock faces.

Route 13 The Kinder Downfall

There are few places in the British hills that are more dramatic than the Downfall on Kinder, a fact which accounts for its immense popularity with walkers. This route is best attempted, therefore, outside the main holiday months or, at any rate, the weekends in them. Even so – except possibly during the foulest weather or in the depths of winter – it is unlikely that you will have the Downfall entirely to yourself.

This walk begins at a small quarry car-park near Hayfield which was used as the starting point for the famous Mass Trespass of 1932. It takes a metalled road to Kinder Reservoir then goes up William Clough to the ridge top of Ashop Head. A short, but steep, climb leads to the edge of the Kinder plateau which is then followed past the Downfall as far as Edale Cross. The final part of the route takes a clear path across pasture land back to the Kinder Road. It is pleasing to record that the area of Kinder is now owned and protected by the National Trust.

A superb walk on which the main attractions are the Downfall, the views from the plateau and the magnificent walk along the edges. But, for many, it will be the historical connection which will appeal most of all.

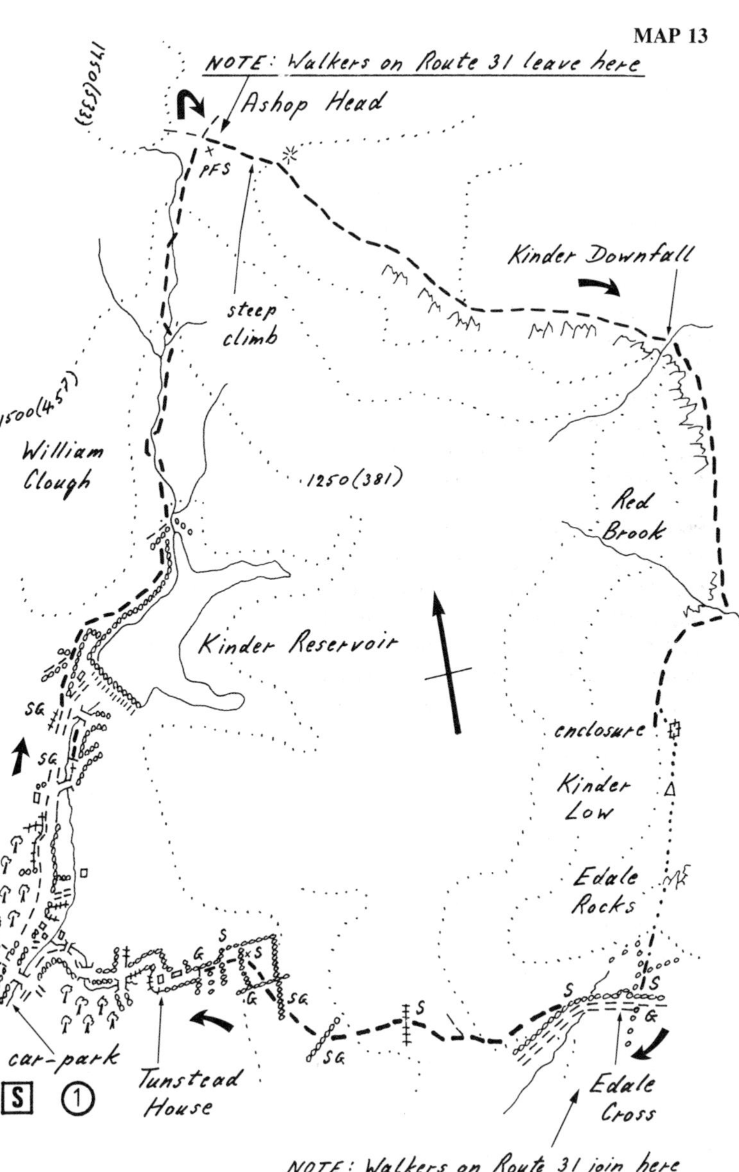
NOTE: Walkers on Route 31 leave here
Ashop Head
1750(533)
PFS
steep climb
Kinder Downfall
1500(457)
William Clough
1250(381)
Red Brook
Kinder Reservoir
SG
SG
enclosure
Kinder Low
Edale Rocks
S
S
G
SG
G
S
SG
S
S
G
car-park
Tunstead House
Edale Cross
S
1
NOTE: Walkers on Route 31 join here

Length: 8½ miles (14 km).

Ascent: 1200 ft (370 m).

Starting and finishing point: A small car-park on the Kinder Road opposite Bowden Bridge about 1 mile (1.6 km) from Hayfield (110-049870).

Maps: Landranger 110; Outdoor Leisure The Dark Peak.

Route description (Map 13)
All ramblers worthy of the name will pause before starting their day's walking to inspect and pay homage at a small plaque on the back wall of the car-park quarry. It commemorates one of the greatest events in the history of the walking movement. See (1) The Mass Trespass.

Leave the car-park into the road and turn L. After about ½ mile (800 m) the road bends R over a bridge. Cross and after a few yards leave the road through a small gate and go along a footpath to the R of the river. Soon cross the river over a bridge to the L and reach a minor road (the dam of Kinder Reservoir is over to the R). Turn R and go through a small gate to the L of the main gates leading to the dam and the waterworks buildings. A clear path rises up the hillside and then later parallel with the water's edge; follow this past the dam to the far end of the reservoir (ignore any paths going up to the L). At this point you reach open country; keep in the same general direction following the path on the L-hand side of the stream which comes down into the reservoir. The path crosses and recrosses the stream several times; where the stream divides take the R-hand branch. Eventually after 1 mile (1.6 km) from the reservoir reach the top of the ridge (Ashop Head) at a PFS where two paths cross (the crossing path is the Pennine Way which is now followed as far as the Kinder Downfall).

Turn R and after a short distance climb steeply up to the edge of

Kinder Scout from Ashop Head. The route goes straight up the steep slope to the edge of the plateau.

the Kinder plateau. On reaching the top of the steep rise at a large cairn continue on the path which goes half R along the edge. Continue along this for about 1½ miles (2.5 km) to reach the Downfall. Those who have never previously visited the Downfall should recognise it easily – at this point the edge turns to the R to form a huge and spectacular amphitheatre; the Kinder River reaches the edge here and descends down the rocks in a waterfall.

Cross the stream – safely away from the edge of the rocks – and continue to follow the edge (but now heading south). There is a good path at the start, but later this tends to disappear. After ⅔ mile (1.1 km) you will reach a stream and ½ mile (800 m) further you should see an Ordnance Survey obelisk up to the L. Rise up the moor to reach the obelisk – this is an extremely eroded part of the plateau – and then continue keeping in the same direction as before. Just before the obelisk there is a fenced area where trials are being carried out on regeneration of the moor surface by the National Trust High Peak Estate – PLEASE DO NOT ENTER. Soon reach a prominent outcrop – Edale Rocks – and keep on now slightly R. With luck a footpath will be found which goes over the moor to a wall. Keep the wall on your R as you descend to a wide stile in a crossing wall.

Cross the stile and turn R through a gateway – notice the old cross on the R – see page 158. Follow the farm road down keeping to the L of a wall. After just over ¼ mile (400 m), where a stream comes on the L, go over a stile to the R and follow the clear path across the hillside. At the end the path curves to the R and starts descending. Go L at a path junction and continue down to a ladder stile. From the stile continue to follow the path as it slowly descends across four fields crossing walls on the way at small gates. In the fourth field turn L over a stile by a PFS and go down towards a farm. Pass in front of the farmhouse bending to the R just beyond down a footpath. This leads to the minor road leading up to the farm. Turn L and walk down the road to a crossroads. Go straight ahead, soon reaching the car-park.

Kinder Downfall under summer conditions.

(1) *The Mass Trespass*
The idea of the trespass probably originated a short time before in an incident in which a party of ramblers from Rowarth was stopped by gamekeepers, although resentment at being denied access to large areas of the Peak District moors had been simmering for a long time as had frustration at the slow progress being made to alter the situation. In no way was the trespass a secret affair, in fact just the opposite. Local newspapers ran headlines giving details of it and leaflets were distributed; news of the plans was also, of course, passed from rambler to rambler by word of mouth. This had the desired effect of bringing ramblers to the correct place at the correct time, but it also enabled local landowners and police to prepare themselves for the event. As is still the case today on similar occasions, estimates of the numbers involved varied considerably. The number of ramblers was put between 200 and 800, the opposition in the form of gamekeepers at eighteen to sixty (outnumbered, but unlike the ramblers well armed with hefty sticks!) and the police at about thirty.

An injunction had been taken out on one of the leaders, Bernard Rothman, but this could not be served despite a police presence at the railway stations at both Manchester and Hayfield as he had reached the latter by bicycle. A meeting was held in the disused quarry used for the start of this route and then the crowd of ramblers started up the path in William Clough. At a high point the group left the track and climbed directly up the face of Kinder to meet there other walkers who had come across the plateau. For the vast majority of ramblers the trespass passed off peacefully enough, but a few encountered violence on the part of some of the keepers. On their return down the Kinder Road the party was stopped and six arrested.

The trial of the six was held at Derby on 7 and 8 July 1932. The charge brought against all of them was of riotously assembling to disturb the peace; in addition one of the group was charged with inflicting grievous bodily harm on one of the keepers. All but one

Trial enclosures being established just to the north of Kinder Low during the summer of 1987.

were found guilty and received a total of seventeen months' imprisonment. From accounts there were, it seems, a number of disquieting features about the trial.

Opinions differed considerably at the time as to the advisability of the trespass and afterwards as to what was gained from it. Even today the subject can arouse some heat! Although in the short term the Mass Trespass probably achieved little – there are some who will maintain that it made things worse – in the long term it hardened people's determination to bring about changes and increased public awareness of the problems. If that is so, then it played a worthwhile part in whatever success was eventually achieved.

Route 14 The Southern Edges of Kinder

Of all villages in the Peak District Edale has by far the closest association with walking and with walkers. It is not therefore inappropriate that two of the routes given in this book should start from there. This route – the shortest and easiest of the five – falls into two distinct sections: the first is fairly easy, going westwards from Edale along the valley on footpaths and farm roads as far as Jacob's Ladder followed by a climb to the southern edge of the Kinder plateau; the second section is harder, along the edge to Grindslow Knoll and the final descent back to Edale. The only serious climbing is from Jacob's Ladder to the edge. The route throughout follows reasonably well-marked paths which in clear conditions should be fairly easy to follow; in thick mist some difficulty may be found at one or two points on the edge (the striking-off point for the head of Grindsbrook Clough, for example) and there some care is necessary. (This crosses an access area – see page 54.)

Length: 8 miles (13 km).

Ascent: 1650 ft (500 m).

Starting and finishing point: The car-park at Edale (110-124853).

Maps: Landranger 110; Outdoor Leisure The Dark Peak.

Route description (Map 14)

Before leaving on your walk read about the history of the village and the valley – see (1) Edale. Leave the car-park to the L of the toilet block and turn R in the road. Go under the railway bridge and walk up the road to the top of the village by The Old Nags Head. Opposite the school turn L, i.e. to the R of the caravan park entrance, to a small gate (PFS 'Upper Booth and Hayfield'). Continue for about 300 yds (275 m) and then turn L over a stile (PFS). Cross the narrow field to a second PFS on the opposite side and turn R. Keep by the hedge until it meets a wall; there cross a stile to the L and head across the field beyond. Keeping in the same direction cross six fields, crossing walls at stiles on the way, until you reach a fence. Turn L down to a stile (the one to the R is an access point to open country) and continue down the field to a stile in a broken wall at the bottom. Cut the corner beyond to another stile and then down a long field to the bottom R-hand corner where you can enter a farm road through a gate. Go down the farm road until you reach a farm; there bend L, then R to a gate and stile. Go half L through the farmyard to a minor road by a bridge.

Turn R and follow the road for nearly ½ mile (800 m) to Lee Farm – there is a National Trust Information Point here – see (2) The Kinder Estate. Continue on the farm road past the farm for another ½ mile (800 m) to a small bridge. Climb the steep slope to the R on the opposite side keeping to R of the fence. At the top follow the very obvious path slowly climbing until you eventually reach a gate. Go through and continue in the same direction keeping to the L of a wall until you reach another gate. Go through the gate and have a look at the lovely old cross on the R – see (3) Edale Cross. Go back through the gate and turn L over a wide stile, i.e. to the R from your original direction. Go up the moor with a broken wall on your L until, after 130 yds (120 m), another broken wall joins it from the R. Here turn R and follow a path which keeps to the L of this second wall.

After ½ mile (800 m) reach a prominent rock (the Noe Stool) and a cairn; just beyond, the wall bends to the R. Do not bend with it,

MAP 14

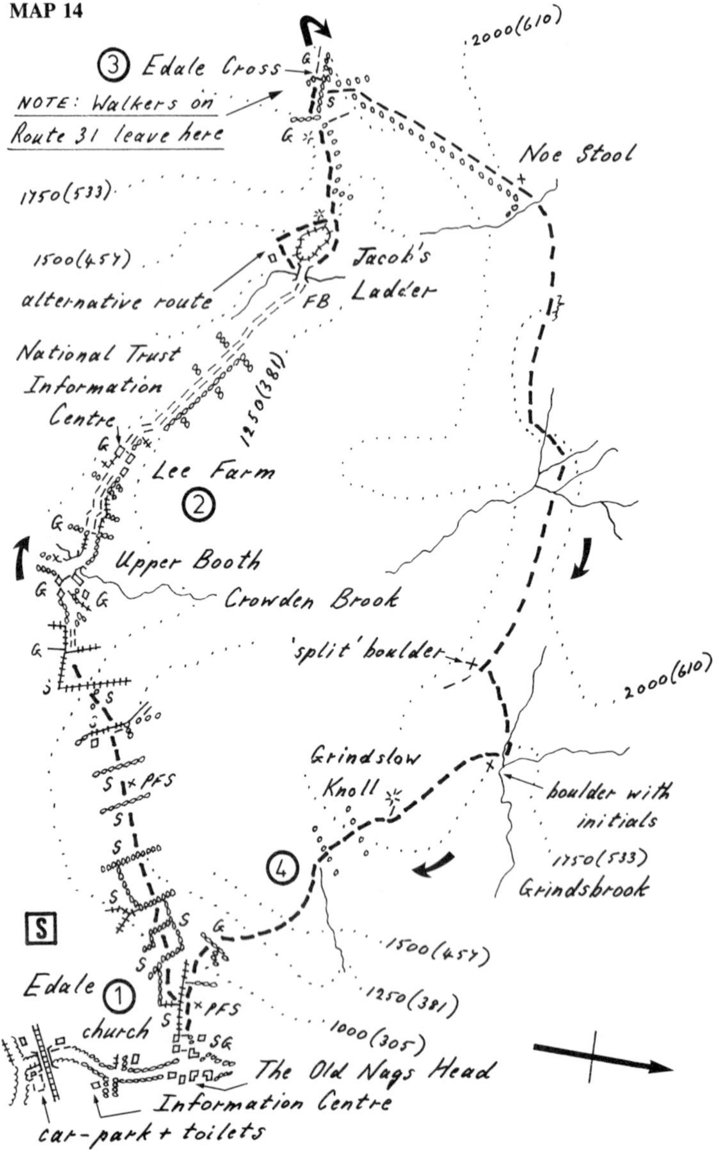

③ Edale Cross

NOTE: Walkers on Route 31 leave here

2000(610)

Noe Stool

1750(533)

1500(457)

Jacob's Ladder

alternative route

FB

National Trust Information Centre

1250(381)

Lee Farm

②

Upper Booth

Crowden Brook

'split' boulder

2000(610)

Grindslow Knoll

boulder with initials

1750(533)

Grindsbrook

④

S

1500(457)

Edale ①

PFS

church

1250(381)

SG

1000(305)

The Old Nags Head

Information Centre

car-park + toilets

but cross the small stream ahead and follow the path bending slightly R along the edge. About ¾ mile (1.2 km) from the Noe Stool you will reach a clough – along the way are other prominent rocks: Pym Chair and the Wool Packs. At the end the path bends L down to a stream. Cross and rise up on the opposite side bending to the R over a small side tributary. Follow the path which continues to follow the edge for just over ½ mile (800 m) until you reach a curious boulder on the R; this has a vertical crack breaking it into two parts resembling two horns. Here the path divides; take the L fork which goes across the open moor. Soon you will reach the head of a prominent clough, Grindsbrook, between two tributaries. Go up to the R towards some rocks – one of these has a curious 'mushroom' shape and has initials scratched into the rock. Here pick up a very clear path which keeps along the edge with a steep drop down to the L. Follow this for ¼ mile (400 m) until it reaches a ridge top – climb a few yards up the ridge to the R to a summit cairn, this is Grindslow Knoll. Go back down the ridge to the path and turn to the R, i.e. apart from the detour to the summit, you will be crossing the ridge and dropping down the opposite side keeping in the same direction. This is an old way down from the moor – see (4) The Sled Road.

After a long descent reach a gate in a wall (access point). Beyond continue to descend following a very obvious hollow-way; this goes ahead and then bends to the L following the R-hand side of the field. At the bottom go through a wall gap and on for a few yards to join your outward path. Follow this back to Edale. In the village turn R for the car-park.

(1) *Edale (110-124857)*

The name Edale was being used by 1362, earlier forms being Aidele and Eydale. It is a name best applied to the valley generally rather than to the main village as there are altogether five separate groups of houses: Nether Booth, Ollerbrook Booth, Grindsbrook Booth, Barber Booth and Upper Booth. The common word 'Booth' is Scandinavian in origin and denoted a temporary hut or shelter used by herdsmen. By the sixteenth century these had become farms. They were all on the north side of the valley for in that position maximum light would be obtained; the settlements in other valleys are similar. Although well served by packhorse trails coming into the valley – there were no fewer than five of these – it would probably have been a somewhat isolated community due to the high ground imposing a barrier on three sides. Up to 1633, when the first chapel was built, the devout of Edale had to walk over to Castleton – in whose parish it lay – for services and even the dead had to go the same way, carried on broad shoulders over Hollins Cross, for burial. Reverse flow took place after the 1790s, however, when a cotton mill was built in the valley – this is still there but has now been converted into flats. The railway reached Edale in 1894, emerging from the Cowburn Tunnel near Barber Booth.

Skiing is practised there in the winter months, but walking is undoubtedly the main attraction for the great plateau of Kinder lies just a short distance to the north. It is moreover the start of the Pennine Way, that 'long green trail' first dreamed of by Tom Stephenson over fifty years ago. Rock climbers have their great centres, such as Wasdale Head in the Lakes and the Pen-y-Gwyrd in North Wales; walkers – particularly hard walkers – have Edale.

(2) *The Kinder Estate*
Kinder Scout was formerly part of the Hayfield Estate put up for sale in 1982. Some small areas were purchased by the Peak Park Joint Planning Board and private individuals, but the very substantial area of Kinder Scout itself was secured by the National Trust. About two-thirds of the purchase price was provided by grants from the Countryside Commission and the National Heritage Memorial Fund, leaving £200,000 which was borrowed by the Trust. To meet this heavy burden and also to provide funds for improvement work in the first few years the National Trust Appeal for Kinder Scout was launched. This acquisition became part of the Trust's High Peak Estate which covers not just Kinder itself but also a substantial part of Bleaklow and all of the Howden Moors. The estate comes under the overall direction of the East Midlands Regional Office of the Trust at Worksop, but on the ground is the

The Old Nags Head at Edale.

The Old Nags Head
HIKERS BAR

responsibility of a head warden supported by a team which includes estate wardens and skilled workmen for maintenance/rebuilding work on the estate. The local estate office is at Edale End, near Hope. As it is the firm policy of the Trust to allow public access to its open spaces, subject only to appropriate consideration for local farming and conservation needs, the Trust's ownership and special care of this beautiful area will be welcomed by walkers everywhere.

(3) *Edale Cross (110-077861)*

The fine old cross, now protected on three sides by sturdy walls, at the highest point of the way over from Edale to Hayfield is called Edale Cross. It is about 5 ft (1.5 m) high, of gritstone, with the rough head of a cross set on a sturdy shaft (the left arm is slightly broken); there are the outlines of crosses cut into the face and rear, also a simple one on the square top surface. On the front are initials and the date 1810. It is almost certainly medieval, probably erected both as a guidestone on an old way which came through here and as a marker in the ancient Royal Forest (the three wards of the Forest, Longdendale, Ashop and Edale, and of Champayne met at this point). It was also called Champion Cross, a name probably derived from the name of the latter ward. The date refers to a restoration early last century.

(4) *The Sled Road*

The local inhabitants of the Edale valley had the right to cut peat, for use as fuel, on the area of moor above Grindslow Knoll – known as the right of turbary. When cut, the peat was brought down into the valley on sledges. This practice over a long period of time gradually produced a 'hollow-way' down the hillside which is still clearly visible today. Its name is the Sled Road.

Route 15 The Edge – Kinder Scout

The Edge forms part of the northern boundary of the Kinder Scout plateau owned by the National Trust – little more therefore really needs to be said in its favour for all the edges of Kinder offer magnificent walking with far-reaching views over the surrounding

Edale Cross.

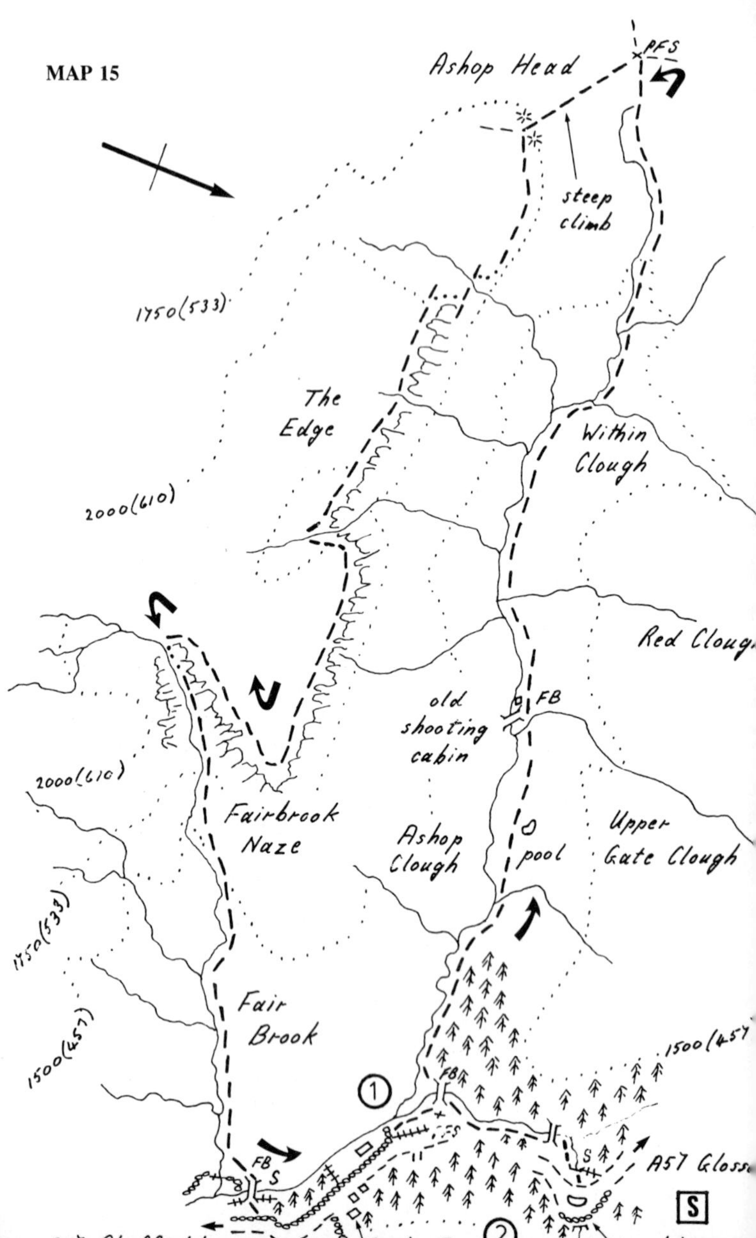

MAP 15
Ashop Head
PFS
steep climb
1750(533)
The Edge
2000(610)
Within Clough
Red Clough
old shooting cabin
FB
2000(610)
Fairbrook Naze
Ashop Clough
pool
Upper Gate Clough
1750(533)
Fair Brook
1500(457)
1500(457)
FB
1
FB
S
PFS
S
A57 Glossop
A57 Sheffield
2
Snake Inn
parking area
S

area. Nor is that all, for the quality of the routes leading to and from the Edge – the Snake Path and the descent by Fair Brook – is very high. From start to finish not one yard of this walk will give anything but sheer pleasure. Clear paths, following well-defined lines such as streams, are used throughout which makes route finding comparatively easy. Gradients are gentle, with the exception of fairly short stretches up to and down from the Edge itself. (This crosses an access area – see page 54.)

Length: 9 miles (14 km).

Ascent: 1100 ft (330 m).

Starting and finishing point: A car-park at Birchen Clough Bridge on the A57, Sheffield–Glossop road, about 2 miles (3 km) south-east from the top of the Snake Pass (110-109914).

Maps: Landranger 110; Outdoor Leisure The Dark Peak.

Route description (Map 15)
From the car-park cross the road and descend steps to a ladder stile. Cross the stream which issues from a tunnel just to the L and walk downstream on the L bank. At a stream junction go L. After a few yards pass a bridge, still keeping in the same direction on the L bank. After 600 yds (550 m) at the end of the forest cross a footbridge over the stream to the right – see (1) The Engineers' Bridge – and take a path which soon bends R. This is the Snake Path.

Follow this clear path up the valley, keeping to the R of the stream, for 3¼ miles (5 km) to an obvious crossing path (the Pennine Way) on a ridge top (PFS) – Ashop Head. Turn L along this path which soon starts to climb steeply up to the edge of the Kinder Scout plateau. On the edge of the plateau at two cairns turn L to follow a path along the edge; down to the L there is a magnificent view of the Snake Path as it comes up the moor and further over a glimpse of cars on the busy Snake Pass road. Where the path fades away strike up the hillside to the R to a higher path;

where that fades strike up again to a third path. This path, which is very clear, keeps along the edge of the plateau above the gritstone cliff.

About 1¼ miles (2 km) from the beginning of the walk along the edge the rocky ravine of the Nether Red Brook will be passed by a diversion to the R and ⅔ mile (1.1 km) further along still the edge bends sharply to the R at Fairbrook Naze. Turn to the R with the edge, keeping with it for about 750 yds (700 m) until it bends again, this time to the L at a clough. There, leave the edge by dropping down to the L to the clough stream. Turn L and follow the stream down over boulders until you reach a path. The way down is now along this path to the L of the stream. Continue to descend for 1⅔ miles (2.5 km) with the stream to your R until you reach a wall. Here, follow the path to the L by the wall to a footbridge. Cross the bridge, then the stile beyond and follow a path into the wood. This soon bends L to the road (A57).

Turn L along the road for 700 yds (650 m), passing the Snake Inn – see (2) below – until the forest recommences on the L. A few yards later go L over a ladder stile (by a Forestry Commission sign) and down a path to the river. Do not cross at the footbridge, but instead turn R to keep on the R side of the river. This is the path taken earlier and leads back to the car-park.

(1) *The Engineers' Bridge (110-107908)*
The sturdy footbridge, which carries the Snake Path over the brook through Lady Clough, was constructed in 1977 by Sheffield University Officer Training Corps, Royal Engineer Troop.

(2) *The Snake Inn (110-113906)*
This well-known inn, which stands at a height of about 1000 ft (305 m) on the A57, was built in 1821 to serve traffic on the new turnpike constructed by Thomas Telford over the Snake Pass. Originally named Lady Clough House – after the nearby clough – it became the Snake Inn in honour of the Duke of Devonshire, whose crest was and still is a snake, and who at that time was the owner of the inn as well as a vast area of local moorland.

Route 16 The Roaches

The Roaches, with Hen Cloud and Ramshaw Rocks, mark both the western boundary of the Peak District National Park and the southern extremity of the hill areas of England. The name is probably derived from the French word *roche* meaning rock, a singularly appropriate name to describe the great gritstone rampart, arranged in two tiers, which faces out over the Cheshire plain. The Roaches – originally part of the Swythamley Estate – were purchased in 1980 by the National Park Authority. One unusual – and rare – inhabitant of the area is the wallaby which was introduced there, along with other animals, in a private zoo which is now no longer in existence. The cliff is, of course, also noted for rock climbing and some of the pioneers, such as Joe Brown and Don Whillans, put up new climbs there. This route goes along the Roaches and around the valley of the Black Brook, a tributary of the Dane.

Length: 8½ miles (14 km).

Ascent: 1550 ft (470 m).

Starting and finishing point: A lay-by on the minor road which runs to the north-west from the village of Upper Hulme. Upper Hulme is on the A53, Leek-Buxton road (119-004621).

Maps: Landranger 118 and 119; Outdoor Leisure The White Peak (West Sheet).

Route description (Map 16)
Facing the lay-by go through a small gate on the R and up a broad track on to the Roaches Estate (PFS to the Roaches). After 125 yds (115 m) turn L on to a minor track which rises up towards the rocks and a cottage (Rockhall). At a wall in front of the cottage turn L for a few yards then R through a gap. Climb straight up the hillside towards the rocks to reach the bottom of a flight of stone steps which will take you up to the top of the first tier of rocks. At the top

MAP 16

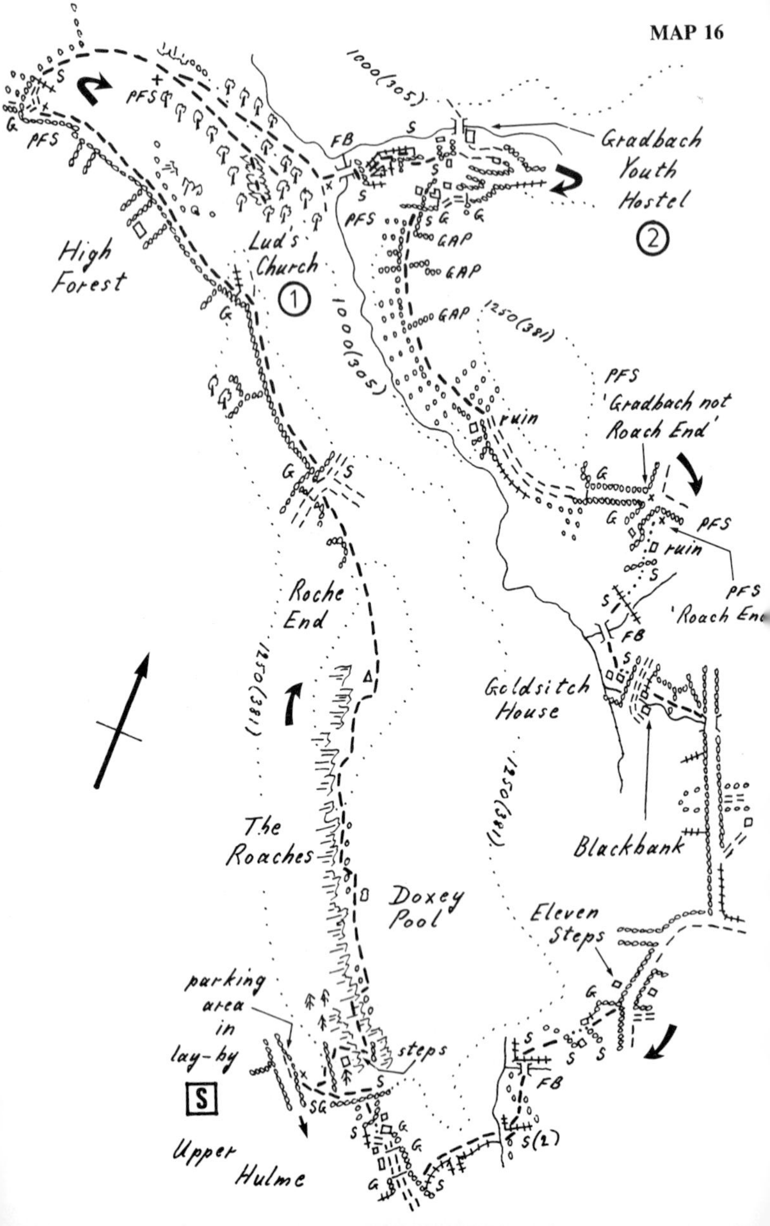

Gradbach Youth Hostel

②

Lud's Church

①

High Forest

1000(305)

1250(381)

PFS

FB

GAP

GAP

GAP

ruin

PFS 'Gradbach not Roach End'

PFS

ruin

PFS 'Roach End'

FB

Roche End

Goldsitch House

Blackbank

The Roaches

Doxey Pool

Eleven Steps

parking area in lay-by

steps

FB

S(2)

S

Upper Hulme

at a stone wall turn L and follow a path along a broad terrace. After 250 yds (225 m) the path bends R and climbs up to the top of the ridge. There cross a broken wall and turn L along a clear path; this runs for 1 mile (1.6 km) to an OS obelisk at the highest point of the fell. Along the way you will pass a small but lovely pool – Doxey Pool.

Keep on the path beyond the summit as it curves to the L and drops down to a road. Cross to a stile opposite and go up by a wall to a gate. Keep in the same direction along the ridge with a wall to the L. Pass a small wood to the L and, shortly afterwards, where the wall bends L and descends, keep with it. Continue along the path by the wall for nearly ⅔ mile (1.1 km) to a gate at a wall corner. Do not go through but turn R up a farm road (PFS). After 200 yds (180 m) at a corner go over a fence at a stile (PFS) and continue in the same direction down a path in a well-defined hollow-way. After 700 yds (650 m) reach a path junction at a sign 'Lud's Church' (there is a superb viewpoint from the rocks over to the L). Take the branch to the R which leads in about 250 yds (225 m) to the entrance of a deep ravine. This is Lud's Church – see (1).

After inspecting the ravine, return along the path to the junction. There turn back half R (i.e. the L-branch from your original direction) and descend down through the wood on a beautiful path. At a PFS go down to the L to a footbridge. Cross and go up half R. After 60 yds (55 m) turn L over a stile and take the path which goes down half L between fences. At a gate ('Private' notice) go R over a stile and continue in the same direction to a further stile. A few yards away are gates made from cart-wheels which lead into the forecourt of a large building – see (2) Gradbach Mill. Go up the drive to the R of the building to reach a road. Turn R.

After 250 yds (225 m) leave the road to the L up a rough lane. (Before going up the lane pay a visit to the Scouts' Camp Chapel on the L.) At a farm the farm road bends to the L to a gate by a barn. After a few yards go L over a stile and by the wall (i.e. the wall will be on your R) to a gap. Go through the gap and turn L. Go up the L-hand side of the field to a gateway in the corner where you can change to the L-hand side of the wall. Keep on this side for ⅔ mile (1.1 km) to an old ruin (Cloughhead). Pass it to the L to reach a rough farm road. Follow this to a metalled road. Immediately leave it again over a stile on the R (PFS 'Roach End').

Head across the moor (no path) to pass between two stone pillars to the L of a wall corner and on to a stile in a wall. After a few yards turn R to a gap and then half L to a stile in a fence. Here pick up a path which crosses a footbridge and heads towards the L side of a farmhouse (Goldsitch House). Pass the farm, cross a farm road and then go half L to a stile which leads into a second farm road. Go through the gap ahead, past a ruin and continue in the same direction over two fields to a road. There turn R. Shortly go R at a junction and L at a fork soon afterwards. 125 yds (115 m) after the cottage (Eleven Steps) leave the road through a gate on the R and go towards a house. Cross two stiles to the L of the house and then a third just beyond. Gradually descend to a footbridge over a small stream (i.e. a side stream to the main one which is over to your R). Continue parallel to the main stream until you can cross it after two more stiles. The path rises on the far side to the R of a fence. Pass a fence corner and continue across to a second corner, then follow the fence as it curves L to reach a stile in a wall.

Turn R in the farm road beyond, soon passing through a gate into a further farmyard. Cross a second gate. At the end by a barn go through a third gate and then turn R to a stile by a small hut. Go across the field beyond to a further stile in a wall. This leads into a farm road. Turn L along it back to the parking place.

(1) *Lud's Church (118-987656)*
Lud's Church is a long, deep but narrow cleft in Forest Wood on the slopes of Back Forest above the Dane valley, probably formed by a great land-slip along the hillside. The walls are precipitous gritstone, fern- and moss-covered, overhung by trees. A quiet place, a secret place, a place of magic. Any tale told about Lud's Church can readily be believed.

The name is said to be derived from that of Walter de Ludank, a fourteenth-century Lollard who met here to worship with others of similar faith but was captured after a fight. The Lollards are often

The Roaches with Hen Cloud in the background.

thought of as followers of John Wyclif, although actually the name preceded him. They were a dissenting group who called not merely for changes in the teachings of the established Church, but also for widespread structural reforms. It is scarcely surprising that such views would attract opposition and from 1400 statutes began to be introduced with the intention of suppressing them. Some prominent Lollards were burned at the stake. It continued, however, as an organised sect until early in the sixteenth century.

In those days the deep ravine on the lonely western moorlands would have offered the Lollards a suitable place for secret gatherings.

(2) *Gradbach Mill (118-994661)*

The large and robust, but somewhat plain, building on the south-east side of the Dane valley, now a youth hostel, was built by Thomas Dakeyne of Darley Dale in 1785 to replace an earlier mill which had been destroyed by fire. It was used for flax spinning until 1837 when it was sold due to the bankruptcy of the owner; afterwards it was used for silk spinning. It was vacant, however, by 1862 and remained so until bought by Sir John Harpur Crewe of Calke Abbey near Derby in about 1885 for use as an estate sawmill. For most of this century up to 1977 the mill was used as a barn for farming purposes with the mill pond employed as a watercress bed. It was purchased by the Youth Hostels Association in 1978, opening after considerable conversion work three years later.

Route 17 Miller's Dale

Water-cum-Jolly Dale has far too intriguing a name to be ignored by any visitor to the Peak District – it also happens to be extremely beautiful. In addition to Water-cum-Jolly this route brings together four other dales: Miller's, Ravensdale, Tansley and Monk's, each of which – with the exception perhaps of Tansley, which is very short – would be worth walking in its own right. Tideswell makes an excellent midday stopping point and there are also two cafés back at the finish at Miller's Dale station.

Gradbach Mill.

MAP 17

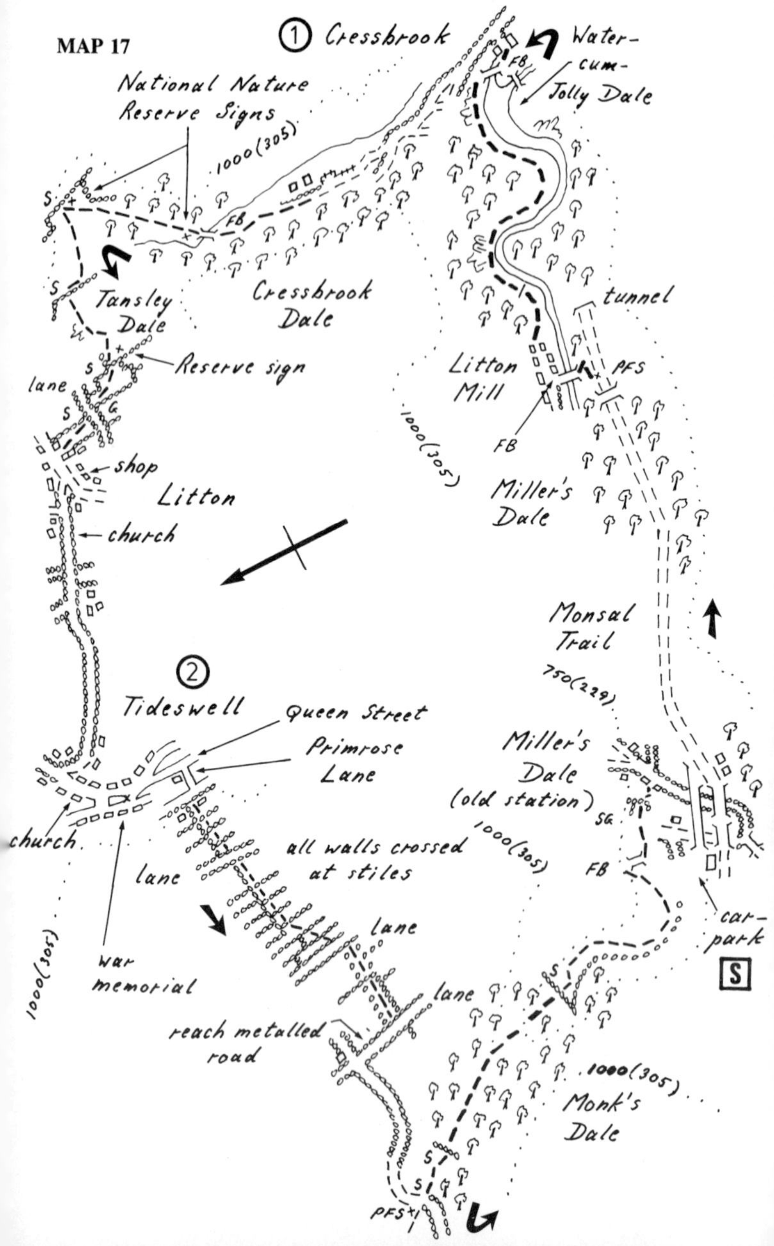

① Cressbrook

National Nature Reserve Signs

Water-cum-Jolly Dale

FB

1000(305)

S

S

FB

Tansley Dale

Cressbrook Dale

tunnel

Reserve sign

S

lane

S

G

Litton Mill

PFS

FB

shop

Litton

1000(305)

Miller's Dale

church

Monsal Trail

② Tideswell

750(229)

Queen Street

Primrose Lane

Miller's Dale (old station)

church

SG

all walls crossed at stiles

1000(305)

lane

FB

car-park

lane

war memorial

S

1000(305)

lane

S

reach metalled road

1000(305)

Monk's Dale

S

S

PFS

Length: 9½ miles (15 km).

Ascent: 1050 ft (320 m).

Starting and finishing point: The car-park at the Old Miller's Dale station on the Monsal Trail (119-139733).

Maps: Landranger 119; Outdoor Leisure The White Peak (West and East Sheets).

Route description (Map 17)
The first part of the route runs along the Monsal Trail – see page 220. From the parking area go on to the track and turn L over the viaduct. You will soon pass some old lime kilns on the R. After 1½ miles (2.5 km), immediately after a bridge, go L through a gap and down to a footbridge (a sign indicates that there is a blocked tunnel ahead). In the road beyond turn R and go through the gates of Litton Mills. Go ahead between the tall buildings of the mill (this is a concessionary path only), turning R at the end to reach the river bank. Follow a lovely path through woods keeping on the L-hand side of the river. Later the river widens and bends to the R with tall limestone cliffs on each side – this section is particularly beautiful and known as Water-cum-Jolly Dale.

At the end go over a footbridge into a stoneyard. Continue ahead bending L between buildings to a road – see (1) Cressbrook Mill. Turn L and immediately R at a junction. The road climbs steeply. After 600 yds (550 m) go L down a side road (sign 'Ravensdale'). Soon pass to the L of some cottages on a footpath and enter a wood. The path goes through the wood, crosses a footbridge and then starts to climb slowly up the R-hand side of the valley. Eventually you will reach a stile at the top by a National Nature Reserve notice; do not cross this stile, but turn L on a path which immediately descends back again into the valley. The climb followed immediately by a steep descent back into the same valley may seem like a waste of a great deal of effort – and it is – but there is no right of way along the valley itself.

At the bottom keep to the R of a wall for 130 yds (120 m), then go

L over a stile. Follow the path up into the minor dale which comes in here – this is Tansley Dale. At the end go up some steps to a stile in a wall corner. Go half R in the next field to a stile also in a corner which leads into a lane. Turn L in the lane for 45 yds (40 m) then R over a stile. Cross the field half L to a stile which will bring you into the street at Litton. Turn L through the village. At a road junction turn R past the Red Lion Inn and a little later the church. After ¾ mile (1.2 km) the road bends R and descends into Tideswell – see (2) Tideswell.

Turn L at the main road passing the George Hotel and the exceptionally fine village church. Keep on the main road through the village; just past the War Memorial on the R is Cherry Tree Square. Fork R up Queen Street by the Horse and Jockey public house, then R up a narrow lane, Primrose Lane. At a crossing street go half R to a stile by a gate. Keeping to the R climb slowly up four fields crossing walls at stiles. At the top cross a lane and continue in the same direction over four more fields. In the fifth field go half L to a stile and then in the same direction over two more fields to a green lane. Cross to a stile opposite and continue on the L-hand side of two long fields to enter a third lane (Note: the stile at the end of the second long field is a few yards to the R). Turn R and follow the lane to a crossroads by a house.

Turn L. The road descends steeply into a valley (Monk's Dale). In the valley turn L over a stile and go down into the ravine ahead. The path to be followed is very clear – it is also very rough and in wet weather very slippery and requires care (it runs moreover through a National Nature Reserve and all wildlife in it should therefore be treated with respect – as, of course, it should everywhere). Eventually, after 1½ miles (2.5 km), leave the reserve at a gate and descend to a road. Turn R, soon going under a tall viaduct. Further along, do not cross the road bridge over the Wye, but instead turn R up to the station car-park.

Water-cum-Jolly Dale.

(1) *Cressbrook Mill (119-173727)*
The large building at Cressbrook was originally a cotton mill built in 1815 on a site already occupied by a smaller mill constructed by Richard Arkwright about thirty years earlier. The mill has four floors arranged in twelve bays of which the centre four stand proud supporting a pediment containing a clock. On the roof is a small bellcote; the bell there was used to summon workers to the factory. Some two to three hundred persons worked at the new mill. The wide stretch of water in Water-cum-Jolly Dale was originally a mill pond providing water for the factory and produced by damming the river a short distance upstream from the mill. William Newton (see page 132) was manager at the mill and by all accounts treated his workers well, which is more than can be said for the manager of Litton Mills, higher up the valley. Built in 1782 that mill became notorious for the bad treatment of its labour force. The first effective Factory Act of 1833 had still to be passed, and even when it was it left much to be desired. At the turn of the century – before the formation of trade unions – there was little to protect workers from tyrannical employers who cared much more for their profits than for the welfare of their workers. Litton Mills was destroyed by fire in about 1870 and rebuilt some four years later.
(2) *Tideswell*
The village was called Tidesuuelle at the time of Domesday Book and Tiddeswell in Pipe Rolls of 1230; the name originally derived from 'Tidi's Stream'. It was a village of some importance even in medieval times, being granted a market in 1251. Visitors should know that the name is pronounced 'Tidzel' and not 'Tides-well'.

It is a large village with public houses, banks, restaurants, a fish and chip take-away and a fair number of shops. It also boasts a superb church, justifiably known both for its size and splendour as the 'Cathedral of the Peak'. Although there are some signs of an earlier building the present church was built in the fifty years between 1340 and about 1390, construction being held up for a few years around 1348 by the advent of the Black Death. Little, however, has changed since then. There is a fine brass to Bishop Robert Pursglove which shows him in full pre-Reformation eucharistic vestments and the tombs of Sir John Foljambe, a generous benefactor of the church, and Sir Sampson Meverill, a local man who probably fought at Agincourt. Much of the woodwork was carved by Advent Hunstone, a local craftsman. In the churchyard is the grave of William Newton, the 'Minstrel of the Peak' whom we have met already.

Route 18 Dovedale

The Dove rises on Axe Edge, to the south-west of Buxton, and leaves the Peak District National Park to the south of Thorpe near Ashbourne. Of this, it is generally accepted that the finest part lies between Milldale and St Mary's Bridge near to its junction with the Manifold. It is difficult to imagine any list of 'best walks' which cannot find a place for that part. Despite this, I was warned off Dovedale several times. 'It isn't what it used to be' and 'It is too overcrowded for me' were some of the comments that I received. With loads of visitors every year – most of whom stay south of Milldale – it is undeniably overcrowded for much of the time. However, enough of that! Whilst those familiar with the Dovedale of old may well lament a paradise lost, the first-time visitor – particularly if he visits it at a quiet time – will still almost certainly come away totally entranced by its beauty. This route goes upstream as far as Milldale, then leaves the river to the east to join the Tissington Trail which is then followed southwards back to Thorpe. Following work by the National Park Authority in collaboration with the National Trust the paths throughout are now in very good condition.

Length: 10 miles (16 km).

Ascent: 900 ft (280 m).

Starting and finishing point: The large car-park on the site of the old railway station at Thorpe, now on the Tissington Trail (119-166503).

Maps: Landranger 119; Outdoor Leisure The White Peak (West and East Sheets).

MAP 18

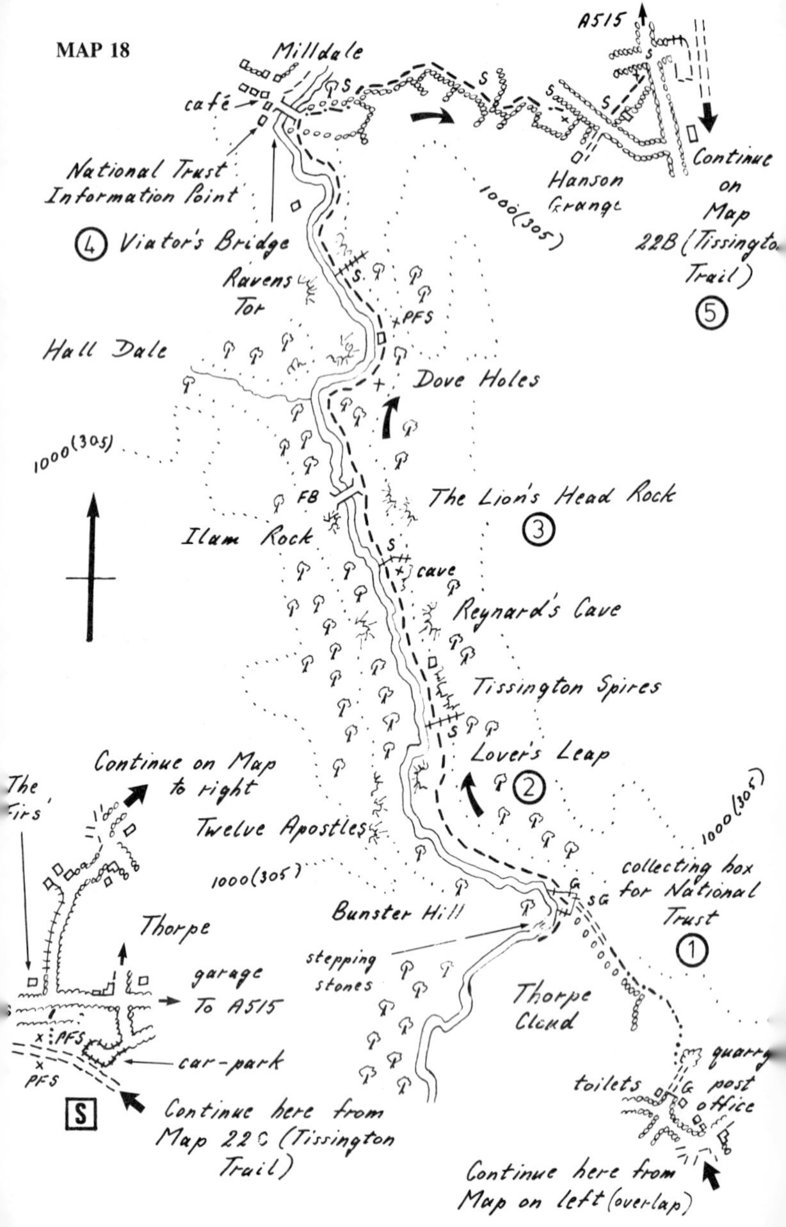

Milldale
café
National Trust Information Point
④ Viator's Bridge
Ravens Tor
Hall Dale
Dove Holes
A515
Hanson Grange
1000 (305)
Continue on Map 22B (Tissington Trail)
⑤
PFS
1000 (305)
FB
The Lion's Head Rock
③
Ilam Rock
cave
Reynard's Cave
Tissington Spires
Lover's Leap
②
1000 (305)
Continue on Map to right
The Firs
Twelve Apostles
1000 (305)
collecting box for National Trust
①
G
SG
Bunster Hill
Thorpe
stepping stones
garage
To A515
Thorpe Cloud
PFS
car-park
PFS
quarry
toilets
G
post office
S
Continue here from Map 22C (Tissington Trail)
Continue here from Map on left (overlap)

Route description (Maps 18, 22B, 22C)

Leave the car-park on to the Tissington Trail and turn R. About 125 yds (115 m) from the far end of the car-park leave the Trail to the R through a small gate (PFS). Go up the field to a stile in a hedge and then, keeping in the same direction, cross a second field to another stile which leads into a road. Cross, and go down the minor road opposite, past The Firs. There is a good view from here of the prominent hill, Thorpe Cloud, over to the R which is passed a little later in the walk. At the farm keep in the same direction on the road, descending steeply to the village of Thorpe. At the main road in the village turn L and follow the road as it climbs and bends to the R.

Where a minor road comes in from the L turn R into a small car-park (toilets and post office). Go through the gate at the far end and up the field beyond on the farm road. Where this ends at a small quarry, skirt round to the L and, keeping in the same direction, drop down the field to a wall corner in the valley. Follow the wall to the L descending into the valley, keeping the wall and the prominent peak (Thorpe Cloud) to your L. This is Lin Dale which leads down to join Dovedale. In the main dale, turn R and follow the broad path to the R of the river. See (1) Dovedale, for an account of the geology of the river.

Further directions should now be unnecessary as a very obvious path keeps to the R of the river until the stone bridge at Milldale is reached. The main features passed along the way are:

(a) Stepping stones. Probably the best-known and most photogenic feature in all Dovedale, these are to the L where Dovedale is joined from Lin Dale.

(b) The hills of Thorpe Cloud and Bunster Hill, separated from each other by a sharp bend of the Dove, form the dramatic skyline to the west during the walk through Lin Dale and lower Dovedale. An ascent of Thorpe Cloud can be made from the stepping stones.

(c) Sharplow Point, Lover's Leap, is the small rocky summit just to the L of the path which offers a superb viewpoint over the Dove. Some steps have to be climbed on the path shortly before the Leap is reached and the path descends on further steps immediately afterwards. The small rock spires on the opposite side of the Dove are called the Twelve Apostles. With a name like Lover's Leap there has to be a story – for it see (2) below.

(d) Tissington Spires. These are the dramatic limestone spires with scree beneath immediately to the R of the path just after the first stile.

(e) The natural arch and Reynard's Cave. A very prominent natural limestone arch will be seen high up to the R about 200 yds (180 m) after the last of the Tissington Spires. It is possible to climb up to the arch; immediately behind is Reynard's Cave. But use care.

(f) The Lion's Head Rock. The rock face, towering over the path soon after Reynard's Cave and before the footbridge is reached, has a strong resemblance to a lion's head when seen from either direction. There is a plaque at the base. See (3) The National Trust in Dovedale.

(g) Ilam Rock. This is the tall rock spire on the opposite bank, i.e. the L bank, by the footbridge.

(h) The Dove Holes. Soon after the footbridge the river swings L then R. At the second bend two large and prominent caves will be seen in the cliffs to the R of the path. These are the Dove Holes.

(i) Viator's Bridge. This is the lovely twin-arched stone bridge at Milldale which marks the end of the section of the Dove explored on this route. For an explanation of its name, see (4).

Do not cross the bridge (except to enjoy the excellent hospitality of the small tea-shop on the corner or to take advantage of the toilets just before or to have a look inside the National Trust Information Barn). Instead, at the end of the bridge, turn R and follow a path which climbs steeply up a hill, keeping to the R of a wood and a broken wall (PFS). Where the steep climb ends go to the L over a stile by a small gate. Follow the clear path beyond to the L of a wall which overlooks and goes parallel to the continuation of the Dove valley down to the L. After just over ½ mile (800 m) cross a stile and go half L still by the wall. Go over the hilltop and then, when the wall bends R, continue down the field in the same direction to a stile which leads into a minor road. Turn R.

Opposite the entrance of the farm road to New Hanson Grange

Dovedale: Tissington Spires.

and Hanson Grange, go L over a stile and cross a large field on a path which runs parallel with the wall to the R. At the end cross a further stile into a main road (A515). Cross and turn L. After a few yards turn R down a rough road into a car-park on the Tissington Trail – see page 205. Go on to the Trail and turn R.

Follow the Trail for 2¾ miles (4.5 km) to reach the old railway station of Tissington where there is a car-park, toilet and picnic tables. This is the first car-park met on the Trail and will be identified by the old platform. The village of Tissington is a short distance away up the lane to the R; if you have time it is worth a visit for it has the twin attractions of being not only one of the most beautiful villages in Derbyshire but also one of the most interesting – see (5) Tissington.

Rejoining the Trail, continue in the same direction for a further 1½ miles (2.5 km) back to the car-park at Thorpe.

(1) *Dovedale*

The Dove rises on Axe Edge to the south-west of Buxton in an area of gritstone – as is the case with most of the principal rivers of the Peak District such as the Derwent, Wye, Dane and Manifold. As far as the general area of Hartington, it flows in a gentle arc over impermeable shales, but then takes an irregular and more southward-inclined course over limestone which it leaves before its junction with the Manifold. The deep ravine of Dovedale has been carved out of this limestone by the river over long periods of time, a tribute to the eroding power of water.

Occasionally, as the river cut down into the limestone, it broke into cave systems and then passed them by leaving cave openings on the valley walls. It is thought that the Dove Holes and Reynard's Cave may owe their existence to this process. Tissington Spires and the Twelve Apostles were formed perhaps in a similar fashion, their present shape the product of much weathering since they were first exposed. Thorpe Cloud and Bunster Hill are reef knolls, formed in the Carboniferous seas (see page 32), their prominence and characteristic shape due to the greater resistance of the limestone

Dovedale: Ilam Rock.

which forms them. The numerous weirs along the river are not natural but man-made; they provide deep pools which encourage fish to gather.

(2) *The legend of Lover's Leap (119-146517)*

Sharplow Point on the Dove is also known as Lover's Leap. It is supposed to mark the spot from which a young lady, the victim of a broken love affair, tried to kill herself. Happily – so the story goes – her fall was broken by bushes and she was able to walk away. During the fall she must have thought better of it, for it is said that she lived contentedly, although singly, for many years afterwards.

(3) *The National Trust in Dovedale*

Large areas on both banks of the Dove between Milldale and its junction with the Manifold are owned by the National Trust. Further substantial areas are held to the north in Mill Dale, Wolfscote Dale and Biggin Dale. All have been acquired since 1934, largely by gifts from Sir Robert McDougall, the Pilgrim Trust and Mr E. H. Kerfoot. On the Lion's Head Rock there is a plaque which reads: 'This dale and adjoining lands became National Trust property through the vision of the late F. A. Holmes, MA, JP of Buxton who planned to that end from 1916 to 1947'. The summit and part of the hillside of High Wheeldon to the north-east of Longnor in the upper Dove valley were given by the family of Mr Holmes in fulfilment of his wishes in memory of the men of Derbyshire and Staffordshire who fell in the war of 1939–45.

(4) *Viator's Bridge (119-139547)*

This famous bridge is mentioned in an addendum to the fifth edition of *The Compleat Angler* by Izaak Walton. This addendum, on 'How to angle for trout and grayling in a clear stream', was written by Charles Cotton, a great friend of Walton, who lived nearby at Beresford Hall. This section in the book is introduced by an imaginary conversation between Piscator Junior (The Angler, Charles Cotton) and Viator (A Traveller) who were journeying together in the district. They descend into Milldale from the east down zigzags and then go on to Alstonefield by Millway Lane. Viator says: 'What's here, a bridge? Do you travel in wheelbarrows

The Hall at Tissington.

in this county? This bridge was made for nothing else – 'tis not two fingers broad.' The bridge that he describes is the narrow stone bridge of two arches which still spans the Dove at Milldale. It was originally a packhorse bridge carrying packhorse trains from the market at Alstonefield over the Dove. The parapets have been put up since Cotton's day. The bridge is now widely known as Viator's Bridge.

(5) *Tissington (119-176523)*

In the Domesday Book of 1086, this little village was called Tizinctun but, as is usually the case, other names have been used: Tiscintona in 1141, Ticintona in the Danelaw Charters of Henry II and Tyscinton in 1242. It is Old English meaning 'The village, or homestead, of Tidsige's people'.

At the time of Domesday, the village and the area around were owned by Henry de Ferrers and remained with his descendants until early in the twelfth century when they passed to the Savage family. On the death of William le Savage, the last male heir, in 1259 the estate was divided equally between two female heiresses and through them it came into the families of Meynell and Edensor. One half eventually passed by inheritance into the possession of the FitzHerbert family to which the other half was added three generations later by purchase. Thus, the Manor of Tissington was reunited after about three centuries. Since then, it has remained with the FitzHerbert family who still live in the Hall at the centre of the village.

The original Hall stood within an earthwork opposite the present building and to the north of the church until about 1609 when the construction of the new Hall began. The new Hall was enlarged in 1896 and is now an imposing building which can be seen from the road.

Many of the present buildings in the village were built by Sir Henry FitzHerbert, the third Baronet, and his sister early in the nineteenth century; for that reason many buildings hold dates between 1830 and 1860. One of the features of this activity was the provision of a number of stone rainwater cisterns, each chiselled out of a single block of stone; some of these can still be seen around the village.

Route 19 The Manifold and Hamps

Like many other valleys in the Peak those of the Hamps and Manifold have improved considerably with time for the former was the line taken by a light railway until 1934 and the latter in the nineteenth century was the scene of intensive mining activity, both products of an age when concern for the environment was less apparent than it is today. Free from this noise and bustle they now offer some of the most attractive walking in the southern region of the Park. This route follows the course of the Manifold northwards from Ilam, keeping on the high ground to the east, and then returns down the Hamps where the old railway has been converted into an attractive walking trail.

Length: 10 miles (16 km).

Ascent: 1100 ft (340 m).

Starting and finishing point: The car-park at Ilam Hall near Ilam (119-131506). Ilam is a small village about 4 miles (6.5 km) NW of Ashbourne. (Parking fee.)

Maps: Landranger 119; Outdoor Leisure The White Peak (West Sheet).

Route description (Maps 19A, 19B)
However eager you may be to start this fine walk, you would have to be remarkably lacking in curiosity to do so without at least a brief look at Ilam Estate Country Park and the village nearby – see (1) Ilam and Ilam Hall.

In the car-park at the side of the Hall, facing the National Trust Information Centre and sales office, turn L and walk to the far end; there a path descends to the R down to the river. On the river bank turn R along a clear path. Where you reach the bank notice the water coming out from under the path – see (2) The disappearing rivers. A short distance further along pass an old stone stump in an enclosure on the R – see (3) The Battle Stone. From Ilam Hall,

MAP 19A

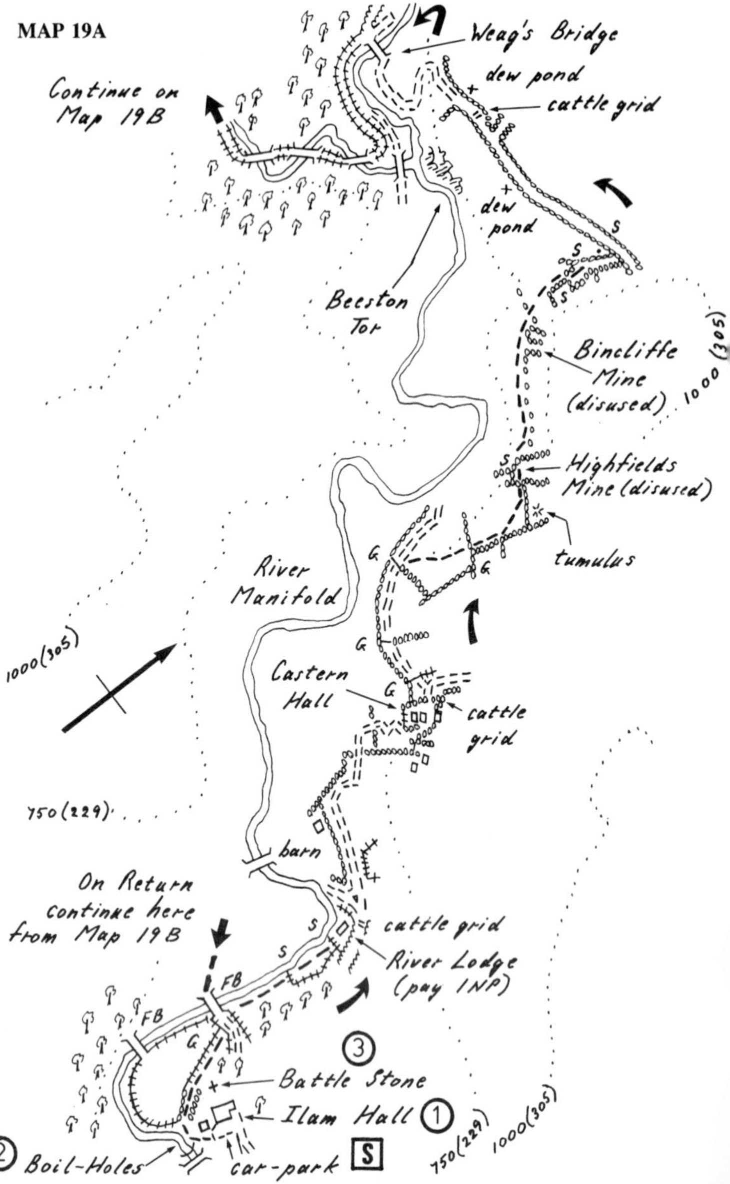
Weag's Bridge
Continue on Map 19B
dew pond
cattle grid
dew pond
S
S
S
Beeston Tor
Bincliffe Mine (disused)
1000 (305)
S
Highfields Mine (disused)
tumulus
G
G
River Manifold
G
1000(305)
Castern Hall
G
cattle grid
750 (229)
barn
On Return continue here from Map 19B
S
cattle grid
S
River Lodge (pay 1NP)
FB
FB
G
3
Battle Stone
Ilam Hall
1
2
Boil-Holes
car-park
S
750 (229)
1000 (305)

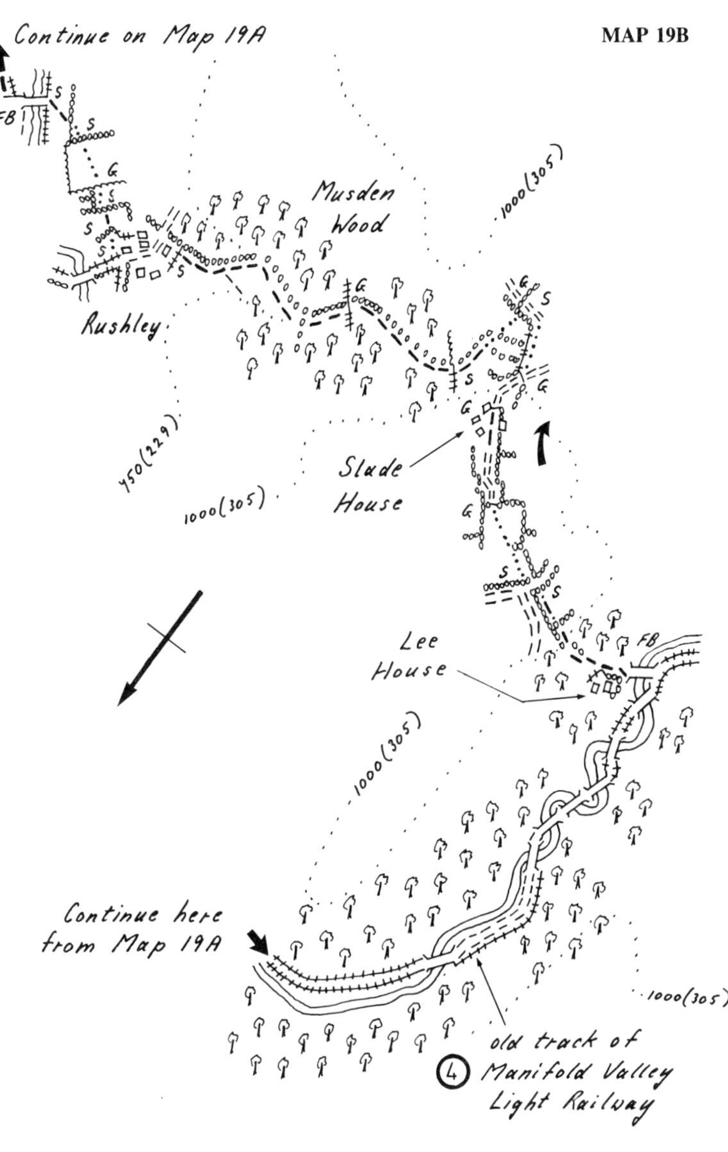
Continue on Map 19A
FB
S
S
G
S
S
S
S
Musden
Wood
1000(305)
G
G
S
G
S
G
Rushley
750(229)
Slade
House
1000(305)
G
S
S
Lee
House
FB
1000(305)
Continue here
from Map 19A
1000(305)
old track of
4
Manifold Valley
Light Railway

keep on the path to the R of the river for about 1 mile (1.6 km) to reach the road at River Lodge. (Along the way you will have passed a notice stating that 'All persons using this road must pay 1 NP at the Lodge'. A small box is provided for this purpose just before the front door.)

Turn L in the road, soon going R at a junction. Follow the road uphill to a large house, Castern Hall. The drive immediately to the R of the Hall goes down the side of the building into a yard; take the farm road to the R of this which bends round to the back to a cattle grid (PFS 'Wetton 2'). After the grid go along the main farm road for a few yards until it turns R towards a farm, Castern; do not turn with it but keep in the same direction along another farm road to a gate, then keep to the R of a wall following it across two fields. In the third field go half R up a lovely grassy track – the farm road continues ahead and then bends down to the L with the wall. The track rises to a gate and stile in the wall at the top of the large field.

Go up the next field on the R-hand side; then at about the half-way point leave the wall half L and cross the field to a gate. Beyond is an old mining area, Highfields Mine. Cross to the far wall and turn L to a stile (at present there is a caravan by the stile). The view into the valley of the Manifold is breath-taking. Cross and turn R, following a path along the edge of the hillside by a wall; to the L is a steep wooded slope dropping down to the Manifold far below. Soon pass a second mine (on your R), Bincliff Mines – this was an old lead mine. After this, the path swings R to a stile overlooking a small side valley. Go ahead to where the walls converge after two wall corners; a few yards further there is a stile on the L. Go up the field beyond to a lane. Turn L and follow the lane for 1 mile (1.6 km) down to a small narrow bridge over the Manifold, Weag's Bridge.

Turn L along the road furthest from the river. Follow this through the very beautiful Hamps valley for 2½ miles (4 km) until you reach a farm, Lee House, on your L. (This is the second farm on the L as Beeston Tor Farm will be passed very soon after leaving Weag's Bridge where the Hamps and Manifold meet.) Although the path through the valley is tarmacked throughout the surface is pleasant to walk upon and cars and motor cycles are forbidden. The way is left therefore entirely to the walker, who can enjoy the beauty of the Hamps valley in peace – see (4) The Manifold Valley Light Railway.

In front of the farm there is a small footbridge. Cross and take the path which goes up to the R of the house and up a shallow valley into a wood. There is a broken wall by the path, first on the R and then on the L. Higher, the path leaves the wood and continues by the wall on the L-hand side of two fields to reach a road by a cattle grid. Cross to the stile opposite and head half L across the large field beyond. You should touch the end of a short length of wall and reach the diagonally opposite corner of the field at a gate by a dew pond. Go down the farm road past the pond to reach a farm (Slade House).

Cross the farmyard to the gate opposite and continue along the farm road beyond. This goes to a gate in the corner of a field. Go through and immediately leave half L dropping down into the valley to the R of a fence. Towards the bottom the fence is replaced by a wall which bends L. Bend with it. Just before a gate turn L over a stile (i.e. in the bottom of the valley). After a few yards meet a broken wall running through the valley; go to the L of it to a stile. Now follow the path through the valley keeping to the L of the wall for 1½ miles (2.5 km) until a farm, Rushley, is reached. At the farm go to the R of some pens to reach the farm road (PFS). Turn L through the farm.

After the last building on the R a lane swings in from the L; a few yards further go R over a stile in a fence. Cross the small field to a stile in a wall and then up the next field half L to a stile near to a wall corner. Cross the field beyond keeping near to the L-hand side to a further gate and stile. From there drop down keeping in the same direction. Cut across the corner of the next field and then along a path half L to a footbridge. On the opposite bank turn R and walk back to the car-park at Ilam Hall.

(1) *Ilam and Ilam Hall (119-133507)*

Ilam Hall was built by a wealthy manufacturer, Jesse Watts Russell, between 1821 and 1826 on the site of an earlier Hall which Izaak Walton and Charles Cotton often visited. Most of the building was demolished in the 1930s but a substantial section still remains. It was given to the National Trust along with 84 acres (34 ha) of park and woodland by Sir Robert McDougall – who also made over large areas of Dovedale in 1934. Part of the building was leased to the Youth Hostels Association in the same year and, in addition to the hostel, there is also now a National Trust Information Centre and shop. The grounds of Ilam Hall are now a country park.

Not content with the building of the hall, Russell also completely remodelled the nearby village of Ilam. Planned villages – as distinct from the vast majority of villages in England which have tended simply to grow up – are not as rare as might be thought. The first village to be deliberately planned was Chippenham, near Newmarket, which was reconstructed by Lord Orford from 1700. His motives were largely selfish – to improve the appearance of the area surrounding his residence while at the same time ensuring that his tenantry were sufficiently near to be able to work on his estate. Although the villagers themselves had little say in the matter, they probably didn't do too badly out if it. For ordinary folk, country life in the eighteenth and nineteenth centuries was not idyllic.

The architectural style chosen for Ilam is unique in Derbyshire. So also is the tall Gothic cross that Russell erected by the bridge in the middle of the village as a memorial to his wife. Even the church did not escape attention; to the building originally erected in the thirteenth century he added a memorial chapel in 1831. He then arranged for a major restoration in 1855–6. The church is worth a visit: in the churchyard there are two Anglo-Saxon crosses; inside, a Norman font, a thirteenth-century shrine to St Bertram (who is said to have brought Christianity to those parts) and a fine monument showing the deathbed scene of David Pike-Watts, the father-in-law of Jesse Watts Russell.

(2) *The disappearing rivers*

An early name for the Hamps in the twelfth and thirteenth centuries was Hanespe which means 'summer dry'; a singularly appropriate name to describe the river's habit of apparently drying up each summer. What actually happens is that the Hamps sinks into fissures in the river bed and travels underground to reappear near Ilam Hall. Only when there is too high a water-flow for the underground passages does the Hamps use its rocky surface bed to a junction with the Manifold near Beeston Tor.

The behaviour of the Manifold is very similar. It normally disappears just south of Wettonmill to reappear a short distance away from the Hamps at the Boil-Holes. Experiments with corks and dyes have indicated that the two rivers follow different courses underground, the journey taking some 22–24 hours.

The Manifold also has an appropriate name for it means 'winding river' or 'river with many folds', which aptly describes its tortuous course southwards from Wettonmill to Ilam.

(3) *The Battle Stone (119-129506)*

A short way beyond the car-park at Ilam Hall is a small enclosure containing the shaft of an ancient cross. Known as 'The Battle Stone' and dating from the middle of the eleventh century, it was removed from the foundations of a cottage in Ilam during the rebuilding of the village. It owes its name to a local tradition that associates it with the struggles between the Anglo-Saxons and Viking invaders. (Viking attacks under the leadership of Swein and Cnut certainly occurred in the area to the east of the Peak District during the early eleventh century.)

(4) *The Manifold Valley Light Railway*

A light railway, 8¼ miles (13 km) long, with a gauge of 2 ft 6 ins (762 mm) was opened in 1904 along the Hamps and Manifold valleys between Waterhouses and Hulme End, with intermediate stations at Sparrowlee, Beeston Tor, near Grindon, Thor's Cave, Wettonmill, Swainsley and Ecton. At Waterhouses it linked up with a branch line of the North Staffordshire Railway from Leek which used standard gauge and which had opened one year earlier. Two engines operated along the line which carried tourists, some local passengers and milk from the farms of the valley. A proposal to extend the line to Buxton was not developed. The line was never a great success and finally closed on 12 March 1934. In 1937 Staffordshire County Council took up the metals and converted the track into a bridleway.

More Strenuous Routes

Route 20 The Goyt Valley

The Goyt Valley on the eastern side of the National Park is within easy travelling distance of the great Manchester conurbation. It is also a place of considerable beauty. These two factors taken together would, of course, be sufficient to make the valley an intolerable place on summer weekends and Bank Holidays were it not for a very timely traffic scheme introduced by the Park Authority. As in the Derwent Valley further to the north-east, the water authorities have seen fit to drown part of it by the construction of two reservoirs. Without doubt these have destroyed some of the beauty which once was there; but at the same time they have added another dimension to it. This route passes through some of the very best of the valley and also includes a traverse of the magnificent ridge to Shining Tor which lies to the west.

Length: 10 miles (16 km).

Ascent: 1700 ft (520 m).

Starting and finishing point: Car-park on the east side of Errwood Reservoir in the Goyt Valley (119-012748).

Maps: Landranger 119 and 118; Outdoor Leisure The White Peak.

Route description (Maps 20A, 20B)
See (1) The Goyt Valley, for information on the area before starting the walk. Leave the car-park into the road and turn L. Follow the road to a junction just above the dam of Errwood Reservoir, there go to the R. About half-way down at a PFS leave the road half L on a clear path. After 50 yds (45 m) at a second PFS go half R. Do not descend to the bottom of the dam, but follow the path which runs to the L across the hillside. Go through a gap and descend through the woods to reach the edge of the reservoir (Fernilee) at a ladder stile. Keep by the water for about ⅔ mile (1.1 km); there the path crosses

MAP 20A

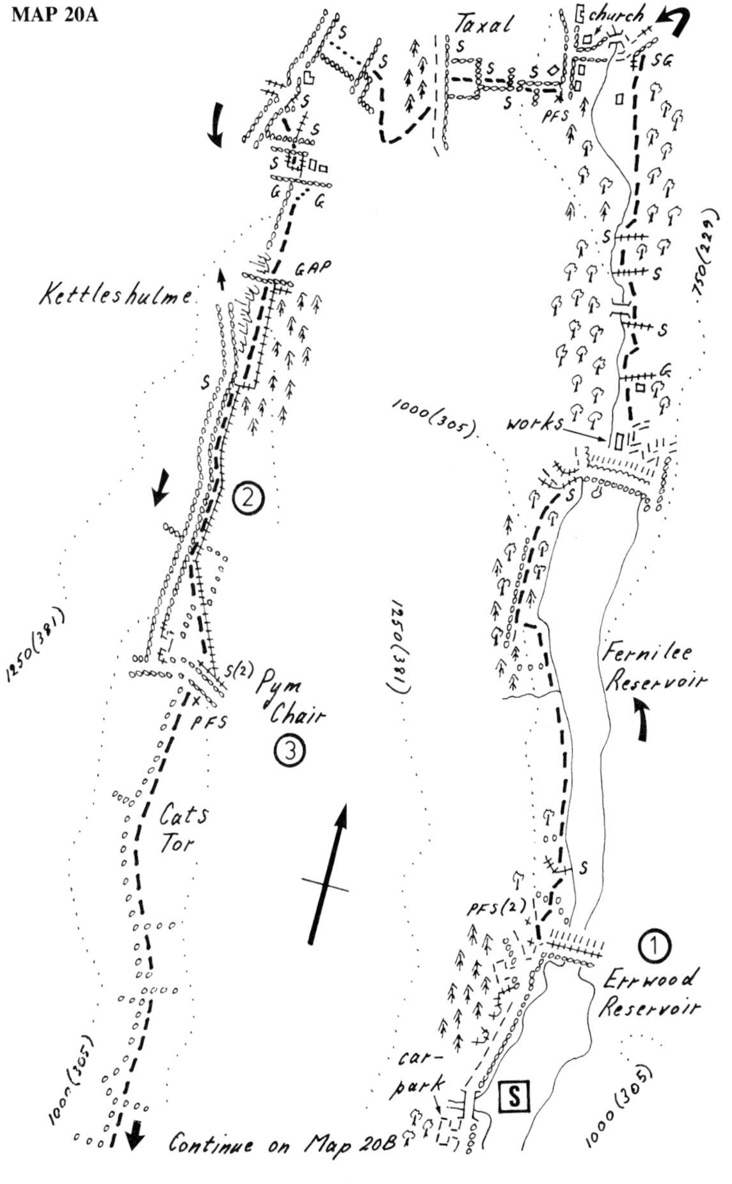

Taxal
church
S
SG
PFS
G
GAP
Kettleshulme
750(229)
1000(305)
works
2
1250(381)
1250(381)
S(2)
Pym Chair
PFS
3
Fernilee Reservoir
Cats Tor
PFS(2)
1
Errwood Reservoir
car-park
S
1000(305)
1000(305)

Continue on Map 20B

MAP 20B

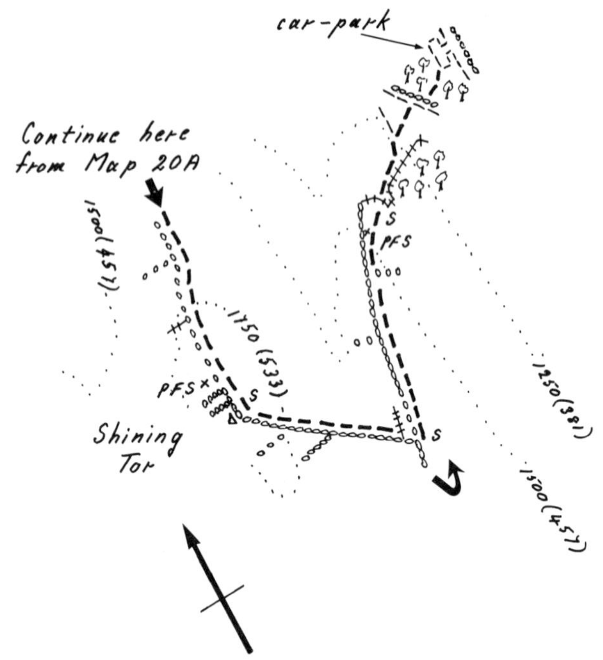

car-park
Continue here from Map 20A
1500(457)
1750(533)
S
PFS
Shining Tor
1250(381)
1500(457)

a small stream (Deep Clough) and then a little later swings L uphill to a cross-track. Turn R along this for about 700 yds (650 m) to a road.

Turn R down the road to the dam and across to the opposite side. At the T-junction there go L and 90 yds (80 m) further turn back half L down a minor road. Follow this through zigzags and past some works buildings to the river bank. Keep on a path by the river crossing several stiles for nearly 1½ miles (2.5 km) to a small gate leading into a farm road. Turn L, cross the river at a bridge and go up a rough lane to Taxal church.

Turn L and immediately after the Rectory R over a stile (PFS 'Taxal Edge'). Keep to the R-hand side of the first two fields, the L side of the next and finally straight across the fourth to reach a road. Turn L. Where the wood ends leave the road along a path half R and climb up the hillside. Towards the top the path curves R, then L to a ladder stile in a wall corner. Cross and go straight down the field ahead to a road. Turn L for 175 yds (160 m) to a junction, then 60 yds (55 m) further L over a stile (PFS). Go diagonally up the field to the top R-hand corner and then straight on towards a farmhouse. Pass the farm to the R (several stiles and small gates) to reach the farm road.

Turn L and through a gate in front of the house. Take the first gate to the R and go up the fields keeping to the L of the wall. At the top go through a gap and continue along the edge of a cliff (Windgather Rocks). The long ridge now stretching before you was the route taken by travellers in the Middle Ages – see (2) The Macclesfield Forest Ridgeway. Beyond the rocks keep to the L of the road between a wall and fence. Where a broken wall comes in on the L go half L by a fence across the moor. Reach the road at Pym Chair over two ladder stiles. At this point you cross the line of an old saltway which came from the brine pits in Cheshire to the large towns to the east – see (3) Pym Chair.

Turn R for 40 yds (35 m) and then L at a PFS ('Shining Tor'). Keep climbing slowly to the L of a broken wall for nearly 2 miles (3 km) to the summit of Shining Tor (the OS obelisk is on the other side of the wall). There turn L, still keeping by the wall. After about ½ mile (800 m) cross a fence at a ladder stile and a broken wall immediately afterwards. Again turn L and commence a long descent to the R of the wall. After ⅔ mile (1.1 km) at a PFS ('Errwood car-park') leave the wall half R. Cross a ladder stile and continue to descend around a fence corner. Lower down at a path junction keep descending parallel to the fence on the R to reach a cross-path by a wall. Go R for 20 yds (18 m) then L for the final descent to the car-park.

(1) *The Goyt Valley*
From its source on the high ground to the east of the Cat and Fiddle Inn, the Goyt flows to the north, eventually joining the Mersey on its journey to the Irish Sea. Its early course is predominantly over Millstone Grit, a hard impermeable rock, folded into a syncline, i.e. a downward fold of the rocks to form a trough, which makes it ideal for water collection. This fact was not, of course, lost on the water authorities and two reservoirs now grace the valley, the Fernilee and the Errwood. The Fernilee, the more northerly of the two, was the first to be built, in 1938, while the Errwood was constructed about twenty years later. Between them they supply an average of 7–8 million gallons (32–36 megalitres) each day to the citizens of Stockport.

One of the casualties of the construction of the Fernilee was Errwood Hall, as well as several other buildings in the valley. Built in the 1830s it was the home of the Grimshawe family who lived there in great style. In 1930 it was sold to Stockport Corporation to become a youth hostel for four years until its demolition when the reservoir was constructed. Old drawings of the Hall in its heyday show it to have been an impressive building with a large square central tower, surrounded by beautiful gardens which had been well stocked by the Grimshawes from their travels abroad.

In order to preserve the peace of the Goyt Valley for the enjoyment of visitors, a traffic control scheme has been devised which is in operation at times of maximum pressure, i.e. on Sundays and Bank Holiday Mondays from early May to late September. This involves the closing of the road from Derbyshire Bridge to The

Street – except to a few official vehicles – between the hours of 10.30 and 5.30. There are free car-parks at each end where visitors may leave their cars.

(2) *The Macclesfield Forest Ridgeway*

The long ridge from Shining Tor over The Tors, Cats Tor, Pym Chair and Windgather Rocks to the A5002 (Macclesfield-Whaley Bridge road) and then on over Black Hill to near Newtown was the route taken by an old way in use during the Middle Ages. It probably provided a link between another old way between Leek and Macclesfield to the south and the Roman road from Buxton to Manchester to the north.

(3) *Pym Chair (118-996767)*

At Pym Chair the route crosses the line of a Roman road (The Street) which ran from Buxton towards Stockport. It was also the line taken by a saltway from Northwich or Middlewich through Macclesfield to Sheffield and Chesterfield. In the Middle Ages it was normal practice to slaughter a high proportion of domestic livestock each autumn as it was impossible to store sufficient fodder to keep more than a few beasts alive through the long winter months. Although part of the meat would be eaten immediately, most would be salted down to preserve it for as long as possible. The trade in salt, therefore, from the pits in Cheshire to towns and villages was an important – and indeed essential – commercial activity. Over long distances and in hilly country the salt was carried by packhorse train, the regular routes taken by them becoming known as saltways. One such way ran through Taxal across the northern end of the Goyt valley and a second one, as mentioned above, over Pym Chair.

Previous pages

Left: The descent from the Shining Tor ridge towards Errwood Reservoir.

Right: Fernilee Reservoir in the Goyt Valley.

Route 21 The Longdendale Edges

Longdendale has had to take more than its fair share of industrial development: early quarrying, a little afforestation, the construction of overhead power lines and a railway track, a vast increase of traffic on the A628 and finally the building of no fewer than five reservoirs have certainly changed it beyond recognition – and probably in the process have robbed it of whatever beauty it may once have had. Most walkers will know it therefore as a welcome stopping post on the long trek up the Pennine Way between the Kinder-Bleaklow section and the traverse of Black Hill, rather than as a valley to be walked along in its own right. This route largely avoids the desecration by using the edges on both the north and south sides. The valley itself is only crossed twice – the first time over the dam of Rhodeswood Reservoir and the second over that of Torside Reservoir. (This crosses an access area – see page 54.)

Length: 9 miles (14 km).

Ascent: 2000 ft (610 m).

Starting and finishing point: The car-park at Crowden on the A628 (110-073993).

Maps: Landranger 110; Outdoor Leisure The Dark Peak.

Route description (Map 21)
For some information on Crowden and the valley, see (1) Longdendale. Leave the car-park from the opposite end to the entrance along a footpath between fences. In a minor road, just in front of a toilet block, turn R. After 100 yds (90 m) turn L at a T-junction and follow the narrow road down to a bridge. After the bridge go through a gate and continue slowly climbing (the surface is now rough). Just before a coniferous wood on the L, turn R at a Pennine Way sign and follow a path up by a fence to a ladder stile. Immediately after the stile turn L and climb up to a broken wall.

MAP 21

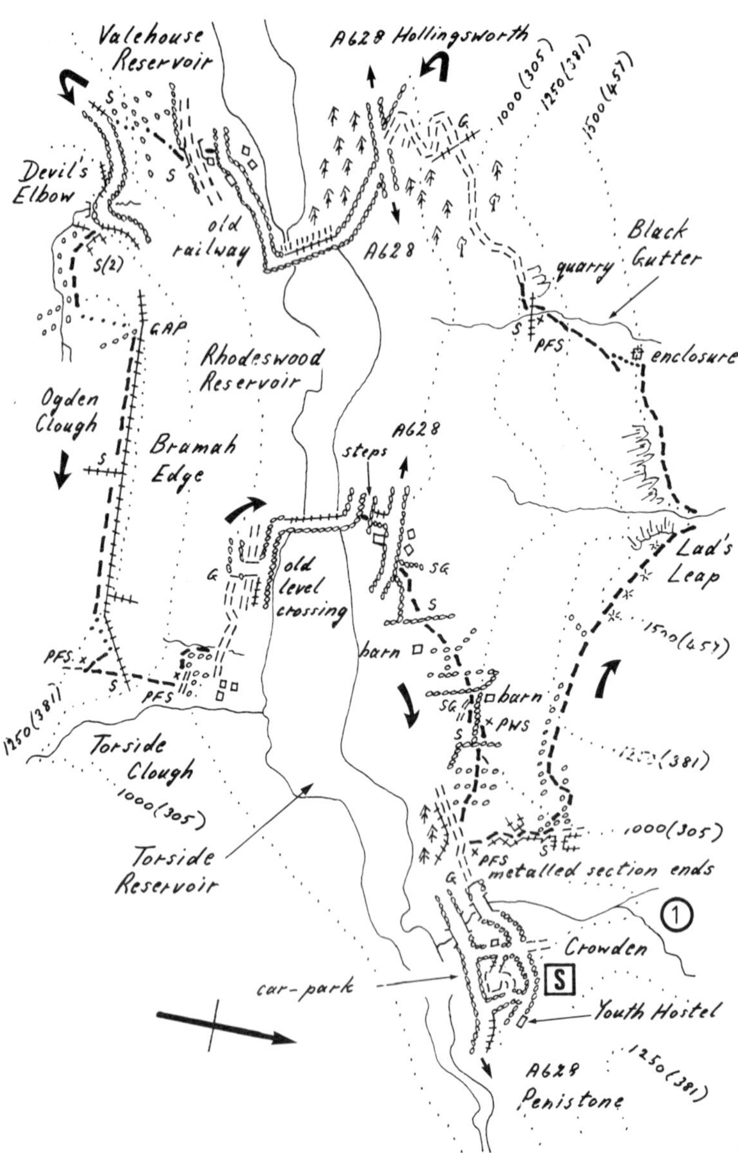

Valehouse Reservoir
A628 Hollingsworth
1000 (305)
1250 (381)
1500 (457)
Devil's Elbow
S
S(2)
G
old railway
A628
quarry
Black Gutter
GAP
Rhodeswood Reservoir
PFS
enclosure
Ogden Clough
Bramah Edge
A628
steps
G
old level crossing
SG
S
Lad's Leap
1500 (457)
barn
PFS
1250 (381)
barn
SG
PWS
Torside Clough
1250 (381)
1000 (305)
1000 (305)
Torside Reservoir
PFS
metalled section ends
G
1
Crowden
S
car-park
Youth Hostel
1250 (381)
A628 Penistone

Over the next 150 yds (140 m) the path crosses to the R and then to the L of a second ruined wall. Soon, still climbing, cross a third wall and then at a fourth wall bend R to keep on its R-hand side. Where this wall ends keep in the same direction over the moor. After 325 yds (300 m) pass the end of a broken wall; beyond the wall the path disappears over stony ground, but if you keep in the same direction you should pick it up again after a few yards. After ⅓ mile (500 m) reach the edge (this point is called Lad's Leap) overlooking Longdendale. Here, the path bends to the R and drops down to a stream (Hollins Clough). On the far side rise up to the L to rejoin the edge.

Continue along the edge for about 600 yds (550 m) until you reach a small fenced enclosure. At the beginning of the enclosure turn down to the L, descending over grassy slopes. After a short distance you should pick up a path – keeping to the L of a stream – which leads down to a ladder stile in a fence at the perimeter of the access area. Beyond the fence the path bends down to the R and soon joins a quarry road (the quarry is over to the R). Follow this splendid way as it slowly descends down the hillside. Eventually go through a gate at the corner of a coniferous wood. Beyond continue to follow the quarry road as it goes through a series of bends to reach the A628.

Cross and turn L, turning half R down a minor road after a few yards. Follow this down to the dam of the Rhodeswood Reservoir and cross. On the far side continue along to a farm (Deepclough). Pass the farm for a short distance until you reach a barn on the L. Turn L just after the barn and go through a tunnel under an old railway track. On the far side go half R up the field to reach a higher road (B6105). Turn L along the road until it bends sharply around a small clough (Devil's Elbow).

Immediately after the bridge in the clough go R up a step and then two stiles. Go up the slope behind the second stile to an upper path and turn R. Follow this path, climbing slowly, to the L of a wall. Eventually where the wall ends turn L (i.e. due north) and strike across the open moor – aim for the junction of a fence and a wall (the fence is on the L of the junction: this will tell you which way to go if you reach one of them in mist). Go through the gap between the fence and the wall and follow the edge keeping to the R of the fence. After about 650 yds (600 m) a fence comes in from the R (cross at a stile) and 600 yds (550 m) further a fence joins from the L. About 225 yds (200 m) further still go half R away from the fence along a hollow track towards a PFS. At the sign you will meet a crossing track – this is the Pennine Way descending from Bleaklow. Turn L and descend down the Way to a ladder stile.

Keep descending to a moor road and turn L. Where this goes through a gap to the R, keep ahead along a footpath to the L of the wall, bending R at a corner above a small clough down to a lower farm road. There turn L and follow it to a road (the B6105). Turn R over a level crossing and then L along a minor road which leads to the dam of Torside Reservoir. Cross the dam and go up steps at the end which lead back to the main road (A628).

Go R for a few yards and then cross to a small gate to the R of a cottage. Follow the path up the field to a wall corner and continue beyond, gradually leaving the wall to the L, until a ladder stile. Continue in roughly the same direction towards a barn crossing several broken walls on the way. Go through a small gate to the R of the barn and after a few yards cross the wall to the L (Pennine Way sign), continuing in the same direction to a ladder stile. At a path junction just beyond the stile go R, crossing the moor to drop down eventually to a farm road by a coniferous wood. Turn L along the farm road and follow it back to the starting point.

(1) *Longdendale*
One of the consequences of the industrial development of Longdendale has been a considerable drop in population. Crowden – now represented by little more than a youth hostel, a campsite and a few cottages – was at one time a thriving community with a public house, a school and several shops. It also had a fine hall, Crowden Hall, which was built in 1692 by the Hatfield family. St James's Chapel, overlooking the dam of Woodhead Reservoir, was founded in 1487. It even enjoyed the services of a railway station which was open from 1860 until 1957.

The building by Manchester Corporation of the five reservoirs, which provide an almost continuous stretch of water some 6 miles

(10 km) in length, took place between 1848 and 1877. Together they supply about 24 million gallons (109 megalitres) each day to the Manchester area.

The railway which ran between Manchester and Sheffield across the northern extremity of the National Park opened in 1845. One feature of it is the Woodhead tunnel, about 3 miles (5 km) long, the driving of which cost the lives of at least thirty-two navvies, some of whom are buried at St James's Chapel. Passenger services ceased on the line in 1970 and goods services a few years later; one reason was the dangerous condition of the tunnels, which now accommodate the power lines that run through the valley.

The youth hostel building at Crowden was originally a row of six cottages used by railway workers; it was converted into a hostel between 1962 and 1965.

Route 22 The Tissington Trail

The railway line from Ashbourne to Buxton, constructed in the 1890s, used part of the Cromford and High Peak Railway between Parsley Hay and Ladmanlow. A victim of progressive rationalisation and cost cutting, it was finally closed in 1967. Instead, however, of suffering the fate of so many other branch lines closed in that period and becoming overgrown and neglected, it was saved by the speedy intervention of the National Park Authority who purchased a considerable section of the line along with its station sites. Over the years since then, work on the old line has produced a walking surface of high quality with car-parks and their attendant facilities at strategic points. The result is a credit to the Board. Nor is that all, for the railway bankings, freed from steam and fumes and the noise of passing trains, have become havens for wildlife. Only the sighing of the wind, the hum of insects and the song of birds will now disturb a walker along the Tissington Trail.

MAP 22A

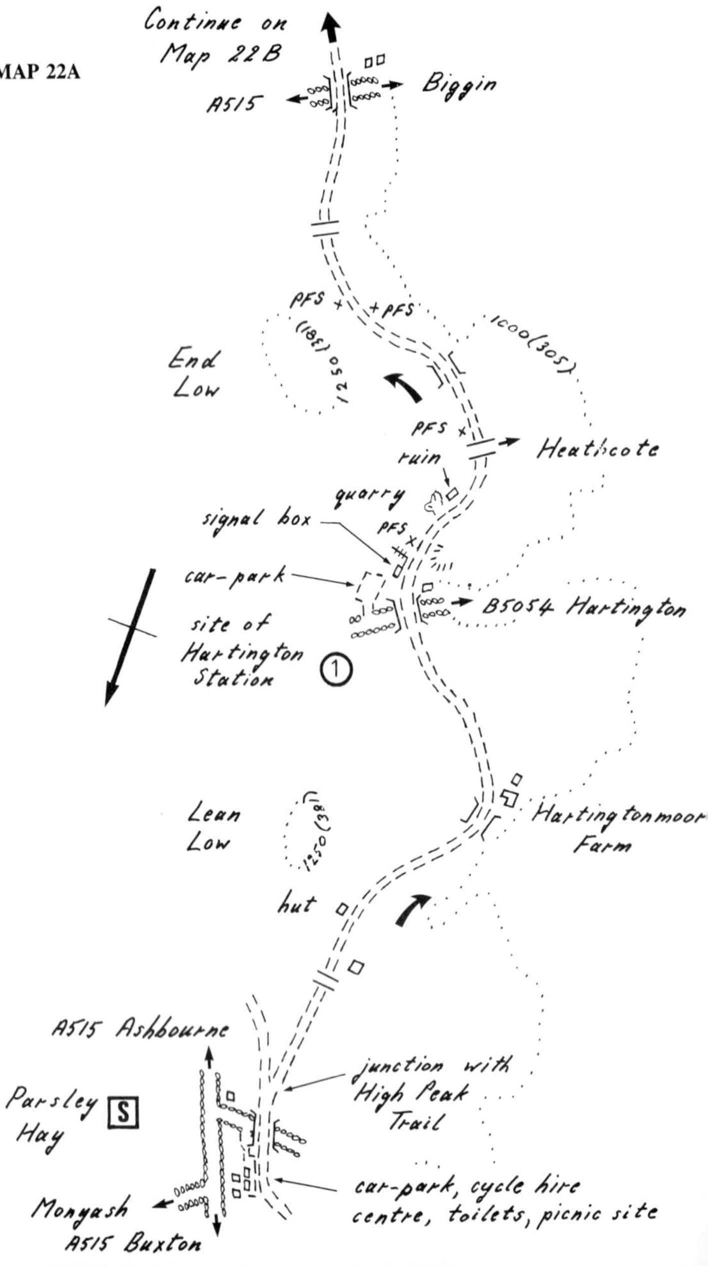

Continue on Map 22B

A515

Biggin

PFS

PFS

1250 (381)

1000 (305)

End Low

PFS

Heathcote

ruin

quarry

signal box

PFS

car-park

B5054 Hartington

site of Hartington Station

1

Lean Low

1250 (381)

Hartingtonmoor Farm

hut

A515 Ashbourne

junction with High Peak Trail

Parsley Hay

S

car-park, cycle hire centre, toilets, picnic site

Monyash

A515 Buxton

MAP 22B

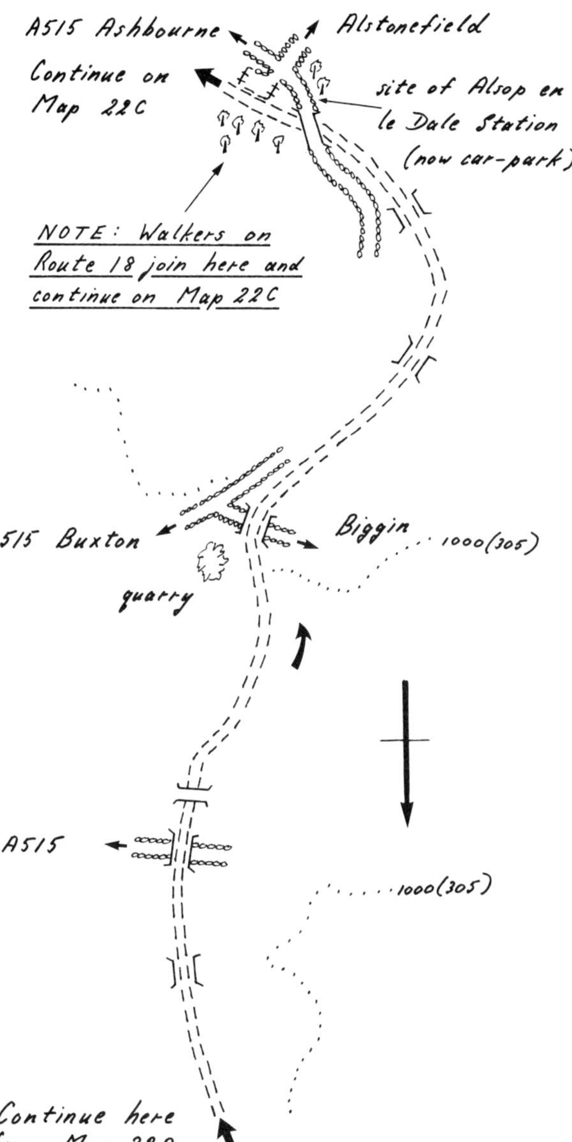

A515 Ashbourne
Alstonefield
Continue on Map 22C
site of Alsop en le Dale Station (now car-park)
NOTE: Walkers on Route 18 join here and continue on Map 22C
A515 Buxton
Biggin
1000(305)
quarry
A515
1000(305)
Continue here from Map 22A

MAP 22C

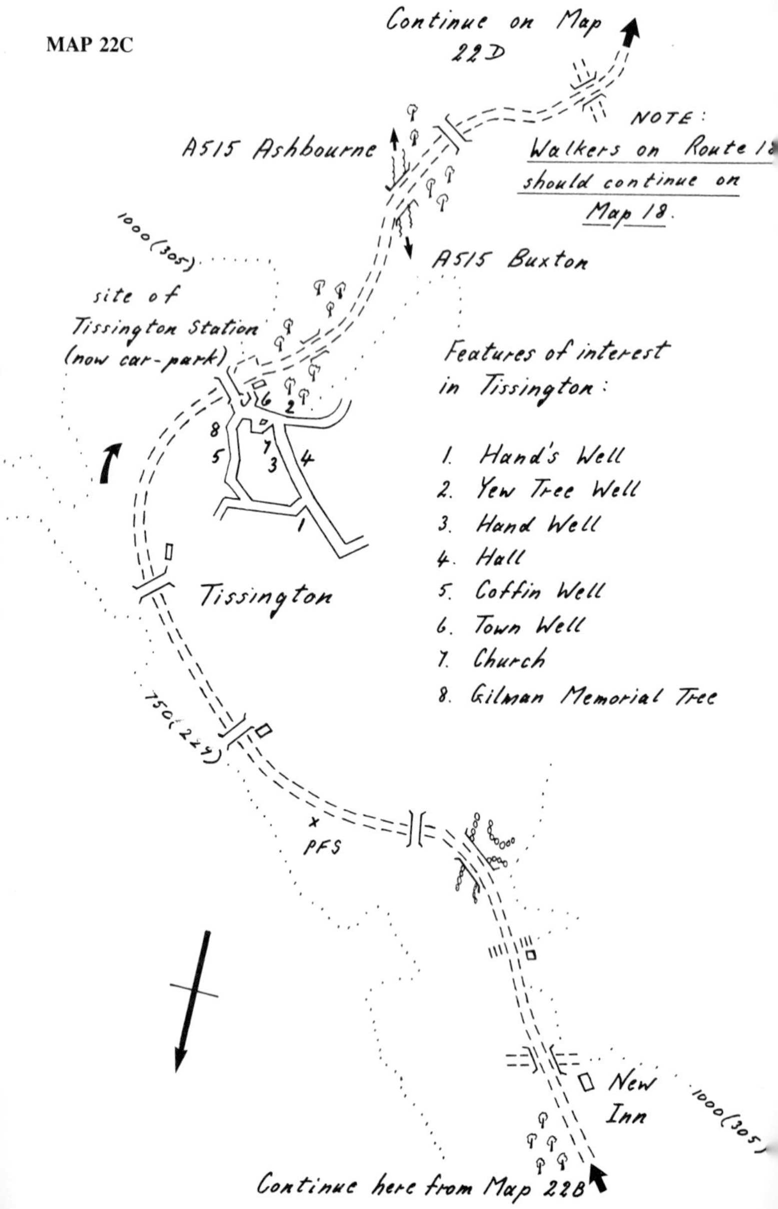

Continue on Map 22D

NOTE:
Walkers on Route 18 should continue on Map 18.

A515 Ashbourne

A515 Buxton

1000(305)

site of Tissington Station (now car-park)

Features of interest in Tissington:

1. Hand's Well
2. Yew Tree Well
3. Hand Well
4. Hall
5. Coffin Well
6. Town Well
7. Church
8. Gilman Memorial Tree

8 5 7 3 4 6 2 1

Tissington

750(229)

PFS

New Inn

1000(305)

Continue here from Map 22B

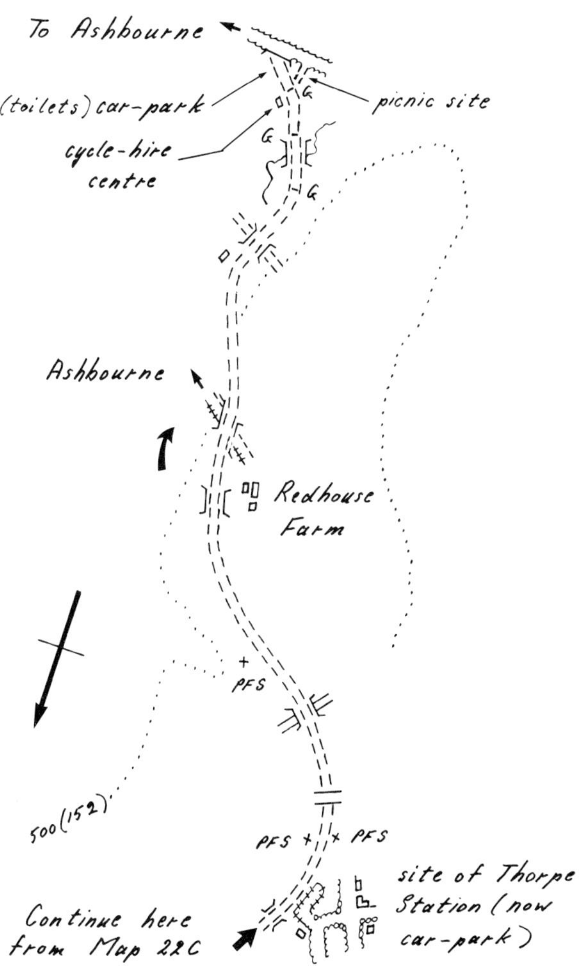
To Ashbourne
(toilets) car-park
picnic site
cycle-hire centre
G
G
G
Ashbourne
Redhouse Farm
PFS
500 (152)
PFS
PFS
site of Thorpe Station (now car-park)
Continue here from Map 22C

Length: 13 miles (21 km).

Ascent: Virtually none, as the railway builders 'ironed out' the landscape by the construction of tall viaducts and the digging out of deep cuttings.

Starting point: The car-park at Parsley Hay, a short distance off the A515, Buxton-Ashbourne road, about 8 miles (13 km) south-east of Buxton (119-147637).

Finishing point: The car-park at Mapleton Lane, Ashbourne (119-176469).

Maps: Landranger 119; Outdoor Leisure The White Peak (West and East Sheets) – part only.

Route description (Maps 22A, 22B, 22C, 22D)
Once a correct decision has been taken at the junction of the Tissington Trail and the High Peak Trail, which is reached within the first few minutes after leaving Parsley Hay, no further route description is necessary. The route is clear throughout with a total absence of junctions where mistakes can occur. It is only necessary therefore to indicate features of interest and car-parks along the way which could provide picking-up points. All distances are from Parsley Hay.

0 miles, 0 km: Parsley Hay. Car-park, toilets, picnic site and cycle-hire. Go on to the trail from the car-park and turn L.

¼ mile, 400 m: The Tissington and High Peak Trails separate here. Take the branch to the R which curves into a deep cutting.

1¾ miles, 3 km: The route crosses the B5054 which gives easy access to Hartington. There are a car-park and toilets at the crossing. A short distance south of the bridge is the Hartington signal box – see (1) below. The high ground over to the R of the track, just before the bridge is reached, was the scene of a skirmish during the Civil War.

The Tissington Trail soon after leaving Parsley Hay on its journey southwards towards Ashbourne.

6½ miles, 10 km: Alsop en le Dale. Car-park and picnic site reached from the A515.

9¼ miles, 15 km: Tissington. Car-park, picnic site and toilets. Tissington is one of the most interesting villages in the Peak District, worth a short detour if time permits on the long trek south. For further information see page 184.

10¾ miles, 17 km: Thorpe. Car-park and picnic site.

13 miles, 21 km: Mapleton Lane, Ashbourne. Car-park, toilets, picnic site, small shop and cycle-hire.

(1) *The Hartington signal box (119-150612)*
This signal box is one of the few relics of the old railway, apart of course from the track itself, which can still be found along the Trail. It has been retained as an Information Point and Ranger Briefing Centre. The lever frame for the signals was restored by volunteers from British Rail.

Previous pages
Left: The Tissington Trail between Alsop en le Dale and Tissington.
Right: The signal box at Hartington Station, now used as an information point on the Tissington Trail.

Route 23 The Monsal Trail

Of the five trails in the Peak District which have been created along the lines of old disused railways the Monsal, which follows the valley of the Wye, is by far the most spectacular. Even the closure of three long tunnels along the way, which has necessitated detours away from the track, has scarcely detracted from it for the alternative paths provided pass through dales, such as Chee and Water-cum-Jolly, which have become bywords for outstanding beauty. Only the somewhat isolated starting and finishing points provide any real grounds for criticism.

Length: 12 miles (19 km).

Ascent: 600 ft (180 m).

Starting point: A car-park off the A6 near Topley Pike Quarry about 3½ miles (5.5 km) east of Buxton (119-104725). Approaching from Buxton the car-park is down a farm road to the L opposite the quarry entrance.

Finishing point: A small bridge about 1 mile (1.6 km) to the south-east of Bakewell (119-230679).

Maps: Landranger 119; Outdoor Leisure The White Peak (West and East Sheets).

Route description (Maps 23A, 23B, 23 C)
Before starting the route see (1) The Monsal Trail, for information on the old railway and trail. From the car-park continue along the farm road going away from the main road (A6). The farm road follows the River Wye as it goes under a great railway viaduct. Shortly afterwards go under a second viaduct. At the third viaduct leave the farm road to the R up some steps which lead on to the track (sign to Monsal Trail). Some cottages can be seen over to the L. Turn R (the viaduct is closed in the opposite direction) and follow the track for nearly a mile (1.6 km) to the end of a *closed* tunnel.

MAP 23A

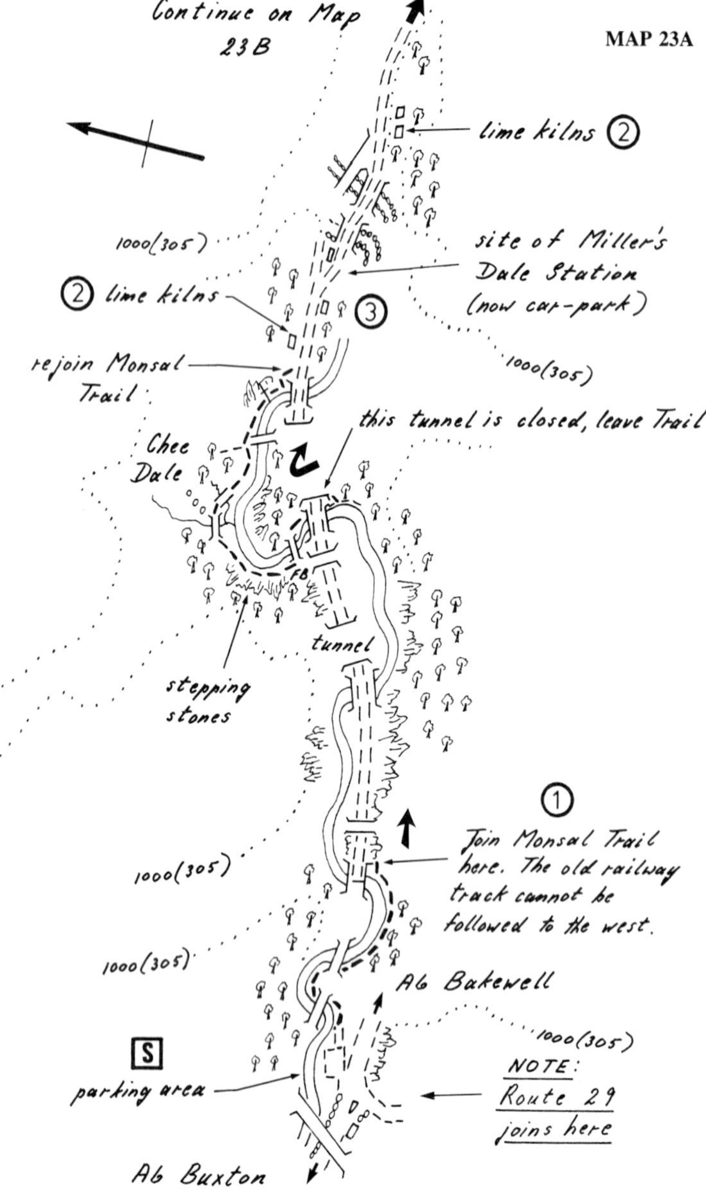

Continue on Map 23B
lime kilns ②
1000(305)
site of Miller's Dale Station (now car-park)
② lime kilns
③
rejoin Monsal Trail
1000(305)
this tunnel is closed, leave Trail
Chee Dale
FB
tunnel
stepping stones
①
Join Monsal Trail here. The old railway track cannot be followed to the west.
1000(305)
1000(305)
A6 Bakewell
1000(305)
S
parking area
NOTE: Route 29 joins here
A6 Buxton

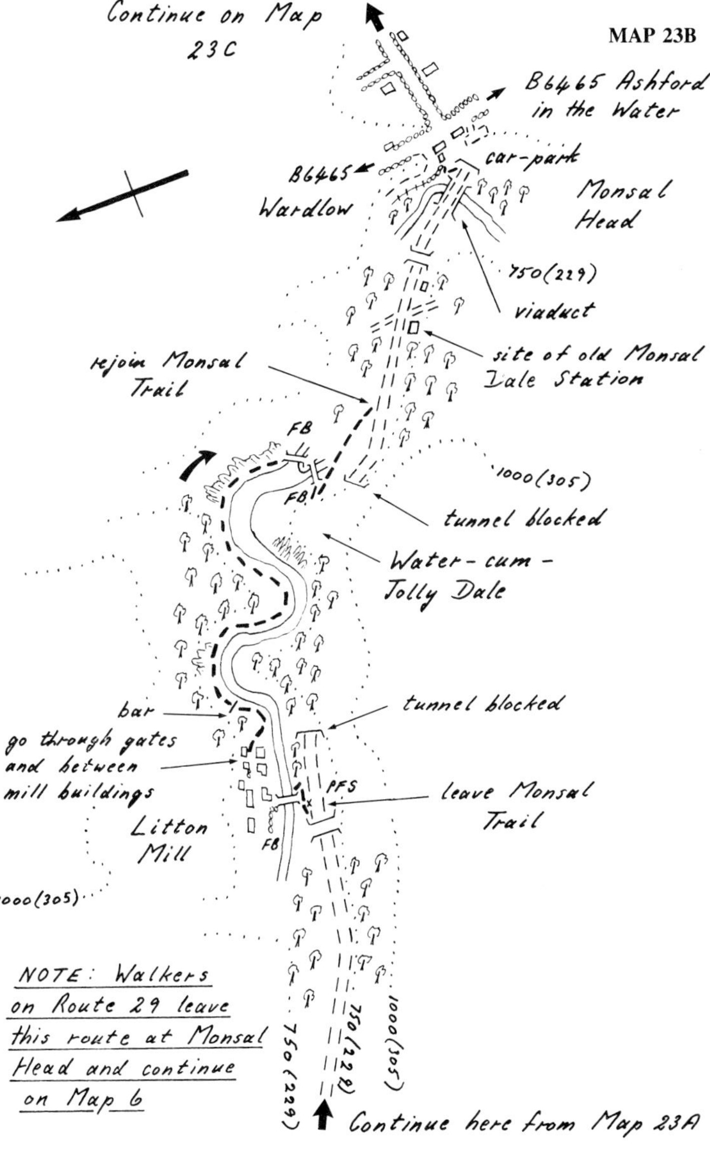
Continue on Map 23C
MAP 23B
B6465 Ashford in the Water
car-park
Monsal Head
B6465 Wardlow
750(229)
viaduct
site of old Monsal Dale Station
rejoin Monsal Trail
FB
1000(305)
FB
tunnel blocked
Water-cum-Jolly Dale
tunnel blocked
bar
go through gates and between mill buildings
PFS
leave Monsal Trail
Litton Mill
FB
1000(305)
NOTE: Walkers on Route 29 leave this route at Monsal Head and continue on Map 6
750(229)
750(229)
1000(305)
Continue here from Map 23A

MAP 23C

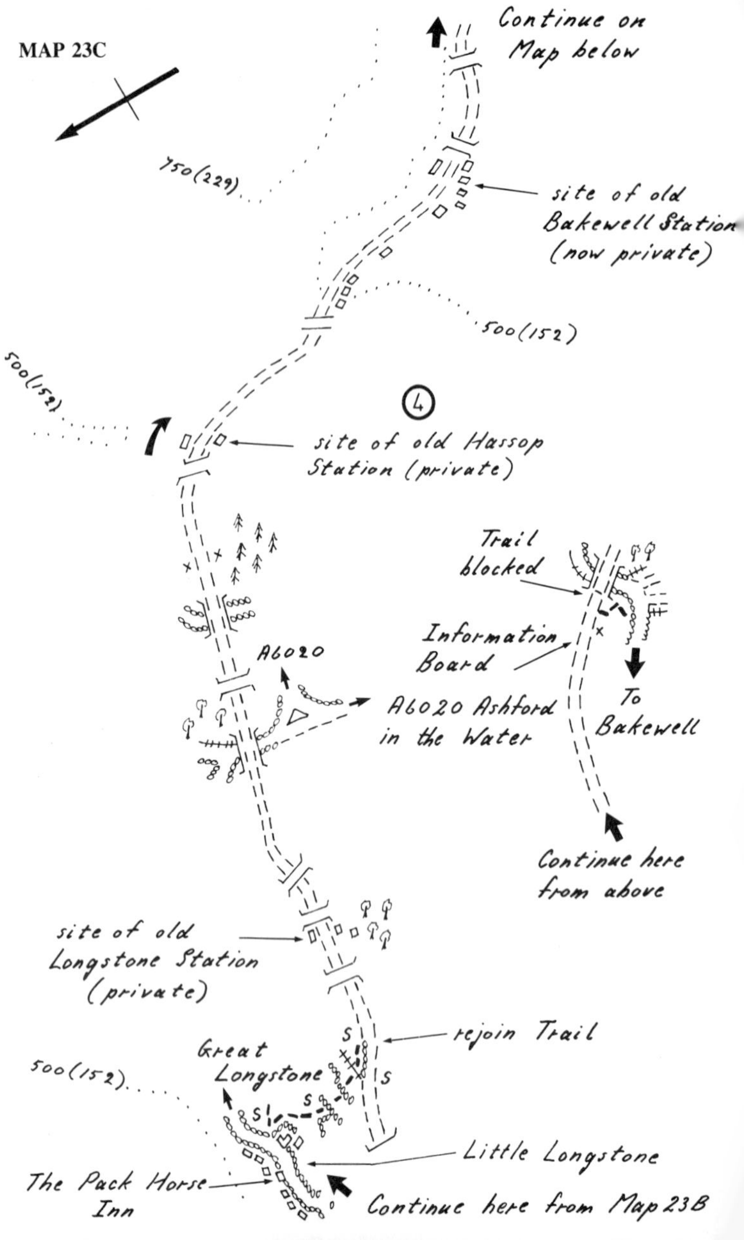

Continue on Map below

750(229)

site of old Bakewell Station (now private)

500(152)

500(152)

4

site of old Hassop Station (private)

Trail blocked

Information Board

To Bakewell

A6020

A6020 Ashford in the Water

Continue here from above

site of old Longstone Station (private)

rejoin Trail

Great Longstone

500(152)

S

S

S

S

Little Longstone

The Pack Horse Inn

Continue here from Map 23B

Go over a stile on the R and down to a crossing path by the river; turn R under the viaduct to a footbridge. The valley ahead is Chee Dale. Cross the bridge and go to the R along the river bank. The way ahead, along a line of stepping stones under the overhangs of a great cliff, is spectacular (this may be impassable at high water). Keep by the river as it runs through this beautiful wooded valley for 1 mile (1.6 km) to a further railway viaduct where you can go up to the L to rejoin the track. Walk along the track as far as the station at Miller's Dale. On the way you will pass a large concrete tower on the L – see (2) Lime kilns.

Pass the platforms – see (3) Miller's Dale station – and continue along the track over a viaduct. There are further lime kilns on the R, but these are an older type – see (2) again. After 1½ miles (2.5 km), immediately after a bridge, go L through a gap and down to a footbridge (a sign indicates that there is a blocked tunnel ahead). In the road beyond turn R and go through the gates of Litton Mills. Go ahead between the tall buildings of the mill (this is a concessionary path only), turning R at the end to reach the river bank. Follow a lovely path through woods keeping on the L-hand side of the river. Later the river widens and curves to the R with tall limestone cliffs on each side – this is the very beautiful and quaintly named Water-cum-Jolly Dale.

At the end go over a footbridge into a stoneyard. Immediately, turn R over a second footbridge and follow a path which rises to the L across the hillside to rejoin the Monsal Trail again. Turn L along the Trail for ¾ mile (1.2 km) to cross the famous viaduct at Monsal Head. The small building and platform passed on the way are the remains of the old Monsal Dale station.

On the far side of the viaduct at a blocked tunnel entrance go L through a small gap and up the hillside. At a crossing path turn R up to the road at Monsal Head; there is a magnificent view from here back over the viaduct and the two dales which meet at this point. Cross over to the main road running past the Monsal Head Inn. Turn R for a few yards, then L along the road opposite. Follow this road to Little Longstone. At the end of the village, immediately after the last house on the R, you will find two stiles; go over the R-hand one and head away at a right angle to the road (PFS

'Ashford' and Monsal Trail sign) soon passing to the L of a wall corner to a stile. Keep in the same direction across two fields; in the third field keep by the wall to a stile which leads back on to the Monsal Trail. Turn L along the railway track.

After 400 yds (375 m) pass an old station and 1⅓ miles (2 km) later a further station near a large roundabout – see (4) Hassop station. Finally, 1 mile (1.6 km) further along, the old buildings at Bakewell station will be reached.

Continue along the track for nearly a mile (1.6 km) to reach the end of the Monsal Trail which is marked by a fence across the track. (If car transport has been arranged it can be met at this point, otherwise the best plan will be to make your way back to Bakewell. There is a bus service from there to Buxton which passes the starting point and also others to local towns and villages.) For the road to Bakewell go down the footpath to the R from the trail. In the road turn R; after ¾ mile (1.2 km) turn R over a bridge into Bakewell.

(1) *The Monsal Trail*

The old railway line through the Wye valley, some sections of which are followed by the Monsal Trail, was originally part of the Midland Railway network and carried trains from St Pancras to Manchester. Authorisation for this line was granted by Act of Parliament on 25 May 1860 and it was opened on 1 June 1863. At its southern end at Rowsley it joined with a line from Ambergate operated by the Manchester, Buxton, Matlock and Midland Junction Railway, which had opened some fourteen years earlier. At its northern end at Buxton a line was built under an arrangement between the Midland and the Manchester, Sheffield and Lincolnshire Railway Company which connected with the latter company's line into Manchester's London Road station (this was replaced later by a line completely under Midland control which ran into Manchester Central).

As might be expected, the forcing of a line through the heart of the Peak District could not be regarded as an easy venture and

The Monsal Trail towards its western end.

necessitated the driving of several long tunnels and the building of some tall viaducts. Of these, the Monsal Head viaduct of six stone arches is undoubtedly the most impressive. Apart from the physical difficulties the enterprise had to contend with some strong criticism. Ruskin deplored it, complaining that 'every fool in Buxton can be at Bakewell in half-an-hour, and every fool in Bakewell at Buxton; which you think a lucrative process of exchange – you Fools everywhere', while the Duke of Rutland insisted that the peace of his home at Haddon Hall should be preserved by a cut-and-cover tunnel.

Despite considerable opposition the line closed in 1968. It is to the considerable credit of the Peak Park Joint Planning Board that they saw fit to purchase some 8½ miles (14 km) of track from Blackwell Mill Junction, east of Buxton, to Coombs Road viaduct, east of Bakewell. This was handed over to the Board by British Rail along with a payment of £154,000 towards the cost of restoration work. This and financial allocations from the Board itself enabled about 6½ miles (10.5 km) of track to be opened. The cost of maintaining and lighting the longer tunnels was much too great however and these had to be sealed, although diversionary paths around them were provided.

At the present time cyclists, horse riders and wheelchair users are only allowed on the Bakewell-Longstone section.

(2) *Lime kilns (119-132733 and 119-141732)*

Two groups of lime kilns will be passed along the Monsal Trail; the first, of fairly recent type, is passed a short distance before Miller's Dale station where the Trail is rejoined after Chee Dale and the second, of an older type, is immediately after the viaduct on leaving the station. Information boards have been provided on both.

(3) *Miller's Dale station (119-138733)*

This was a very substantial railway station in its heyday with no fewer than five platforms, sidings and numerous buildings which included a coal office and a house for the station master. Immediately outside the station there are two large viaducts both of which have metal spans supported by masonry piers; the one with

Negotiating the stepping stones in Chee Dale.

curved spans was built in 1863, the one with girders forty years later in 1903.

(4) *Hassop station (119-217707)*

Situated in the country over a mile (1.6 km) from Hassop village, it was built largely for the convenience of the Duke of Devonshire who lived at nearby Chatsworth.

Route 24 Lathkill Dale

There are perhaps a few dales that can start to compare with Lathkill for beauty – every walker will have his own short-list – but there are certainly not many. Its wooded slopes, weirs and wonderfully clear sparkling waters will delight everyone who goes there. It was very appropriate therefore that in 1972 a substantial part of it was taken under the guardianship of the Nature Conservancy Council as a National Nature Reserve. Present day visitors will be surprised to learn, however, that the peace and beauty of the Lathkill are comparatively new features, for the dale was the scene for several hundred years of intensive mining activity, some remains of which can still be seen. This route takes in the whole of the dale from Alport to Monyash with a substantial part of its neighbour, Bradford Dale. The starting and finishing points are joined by a long traverse over the limestone plateau through One Ash Grange and Calling Low.

Length: 12 miles (19 km).

Ascent: 800 ft (240 m).

Starting and finishing point: A parking place at Monyash. Coming from Bakewell on the B5055 turn R at the crossroads at the centre of the village; the parking place is on the L after 150 yds (140 m) (119-150667).

Maps: Landranger 119; Outdoor Leisure The White Peak (East Sheet).

Route description (Maps 24A, 24B)
Walk down to the crossroads, where there is an interesting old cross, and take the road directly opposite (Rakes Road). This soon bends L by a pond, then R. At the R bend leave the road and continue straight ahead on a minor road (PFS 'Limestone Way'). Where this swings R keep in the same direction down a lane (PFS). At the lane end (after ½ mile, 800 m) go over a stile by a gate (note some fossils on the stile as you cross it) and keep to the L of a wall. After 60 yds (55 m) go R over a stile and then half L across the field to a stile. Keep to the L side of the next two fields. At the end of the second field go over a stile in the corner and continue in the same direction but now to the L of the wall. At the end of this field go through a gate and down a farm road. The farm ahead is One Ash Grange Farm – see (1).

Enter the farm area. After the barn on the R turn L at a junction (PFS) and then R at a second junction just behind the farmhouse, to pass between barns to a stile (there are yellow arrows on this section). Descend into the valley beyond. After a stile go down a small ravine and along a shelf under a cliff. At a PFS ('Limestone Way') turn R and descend to the floor of the dale (Cales Dale); there cross a fence and go up some steps to a wall stile at the top. Head across the fields towards a second farm (Calling Low), crossing three broken walls on the way. At the farm bend L to a gate leading into the farmyard.

Turn L at the end to a second gate and then through two more. Leaving the farm, head in the same direction across the field beyond to a stile in the far R-hand corner. Go into a wood and turn L by the wall. At the end of the wood go through a gap and half R to a second gap. Now keep in the same direction across a large field aiming to the R of a wood seen in the distance. At a further broken wall and PFS the path bends half R across another large field to a stile. Cross the corner to the L to a further wall, then parallel with wall on L to a gap; finally go to the far R-hand corner of the next field where the road is reached.

Go L, immediately taking the R junction at a fork. After a few yards just after a small car-park on the R turn R down a lane passing the car-park and picnic site. Soon go through a stile at a wall corner.

MAP 24A

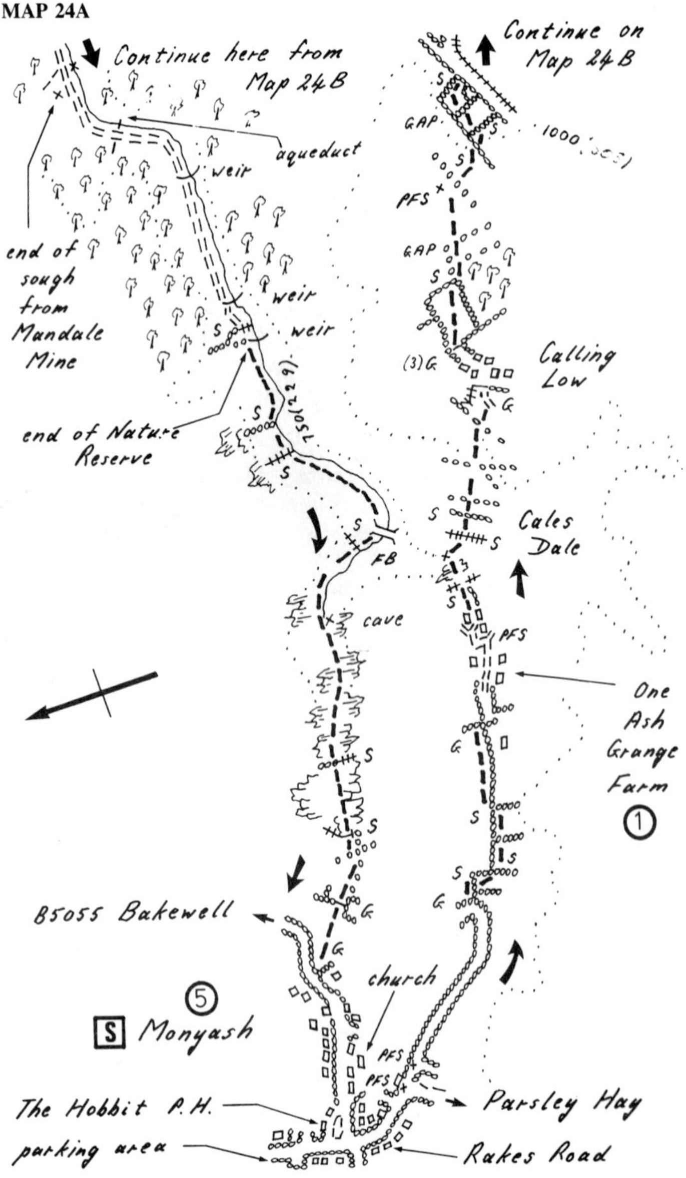

Continue here from Map 24B

Continue on Map 24B

aqueduct

weir

weir

weir

GAP

1000 (305)

PFS

GAP

end of sough from Mandale Mine

end of Nature Reserve

750 (229)

(3) G

Calling Low

Cales Dale

FB

cave

PFS

One Ash Grange Farm

1

B5055 Bakewell

5

S Monyash

church

PFS

PFS

The Hobbit P.H.

Parsley Hay

parking area

Rakes Road

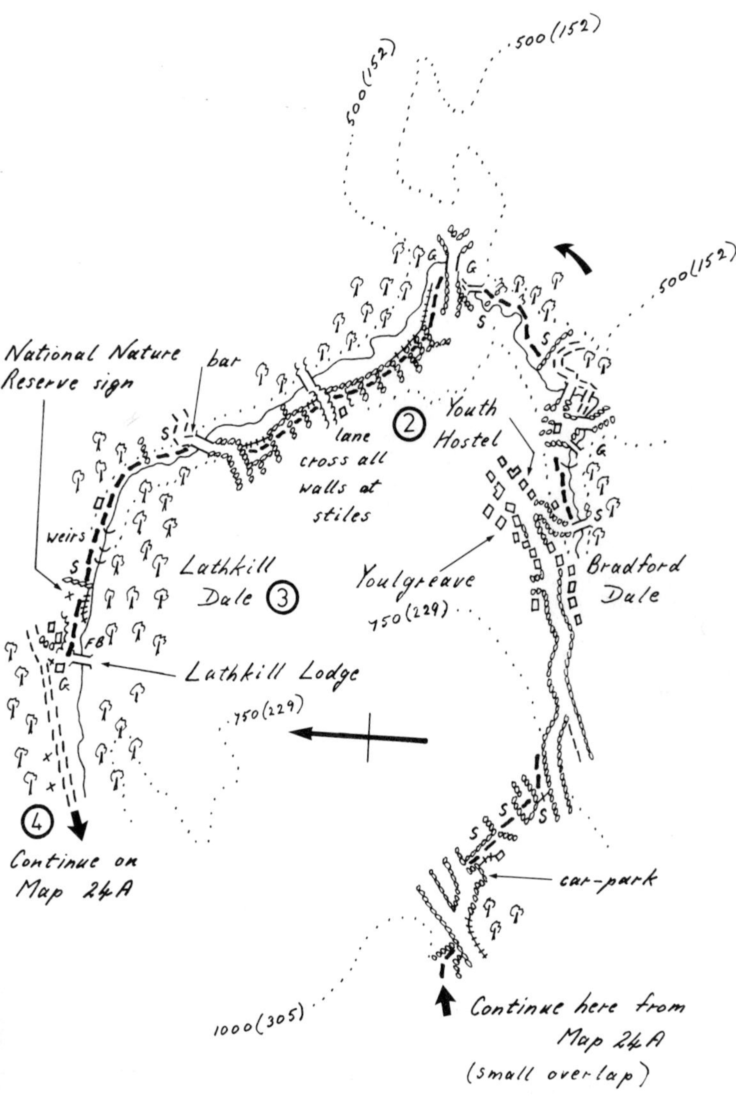
500(152)
500(152)
500(152)
National Nature Reserve sign
bar
G
G
S
S
S
Youth Hostel
2
lane
cross all walls at stiles
weirs
S
Lathkill Dale
3
Youlgreave
Bradford Dale
G
S
FB
Lathkill Lodge
750(229)
750(229)
G
4
Continue on Map 24A
S
S
S
car-park
1000(305)
Continue here from Map 24A (small overlap)

Cross the next field in the same direction. Cross a further stile and descend to the R of a wall. Where this ends keep descending to a stile, then go half L to a road. Turn L. Go along the road, ignoring a road coming in from the R, to enter the village of Youlgreave. Continue through the village to the centre where there is a fountain on the L and a very unusual youth hostel on the R – see (2) Youlgreave Youth Hostel.

Return back along the road for a short distance to a minor road on the L. Turn L down this and descend steeply into the valley. At the river (Bradford Dale) go L over a stile and follow the path on the L bank past a bridge and a weir. At a road, cross over and go down the wide unmade road opposite. This soon bends L with the river on that side. Where this swings R uphill go ahead through a stile and continue down the valley to the R of the stream. Eventually reach a minor road and go along it to reach a main road. Cross to a gate and a stile on the opposite side.

Follow the path which starts by the stream but which gradually leaves it to run alongside a fence and later a wall. Continue for about ½ mile (800 m), crossing a series of stiles, to reach a lane. Cross it to a stile opposite and then continue as before for about ¼ mile (400 m) to reach a road. Turn R and go down to a bridge. Immediately after the bridge turn L through a stile by a bar and follow the path beyond. This section of Lathkill Dale is one of unforgettable beauty, the end product of a useful working relationship between man and nature. Savour it to the full as you proceed – slowly and with, I hope, frequent pauses – over the next ¾ mile (1.2 km) to the road by Lathkill Lodge. This is the start of the Nature Reserve – see (3) Lathkill Dale. Before continuing, examine the slabs of the bridge to the L of the Lodge which contain some well-defined fossils.

Turn R up the road and between the buildings for a few yards, then L through a gate. Follow the very clear path to the R of the stream for about 2½ miles (4 km), first through deciduous woods and then through open country. Some ruins – see (4) Lead mining in Lathkill Dale – are passed after 700 yds (640 m) and the end of the Nature Reserve is reached about 1 mile (1.6 km) later. Cales Dale – crossed earlier in the walk – comes in on the L nearly ¾ mile (1.2

km) after the end of the Reserve. Soon after Cales Dale you will pass a prominent cave on the L: this is the usual source of the River Lathkill although water ceases to flow from it in dry periods.

Finally, leave the dale at a stile, passing a boulder slope on the L, to enter a narrow ravine. Soon cross a further stile and go ahead to a gate. Keep in the same direction up a shallow valley to reach a road. Turn L for ½ mile (800 m) back to the crossroads in Monyash. Monyash has an interesting history (as have most villages in the Peak District) – see (5).

(1) *One Ash Grange Farm (119-169652)*
The farm of One Ash Grange originally supplied the great religious house of Roche Abbey in Yorkshire. Abbeys, founded in the North after the Norman Conquest, followed a deliberate policy of establishing such granges or farms whose produce went to support the parent house. The establishment of a grange was usually carried out with ruthless efficiency involving the wholesale or piecemeal eviction of the local peasantry. Wool was the most important product of the granges, which were worked by converts or hired labourers. Following the Dissolution of the Monasteries most granges were sold off. On a happier note, John Bright, a Quaker mill-owner and statesman, spent his honeymoon at One Ash Grange – nearby Monyash was a strong Quaker centre.

(2) *Youlgreave Youth Hostel (119-210643)*
One of the most attractive features of youth hostelling is the extremely varied nature of the hostels themselves – the hostel at Youlgreave was a Co-operative stores erected in 1887. It is a standard hostel with accommodation for fifty-four persons. (See also the Conduit Head opposite.)

(3) *Lathkill Dale*
In an area famous for its beautiful dales, that of the River Lathkill is undoubtedly outstanding, particularly in the section immediately to the west of Conksbury Bridge. It is appropriate therefore that a substantial part of it has been declared a National Nature Reserve under the guardianship of the Nature Conservancy Council. The Reserve was established in 1972, with additions in 1974 and 1977, and covers 258 acres (104 ha).

Like some other rivers in the White Peak, e.g. the Manifold and Hamps, the Lathkill dries up each summer for most of its course, only emerging to the east of Lathkill Lodge at the Bubble Springs; in winter it emerges from Lathkill Head Cave. Its waters, arising entirely on limestone, are reputed to be the clearest in the Peak District. This disappearing trick each year can probably be laid at the door of old lead mine workings – see (4) below – as the Lathkill Dale Mine levels and their associated workings run underneath or close to the river over most of its length. When the mines were being worked this was prevented by giving a 'puddled clay' bed to the river in order to keep the workings as dry as possible; this however has now deteriorated, hence the problem.

One very important inhabitant of Lathkill Dale is *Polemonium caeruleum*, better known as Jacob's Ladder. This plant, which produces beautiful blue flowers, is found only in the limestone areas of the Pennines with its largest colony on the moist southern slopes of the upper Lathkill. Its continuing existence there is our responsibility.

(4) *Lead mining in Lathkill Dale*

As you proceed up the dale from Lathkill Lodge evidence of old lead mining activity can be found at several points. The Mandale Mine was situated to the R just before the river bends to the left and the Lathkill Dale Mine was further along by the river beyond the next bend. The pillars running across the path between the bends were an aqueduct; this originally supported a wooden trough which carried water from a leat, i.e. an artificial stream, on the opposite side to a water wheel at the Mandale Mine which was used for pumping. There was a similar, but smaller, aqueduct serving a water wheel in the Lathkill Dale Mine from the same leat – the water wheel there was exceptionally large with a diameter of 52 ft (16 m). On the L of the path just before the Mandale ruins there is the tail, i.e. the end, of a sough, coming from the Mandale Mine, which discharges by a leat into the Lathkill.

(5) *Monyash (119-150665)*

Like so many other villages in the Peak District, Monyash was granted a charter in the Middle Ages in 1340 which gave it the right to hold a weekly market and a fair twice each year. The old market cross still stands on the green at the centre of the village. Around that time Monyash lay on an old way from Derby to Manchester which linked it with the neighbouring villages of Middleton and Flagg. Later, packhorse trains and drove herds came through Monyash and a saltway from Leek to Bakewell and Chesterfield bypassed it just to the south. It also lay on the 1765 turnpike from Newcastle under Lyme to Hassop which carried chert (a hard silica) from Great Longstone to the potteries in North Staffordshire and their produce back in the opposite direction; one of the tollhouses of the turnpike was situated near the centre of the village.

Route 25 Bleaklow

This is the only route in the book which will lead you onto the great moorland area of Bleaklow, although one or two others cut across corners of its periphery. Even then it will not take you to the summit at Bleaklow Head, although the determined can always reach this by striking out towards the NNW from Hern Clough if they wish. This is, however, a route of tremendous interest, not just for the quality of the walking, which remains high throughout, but for the glimpses that it will give you into one of the wildest and roughest areas of the Peak. (This crosses an access area – see page 54.)

Length: 11 miles (18 km).

Ascent: 1400 ft (430 m).

Starting and finishing point: Car-park at Birchen Clough Bridge on the Snake Road (A57) about 2 miles (3 km) on the Chesterfield side of the Snake Pass (110-109915).

Maps: Landranger 110; Outdoor Leisure The Dark Peak.

Route description (Maps 25A, 25B)
From the car-park cross the main road and descend some steps to a ladder stile. Turn R and follow a path to the R of the river and

MAP 25A

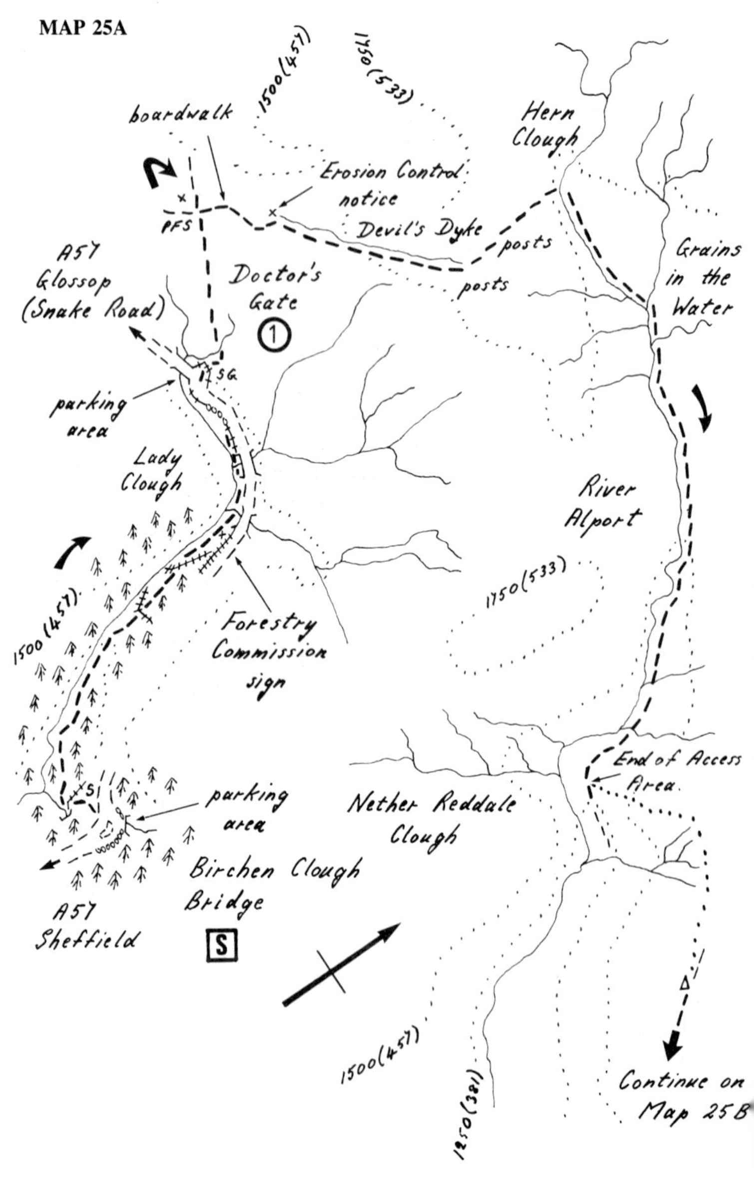

1500(457)
1750(533)
boardwalk
Hern Clough
Erosion Control notice
PFS
Devil's Dyke
posts
Grains in the Water
A57 Glossop (Snake Road)
Doctor's Gate
posts
1
SG
parking area
Lady Clough
River Alport
1750(533)
1500(457)
Forestry Commission sign
End of Access Area
S
parking area
Nether Reddale Clough
Birchen Clough Bridge
A57 Sheffield
S
1500(457)
1250(381)
Continue on Map 25B

parallel with the road for about 1 mile (1.6 km) until the forest ends. (This is a permissive path only.) Beyond the forest the path crosses two streams coming from under the road. After the second stream rise up R to the road and turn L.

After 600 yds (550 m) the road bends R and then L. At this second bend at the end of a parking area leave to the R through a small gate (PFS 'Doctor's Gate Roman Road to Glossop'). Soon the path bends half L to cross the stream. Follow the path (partly paved) over the moor for about 700 yds (650 m) to an obvious crossing-path – see (1) Doctor's Gate. This crossing path is the Pennine Way on its first lap from Edale – or on its last, depending upon your choice of starting point. This section, near to the Snake Pass, has been extensively resurfaced. Turn R.

Follow the resurfaced path to its end at a prominent grough (Devil's Dike) where there is an erosion control notice. (Note the word 'control'; it implies an acceptance that some erosion is inevitable, but a hope that with proper path maintenance and some co-operation from walkers it may at least be kept within acceptable limits.) Keep in the same general direction but now on the firm bed of the grough. Where the grough ends continue up to the top of the moor following a line of posts. From the top the path goes half L, marked as before with posts. Follow these until you reach a stream at a bend (Hern Clough). Cross and turn R to follow the L-hand side of the stream (i.e. downstream). Continue to follow the stream down until a hollow is reached with another stream tributary coming in from the L. At this point the stream being followed bends to the R down a deepening valley. This remote spot is called Grains in the Water: on a warm sunny day a delightful place to rest for a while, eat lunch and enjoy the wild beauty of the country around you.

Continue to follow the main stream down, still keeping on the L bank where there is an excellent path. After about 1⅓ miles (2.1 km) two prominent cloughs (Upper and Nether Reddale) will be seen coming in from the R. About this point the access area ends although the path continues. Leave the path and strike up the hillside to the L. Reach the flat top of the ridge and go half R aiming for a white Ordnance Survey triangulation column. By the column is a path which continues in the same general direction as before.

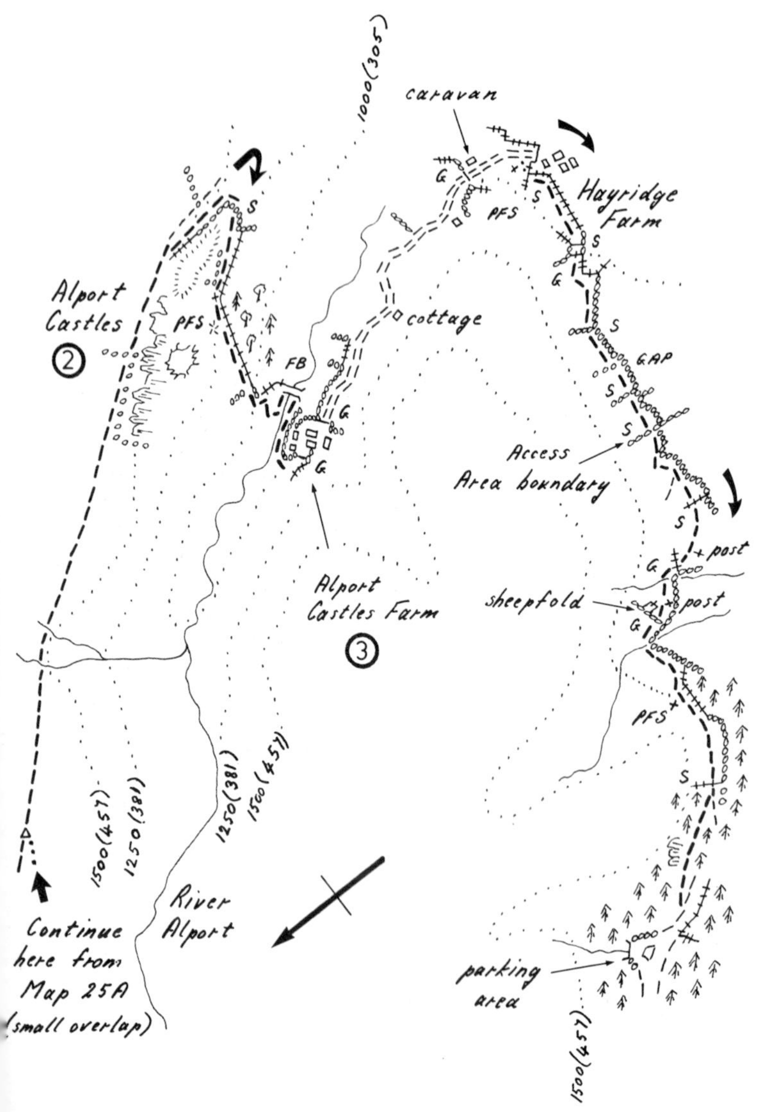
caravan
Hayridge Farm
Alport Castles
②
PFS
S
FB
G
cottage
GAP
Access Area boundary
post
sheepfold
Alport Castles Farm
③
1000(305)
1500(457)
1250(381)
River Alport
parking area
Continue here from Map 25A (small overlap)

Follow this for about 1 mile (1.6 km) to a wall corner at an edge. Continue along the edge keeping to the L of the wall until it ends. At this point the spectacular land-slip of Alport Castles will be seen down to the R – see (2) Alport Castles.

Keep in the same direction walking on the path near to the edge of the cliff. About 200 yds (180 m) before a broken wall comes in to meet the edge take a path which drops steeply down half R into the small valley formed between the main fell and the land-slip. This path goes down the valley to the L of a fence and, after a gap, to the L of a wall. At the end bend R with the wall to a ladder stile. Continue to descend into the main valley with the wall then a fence to your L, eventually reaching a footbridge.

Cross the footbridge and turn R by the river. After about 100 yds (90 m) the path bends to the L to a gate and a stile. Cross and go up a short lane into a farmyard – see (3) The Alport Castles Love Feast. Go between the barns ahead, turning R after the barn on the R (this is a camping barn – see page 24). At the end go L through a gate into a farm road. Keep on this for nearly 1 mile (1.6 km) until a gate is reached with a caravan just beyond. Continue along the farm road for a further 250 yds (225 m) to a fence corner with a farm just ahead. Go ahead to a PFS then leave the farm road half R to a ladder stile. Beyond the stile follow the path by a fence passing the farm on the R, until at the end you can go half R up a sunken farm road. At the top cross a ladder stile, then a gate and finally a stream to continue in the same direction as before to still another ladder stile.

Continue in the same direction with a wall to the L over three fields crossing walls at stiles or gaps. Then, after a long field, cross a stile in a wire fence and follow the path as it curves away to the R to a gate and a stile in a corner. Beyond, the path swings L keeping near to a wall. Go through a gate by a sheepfold and follow the wall down into a clough. Cross the stream in the clough and go steeply up to the L still keeping by the wall to reach a coniferous wood. There turn R and follow the boundary fence of the wood up the steep hillside. Follow the fence as it bends to the L at the top. Shortly the path descends and cuts across the hillside to a stile in a corner.

Go through the stile and enter the forest. After a few yards, at a junction, keep straight ahead. After about 300 yds (275 m) pass to the L of an area of boulders and then to the R of a wall. Descend to meet a road (A57); there turn R for a short distance back to the car-park.

(1) *Doctor's Gate*

From AD78 to 84, during the governorship of Agricola, the Romans established an impressive system of forts and roads over the area of the Peak District. This provided not only the means for controlling the local population, but also a secure base for the supply and support on which the Roman conquest of northern England depended.

One road in this network linked the Roman fort of Navio, situated by the River Noe to the north-west of Brough, with one near Glossop (nowadays usually referred to as Melandra, although this was probably not its real name). Unlike most Roman roads which went in long straight lines, this one followed a more irregular path in order to use the contours of the hills to advantage and to avoid difficult ground.

Like most other Roman roads, however, it was well constructed, with a surface made up from flat gritstone blocks, 6 inches (15 cm) thick, set closely together. At each edge there was a kerbstone which stood proud of the road surface and in the middle a centre stone. Drainage was ensured by deep ditches dug along each side, into which the moor edges were sloped. The effort needed to construct such a road, particularly over the wilder moorlands of the Peak, must have been considerable.

From Hope the road ran generally to the north-west over the ridge into the neighbouring Woodlands valley, where it crossed the River Ashop near its confluence with the Alport. From there it ran along the northern side of the valley, later coinciding with the present line of the Snake Road. Its final stretch was over the ridge of moorland (now the Snake Pass) to Shelf Brook which it followed down to Glossop.

The name of this way came, not from its Roman origin, but – it is said – from its connection with Dr John Talbot, an illegitimate son of the Earl of Shrewsbury and vicar of Glossop for fifty-five years from 1495 until 1550. It is likely that he travelled the road frequently during his long incumbency and so his name became associated with it; the word 'gate' was often used to mean 'road'.

(2) *Alport Castles (110-142914)*

First-time visitors to The Tower at Alport Castles may be forgiven for imagining – both from its name and from the shape of the rock formations there – that man had some hand in its creation. This, however, is not the case; Alport Castles owe their existence to what has been described as the largest land-slip in Britain. It is clear that at several points on the eastern side of the valley massive slippage took place sometime in the past, bringing down huge blocks of gritstone. The name 'castles' obviously arises, not from their origin, but from the appearance of these huge blocks, now clearly separated from the main cliff.

(3) *The Alport Castles Love Feast*

The restoration of Charles II in May 1660 ushered in a period of intense religious intolerance in which Anglican values and practice were vigorously promoted both at local and national level by Act of Parliament. At the end of it the Church of England was totally dominant, supported by and in turn supporting both Monarchy and Government. Anglican priests, required to conform to the doctrine and the use of a revised Prayer Book, were given in return a monopoly of public office. Nonconformists, by comparison, were denied both public office and freedom of worship. Even by the end of 1660 nearly 700 ministers who had served under Cromwell had been ejected from their livings. In all fairness it should be said that this was not of Charles's doing; faults he certainly had in abundance but religious intolerance was not one of them. The demand for these changes came from Parliament, the Church and the masses and they were largely forced upon him.

It is said that in 1662 forty-six clergymen in this area were deprived of their livings. Thereafter, to avoid persecution – for it was illegal to gather together and hold services – they met to worship in secret in a barn in the lonely Alport valley. At that time such a gathering would certainly have been broken up with dire consequences for the participants.

On the first Sunday of each July that meeting is still celebrated in the same barn. The Feast, as it is called, is simple; hymns are sung, prayers said, cake and water form the ingredients of a communion. It is held in memory of those dissenters of 1662 and – much more important – in the name of religious tolerance anywhere and at any time.

The barn is at Alport Castles Farm.

Route 26 Derwent Edge

Derwent Edge – the most northerly of that great line of gritstone edges coming down the eastern flank of the Peak District – lies to the east of the Derwent and the Ladybower Reservoirs. It provides a magnificent walk, particularly when combined with a descent from Back Tor and Lost Lad, at the northern end of the edge, down Abbey Clough and the path along the eastern side of the reservoirs. The route finding should present no problems, with the possible exception of the descent from Back Tor to the top of Abbey Clough if there is thick mist over the moor.

Length: 12 miles (19 km).

Ascent: 1500 ft (460 m).

Starting and finishing point: Fairholmes car-park just below the dam of Derwent Reservoir. Coming from Sheffield along the A57 turn to the R along a minor road immediately after the viaduct over the Ladybower; the car-park is to the R at the end of that reservoir. The road beyond the car-park is closed on Sundays in summer and on Bank Holidays. There is also an information point, toilets and a picnic site at the start (110-173893).

Maps: Landranger 110; Outdoor Leisure The Dark Peak (part only).

Route description (Maps 26A, 26B)

In the car-park facing the front of the toilet block (i.e. by the information boards) turn to the R and follow the path which leaves the car-park along the side of a fence. This soon reaches a road; there go R and across a small bridge. Over to the L you will see the dam of the Derwent Reservoir – this is at its most impressive during the winter months when water cascades over the centre section producing a superb waterfall. Keep following the road as it bends to the R and starts to climb. The black domes that you see at intervals beside the road are for the ventilation of pipes that carry water from the reservoirs to neighbouring towns. Keep on the road until the metalled section ends by Wellhead Farm, then continue in the same general direction along the rough forest road which keeps parallel to and near the reservoir shore. Keep on this as it runs along the full length of the northern section of the Ladybower Reservoir for about 1½ miles (2.5 km). The small bridge just beyond Wellhead Farm is the site of the small hamlet of Derwent which was submerged when the Ladybower Reservoir was constructed – see (1) The lost valley.

At the viaduct which marks the end of the northern part of the Ladybower Reservoir go through a gate and on to the metalled road beyond. Go up to the L by some cottages. The metalled road soon changes to a lovely grassy track which climbs slowly up the hill and then descends (crossing three gates) to reach the back of the Ladybower Inn. Do not go down to the inn, but continue along the track which soon bends to the L to a gate (entrance to Nature Reserve). Go through the gate and keep on the path to a further gate under some power lines. Continue along the same path as it crosses the moor and slowly descends towards a bridge on the road down to the R – see (2) Cutthroat Bridge.

Do not turn down to the bridge but instead follow the L-hand path which drops down slightly L to a small stream; there the path bends to the L to follow the stream on its L bank. After a short distance the path leaves the stream to the L and starts to rise up the moor. Continue to rise for about 1 mile (1.6 km) to the top of the ridge where there is a superb view ahead down into the Derwent valley. This is the meeting place of a number of paths; take the one

MAP 26A

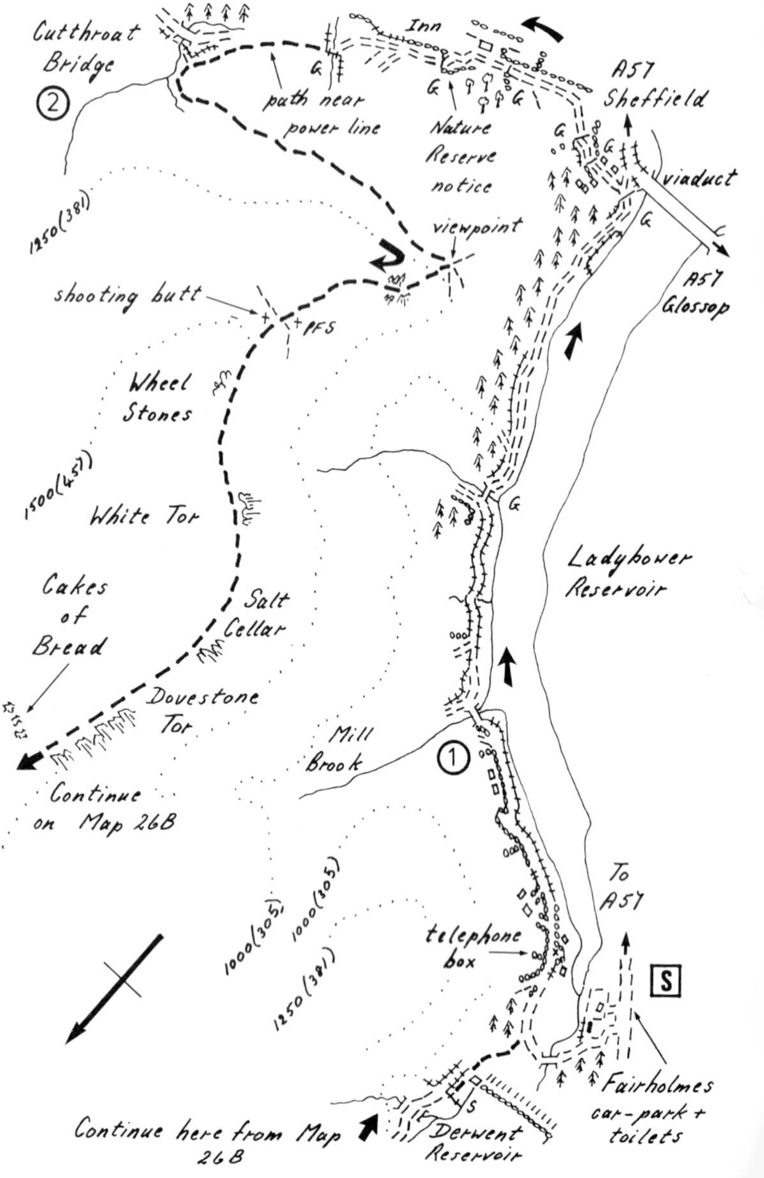

Cutthroat Bridge

2

path near power line

Inn

Nature Reserve notice

A57 Sheffield

viaduct

A57 Glossop

1250(381)

viewpoint

shooting butt

PFS

Wheel Stones

1500(457)

White Tor

Ladybower Reservoir

Cakes of Bread

Salt Cellar

Dovestone Tor

Mill Brook

1

Continue on Map 26B

1000(305)

1000(305)

1250(381)

telephone box

To A57

S

Fairholmes car-park + toilets

Continue here from Map 26B

Derwent Reservoir

MAP 26B

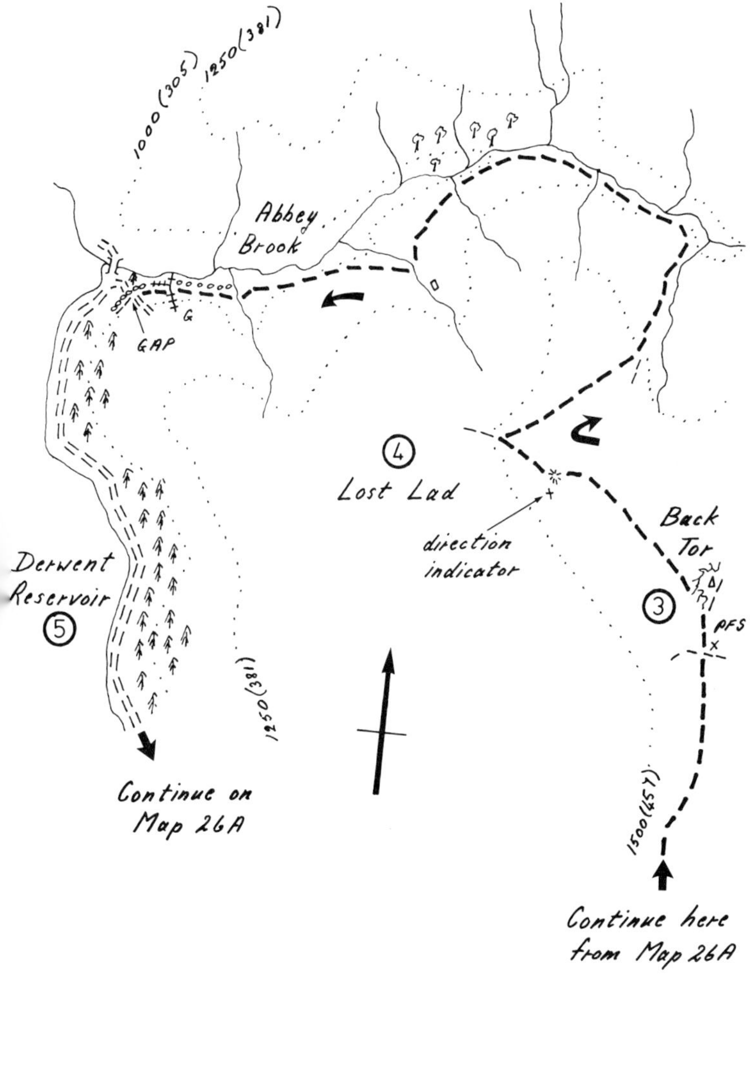

1000 (305)
1250 (381)
Abbey Brook
GAP
G
4
Lost Lad
direction indicator
Back Tor
3
PFS
Derwent Reservoir
5
1250 (381)
1500 (457)
Continue on Map 26A
Continue here from Map 26A

to the R which climbs steeply up the ridge to some rocks. At the rocks the path bends to the R and soon reaches a crossing path by a shooting butt.

Follow the very clear path ahead which runs along the edge of the moor with a steep drop to the L. Keep on this path for about 2 miles (3 km) passing a number of weathered gritstone outcrops – in particular look out for the Salt Cellar and the Cakes of Bread which live up to their names. Eventually you will reach Back Tor – this is unmistakable for there is a white Ordnance Survey obelisk high on the rocks – see (3) The engagement. With care drop down to the L of the obelisk (i.e. leaving the main path which continues to the R of the obelisk) to pick up a pronounced hollow-way which goes across the moor half L from the original route. Follow this hollow-way until it dips and then rises up to a cairn on the top of a small hill, Lost Lad – see (4) below. This is a lovely viewpoint, considerably better than Back Tor.

Still following the hollow-way continue in the same direction beyond the cairn for about 300 yds (275 m) until a second hollow-way comes in from the R; turn back half R along it. This way crosses the moor, slowly dropping down towards a deep stream valley, Abbey Clough. At the clough the path bends to the L and follows it down on its L bank. On the way you will cross a deep side clough which will necessitate a deep descent and then an ascent on the other side. At the top of the rise just after this clough you will catch sight of the Derwent Reservoir. Later cross a further side clough and continue until you reach a gate (the total distance down Abbey Clough is about 2 miles, 3 km). Beyond, keep in the same direction by a fence and then a wall until a gap is reached to the R. Go through this and descend through a wood to reach a lower forest road running alongside the reservoir shore – notice the large dam over to the R; this is the dam of Howden Reservoir. Turn L and follow the broad path by the shore of the reservoir for 1½ miles (2.5 km) until you are almost at the dam of Derwent Reservoir and fences start on both sides. At the start of the fence on the R, go over a stile and follow the path which goes past the end of the dam – see

Gritstone architecture in the Dark Peak – the Wheel Stones.

(5) The Dam Busters, below – and down through a wood. Soon reach the road that you used earlier and turn R along it to return to your starting point.

(1) *The lost valley*
The upper Derwent valley holds three reservoirs – the Howden, Derwent and Ladybower – which together form an almost continuous stretch of water over 6 miles (10 km) in length from its western reach in the Woodlands valley to its northernmost point near Ox Hey. The first of these to be completed, and now the most northerly, was the Howden which took eleven years to build from 1901 to 1912, while the centre one – the Derwent – started a year later, was not completed until 1916. The original authorisation for this work was the Derwent Valley Water Act of 1899 which also allowed the construction of four other reservoirs, two in the Derwent valley and two in the Ashop valley, but these were abandoned in 1920 in favour of a single large reservoir, the Ladybower. The subsequent history of the Ladybower is similar to that of Haweswater further to the north in the Lake District as both involved the drowning of valleys of considerable beauty with the destruction of their village communities – in the latter case that of Mardale Green and in the former of Derwent and Ashopton.

By any standards neither Derwent nor Ashopton was a large village, but both possessed buildings of considerable character of which Derwent Hall was outstanding. Built by Henry Balguy in 1672 it was extended and considerably improved in the nineteenth century. After a succession of owners the Hall was finally sold in 1927 to the Derwent Valley Water Board. It served as a youth hostel for a few years and as a school for a few more, but from September 1942 systematic stripping and then destruction of the Hall began. By the summer months of 1943 only ruins remained. In addition to the Hall went a much-loved church – the bodies from the churchyard were re-interred at Bamford – a fine coaching house (the Ashopton Inn) and a Methodist Chapel, besides a number of farms, shops and cottages. From 1943 onwards the valleys slowly

Back Tor.

filled and the ruins of both villages had disappeared by the end of the Second World War.

(2) *Cutthroat Bridge (110-214874)*

This bridge, built about 1821, owes its sinister name to the discovery in 1635 of a man with his throat cut a short distance away.

(3) *The engagement (110-198910)*

Many years ago one 5 March Mary and Jack became engaged on Back Tor and thought it appropriate to record the fact for posterity by chiselling an announcement about it on to a convenient rock face. It will be found just below the Ordnance Survey obelisk on the south-east corner of the rocks.

(4) *Lost Lad (110-193912)*

By the cairn on Lost Lad there is a direction indicator which is inscribed to the memory of W. H. Baxby (1901–1977).

The cairn is said to mark the spot where the body of a young shepherd boy was found; he had become lost while gathering sheep in bad conditions and had died of exposure. The body was found some time later by a shepherd who was crossing the area and noticed the words 'lost lad' scratched on a rock face.

(5) *The Dam Busters*

In 1943 the Derwent Reservoir dam was used for practice runs by Lancaster bombers of 617 Squadron who were training for their operation against the Eder and Mohne dams. A film about this episode – *The Dam Busters* – was also made in this area.

Route 27 The Ladybower Ridge

The Ladybower Reservoir is in the form of an inclined – but somewhat distorted – letter Y, with arms that point directly towards the great Bleaklow massif to the north-west. The long ridge in between the two arms offers the possibility of superb walking. This route, which takes in some of the most attractive features of the ridge, falls into three distinct parts: the first along the spine of the ridge and then down to the Derwent Reservoir, the second from the Derwent over the ridge again by Alport Castles into the Woodlands

The dam of Derwent Reservoir.

valley, and the third along the old Roman road to the south by Hope Cross. The paths are all good, the views breath-taking, the variety of landscape refreshing. Undoubtedly, however, the highlight of the walk is the view of the great land-slip of Alport Castles revealed suddenly and dramatically during the second crossing of the ridge at the end of the long rise up Birchinlee Pasture.

Length: 12½ miles (20 km).

Ascent: 1950 ft (600 m).

Starting and finishing point: A small parking place on the A57 towards the end of the western arm of the Ladybower Reservoir (110-172872). The space here is very limited, but there are further parking places within easy reach in both directions.

Maps: Landranger 110; Outdoor Leisure The Dark Peak.

Route description (Maps 27A, 27B)
Cross the road and turn R for a few yards. Just after the start of the forest go L through a gate and follow a bridleway up into the trees. The way soon bends to the R and climbs up the hillside. After about ½ mile (800 m) pass through a gateway and a short distance further a gate. Continue ahead for 50 yds (45 m) and then turn back half L along a path which soon bends R to run parallel to a wall. At the top go through a gate about 140 yds (130 m) to the R of a wall corner, and follow a path to the L. Do not go through the gate ahead ('private' sign) but turn R to a ladder stile. Follow the path which rises slightly L to a small gate, then in the same direction to a second small gate. Finally, cross a third field to reach a forest.

Keep to the L of the forest boundary for ¾ mile (1.2 km) until the forest ends at the junction of three farm roads. Turn R along one of them keeping the forest on your R, and follow that past

The Upper Derwent Valley. The Ladybower Ridge which is crossed and then recrossed on Route 27 lies to the left of the reservoir.

MAP 27A

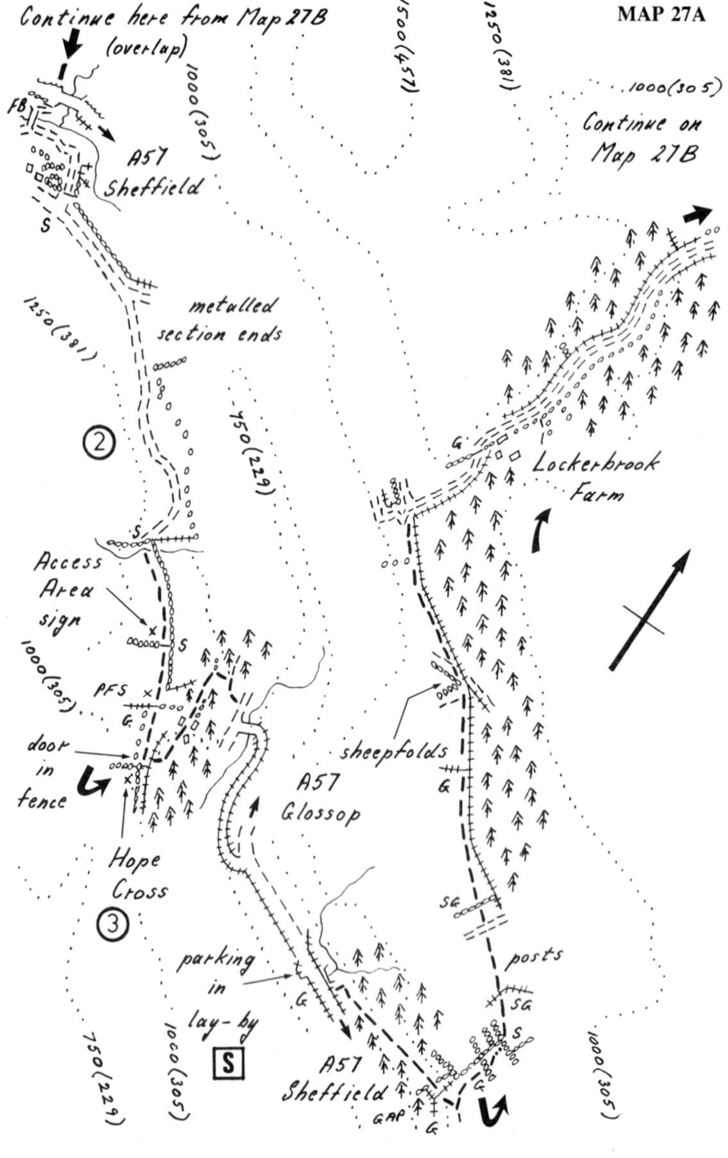

Continue here from Map 27B
(overlap)
FB
A57
Sheffield
S
1000(305)
1500(457)
1250(381)
1000(305)
Continue on
Map 27B
1250(381)
metalled
section ends
750(229)
2
G
Lockerbrook
Farm
S
Access
Area
sign
S
1000(305)
PFS
G
door
in
fence
sheepfolds
A57
Glossop
G
Hope
Cross
SG
3
parking
in
lay-by
G
posts
SG
S
S
750(229)
1000(305)
A57
Sheffield
GAP
G
G
1000(305)

MAP 27B

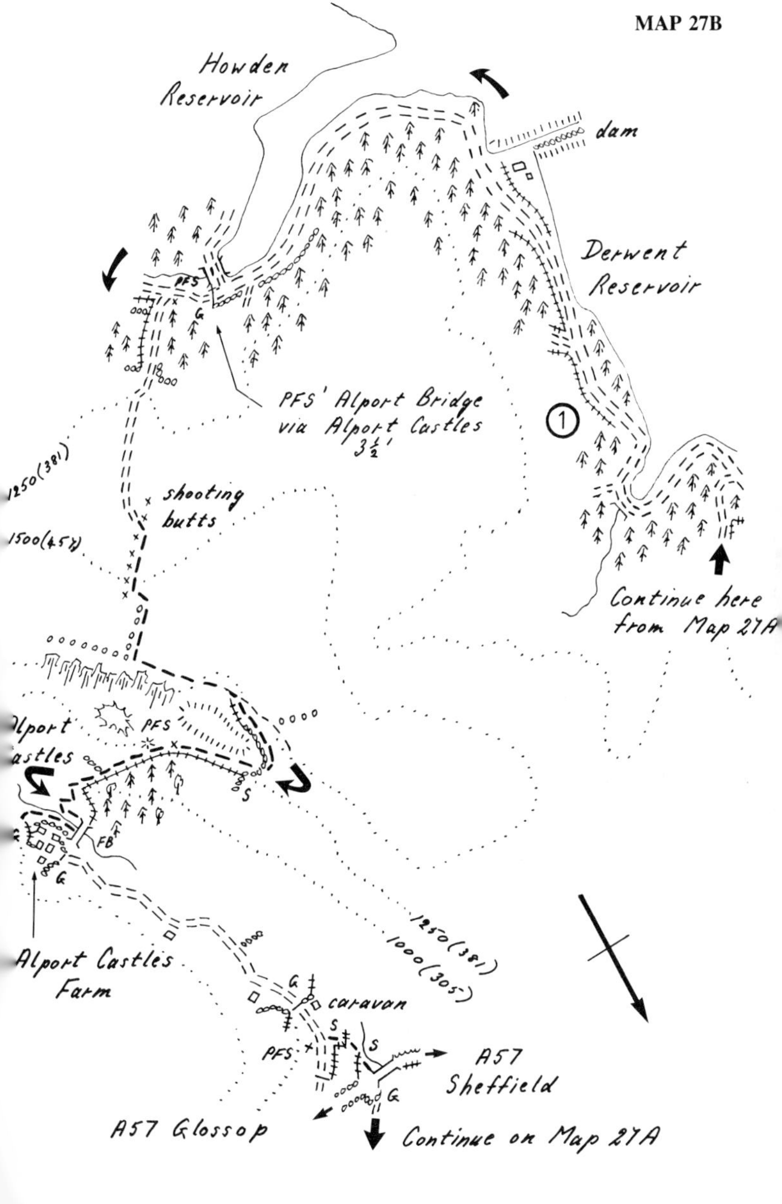

Howden Reservoir

dam

Derwent Reservoir

PFS

G

PFS' Alport Bridge via Alport Castles 3½'

1250(381)

shooting butts

1500(457)

Continue here from Map 27A

Alport Castles

PFS

S

FB

G

Alport Castles Farm

1250(381)

1000(305)

G

caravan

S

S

PFS

A57 Sheffield

G

A57 Glossop

Continue on Map 27A

Lockerbrook Farm for 1½ miles (2.4 km) to a road in the Derwent valley. Turn L. The road goes around a small spur of the Derwent Reservoir; immediately after the spur is the site of a temporary village erected when the reservoirs were being built – see (1) Birchinlee below. Later pass the Howden Dam. Shortly after the dam the road bends L and runs along a long side arm of Howden Reservoir. About 1 mile (1.6 km) after the bend the road bends R over a bridge and runs along the opposite side of the arm. Do not go with it, but keep in the same direction through a gate (PFS 'Alport Bridge via Alport Castles 3½').

Go up the forest road which soon bends R then L. Immediately afterwards at a fork (PFS) go L, climbing into the forest. After about 600 yds (550 m) leave the forest and continue up the moor on a superb grassy track. The path rises slowly for about ¾ mile (1.2 km) past two rows of shooting butts to reach a wall and the edge of a cliff. Directly ahead and to the L is the scene of a gigantic land-slip, Alport Castles – see page 237.

Turn L to walk along the path near the edge of the cliff. About 200 yds (180 m) before a broken wall comes in to meet the edge, take a path which drops steeply down half R into the small valley between the moor top and the land-slip. This path goes down the valley to the L of a fence and a wall. Bend R with the wall to a ladder stile. Continue to descend with the wall, then a fence, to your L. Eventually reach a footbridge in the valley.

Cross the footbridge and turn R. After about 100 yds (90 m) the path bends to the L to a gate and a stile. Cross and go up into a farmyard (Alport Castles Farm). Go between the barns ahead, turning R after the barn on the R. At the end go to the L through a gate into a farmroad. Keep on this for nearly 1 mile (1.6 km) until a gate is reached (a caravan just beyond). Continue for a further 250 yds (225 m) to a fence corner with a farm directly ahead. Leave the farm road half L to a stile, then more steeply into a road (A57).

Cross the road and go down to a gate to the R of the stream. This leads to a ford which can be crossed if safe (if not, use the footbridge nearby). Follow the rough farm road which goes off to the L – this is the line of an old Roman road – see (2) Doctor's Gate. After ¼ mile (400 m) cross a ladder stile by a gate to the L of a farm, Upper Ashop. The farm road now swings L to join another coming in from the farm. Continue in the same direction to a fork. There take the branch to the R, climbing slowly up the hillside. At the top go around a clough, Blackley Clough, crossing a stile just before the stream. Keep in the same direction to leave the access area at a further stile. 300 yds (275 m) later go through a gate (PFS) and to the L of a broken wall to a wall by a wood (there is a tall monolith on the opposite side of the wall – see (3) Hope Cross). Do not cross the wall to the monolith, but instead turn L into the wood through a wooden doorway!

Follow a lovely path through the wood with occasional good views over Ladybower Reservoir to the R. At a ruin keep in the same direction by a short length of broken wall. Later, at a further broken wall and junction, go down to the R. Shortly, turn R on a forest road and after a few yards leave the forest at a T-junction; turn L soon crossing a bridge. Follow the rough road between fences to the main road (A57). Turn R and walk a short distance back to the parking place.

(1) *Birchinlee (110-165931)*
The hillside on the shore of Derwent Reservoir, just beyond the small spur of the reservoir where the waters of Ouzleden Clough come in from the left, was the site of a temporary village early this century. It was built in 1901 to house the workers who were constructing the Howden and Derwent Reservoirs and was dismantled when that work was complete. The village took its name from a nearby farm. Birchinlee – unlike many other temporary villages built in similar circumstances – was no shanty town but a well-organised community. A school, hospitals, police station, baths, Mission Hall and shops were some of the amenities provided.

(2) *Doctor's Gate*
The moor road followed from the ford over the River Ashop to Hope Cross coincides with a section of Doctor's Gate, a Roman road, part of which is also followed on Route 25. From Hope Cross it descended to the south-east towards the Roman fort at Brough. See also page 236.

(3) *Hope Cross (110-162875)*
Milestones and guidestones are common in the Peak District. This superb example stands at the crossing point of two old packhorse ways, one coming along the ridge and the other from Jaggers Clough to the west.

Route 28 The High Peak Trail

Out of the five railway trails in the Peak District National Park the High Peak is outstanding in three respects: firstly, it is the longest – some 4½ miles (7 km) more than its nearest rival, the Tissington; secondly, it still retains numerous relics of the old railway; and thirdly, it is far from flat with several steep inclines. With the exception of the Sett Valley Trail – which never gets far away from buildings – it also passes more industry than do the others. Despite the very easy nature of the walking, however, the completion of the High Peak Trail in a single expedition is a fair undertaking. Walkers who are also railway enthusiasts will find it fascinating.

Length: 17½ miles (28 km).

Ascent: The High Peak Trail is substantially flat over most of its distance. There are, however, three long steep inclines which give a total rise of about 850 ft (260 m).

Starting point: High Peak Junction on the A6, 1¼ miles (2 km) south-east of Cromford (119-314560). Cars may be parked at Cromford. The old railway line will be seen going underneath the road. On the east side of the bridge is the Agent's House; go through a stile to the R of this and down to some railway carriages and buildings. Turn L between the carriages and the Ranger Office and along the track.

Finishing point: Near Doolow Farm on the A515 about 5 miles (8 km) south-east of Buxton (119-110673). There is a lay-by for parking near the end.

Hope Cross.

MAP 28A

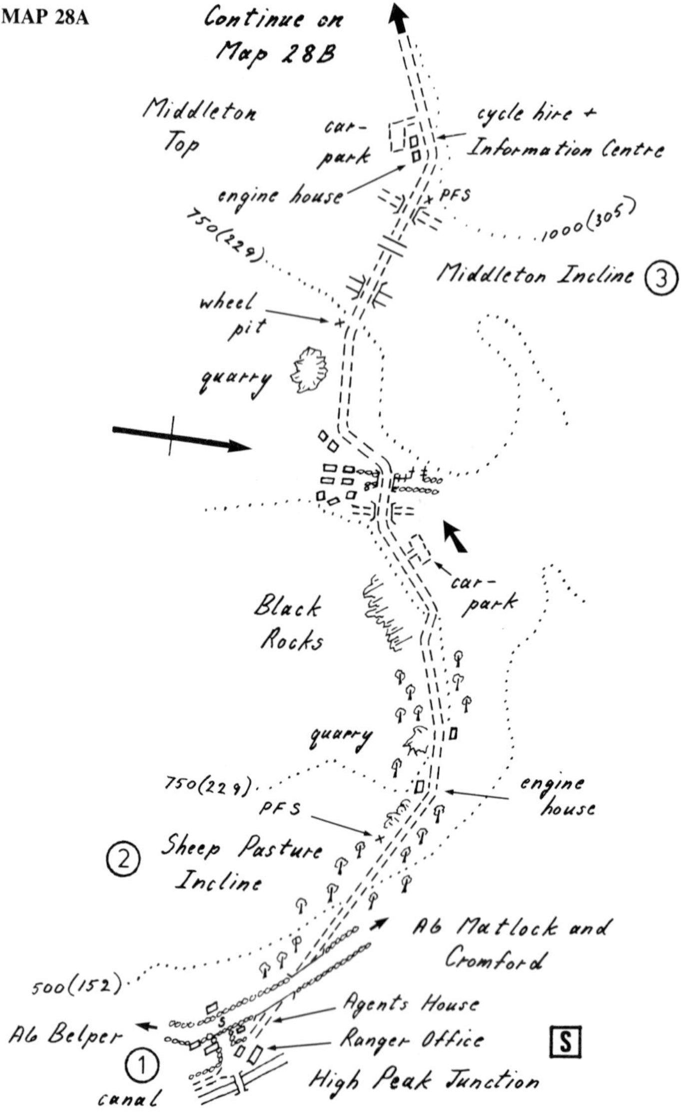

Continue on Map 28B

Middleton Top
car-park
cycle hire + Information Centre
engine house
PFS
1000(305)
750(229)
Middleton Incline ③
wheel pit
quarry
car-park
Black Rocks
quarry
750(229)
engine house
PFS
② Sheep Pasture Incline
A6 Matlock and Cromford
500(152)
Agents House
A6 Belper
Ranger Office
S
① canal
High Peak Junction

MAP 28B

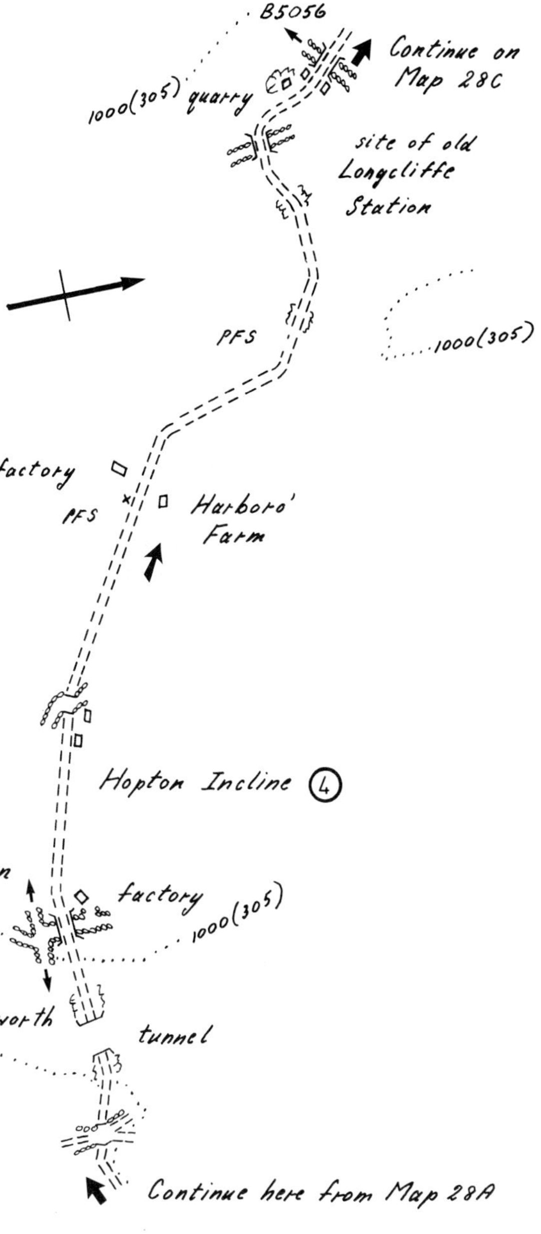

B5056
Continue on Map 28C
1000(305) quarry
site of old Longcliffe Station
PFS
1000(305)
factory
PFS
Harboro' Farm
Hopton Incline 4
Brassington
factory
1000(305)
Wirksworth
tunnel
Continue here from Map 28A

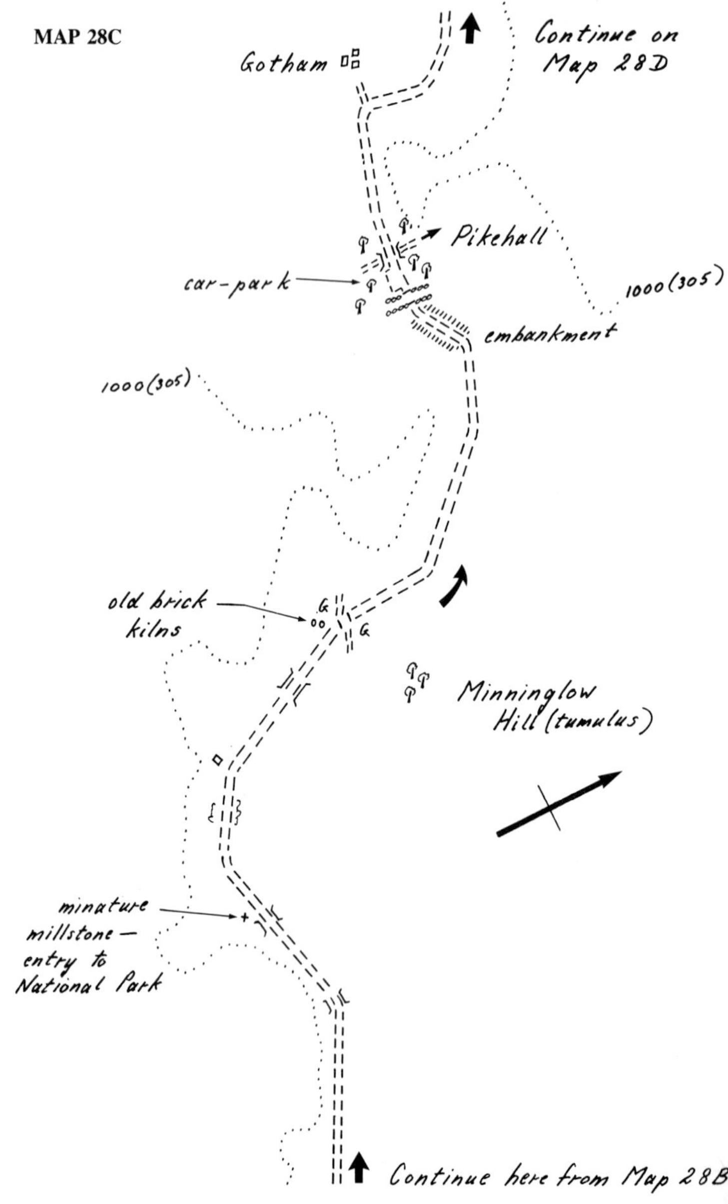
MAP 28C
Gotham
Continue on
Map 28D
Pikehall
car-park
1000(305)
embankment
1000(305)
old brick
kilns
Minninglow
Hill (tumulus)
minature
millstone —
entry to
National Park
Continue here from Map 28B

MAP 28D

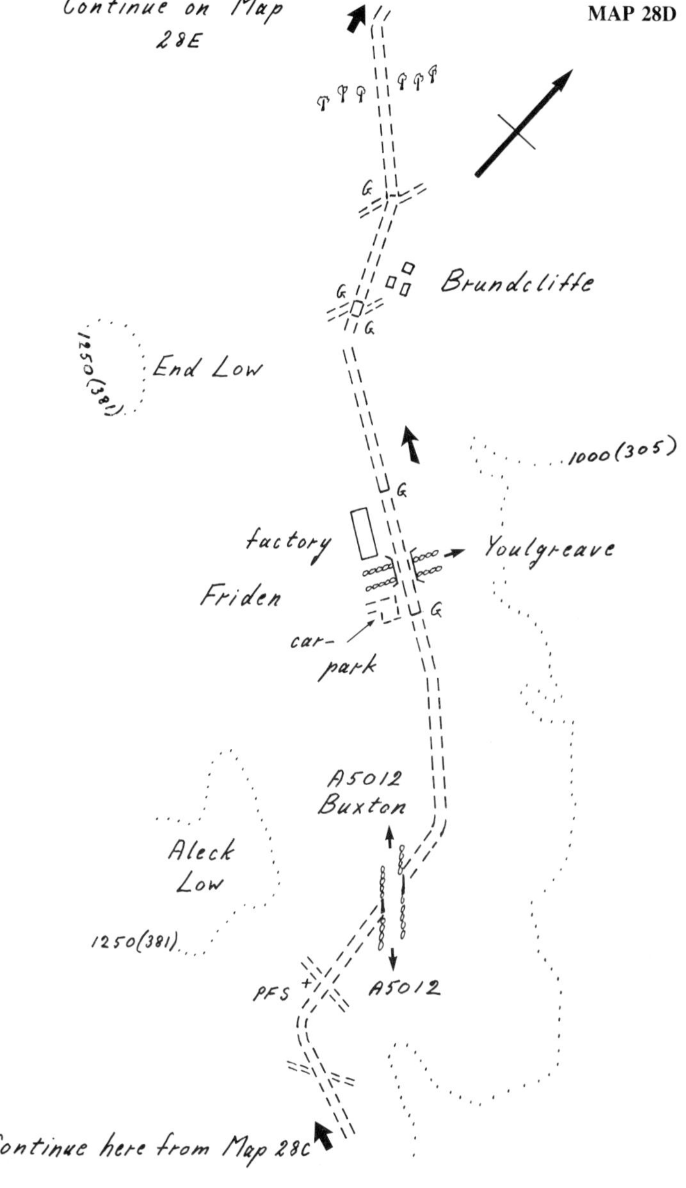
Continue on Map 28E
G
Brundcliffe
G
G
1250(381)
End Low
1000(305)
G
factory
Youlgreave
Friden
G
car-park
A5012
Buxton
Aleck
Low
1250(381)
PFS
A5012
Continue here from Map 28C

MAP 28E

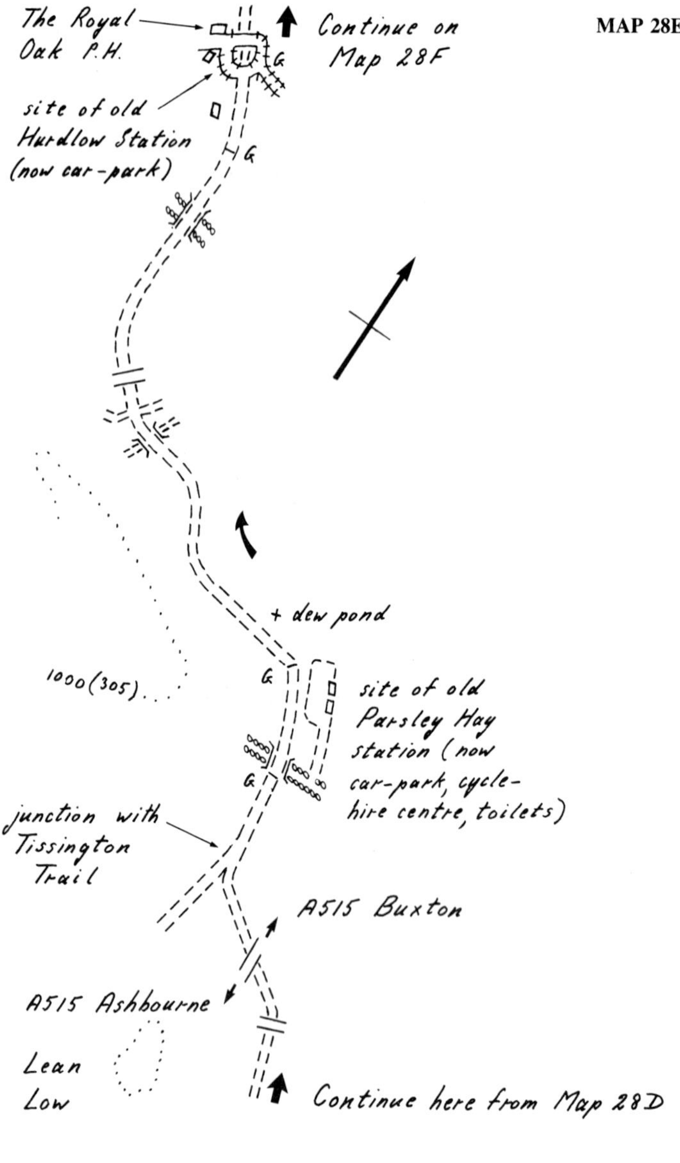

The Royal Oak P.H.
Continue on Map 28F
G
site of old Hurdlow Station (now car-park)
G
+ dew pond
1000(305)
G
site of old Parsley Hay station (now car-park, cycle-hire centre, toilets)
G
junction with Tissington Trail
A515 Buxton
A515 Ashbourne
Lean Low
Continue here from Map 28D

MAP 28F

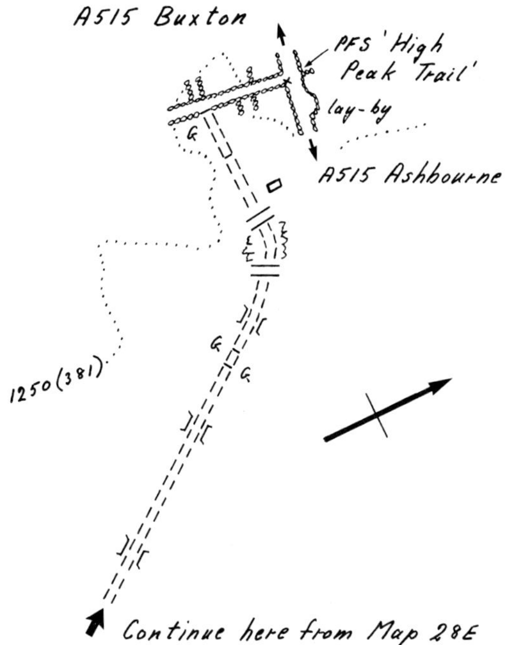

A515 Buxton
PFS 'High Peak Trail'
lay-by
A515 Ashbourne
G
G
G
1250(381)
Continue here from Map 28E

Maps: Landranger 119; Outdoor Leisure The White Peak.

Route description (Maps 28A, 28B, 28C, 28D, 28E, 28F)
Once you have embarked on the way, any route description is superfluous as there is nowhere else to go except straight on. As with the Tissington Trail, therefore, this section is restricted purely to mentioning places of interest and possible picking-up points. All the distances given are taken from the starting point at High Peak Junction. Before starting, read (1) The High Peak Trail.

0 miles, 0 km: High Peak Junction. Goods brought by canal to this point were transferred from narrow canal boats on to railway trucks. Locomotives were overhauled in the workshop there.

¾ mile, 1.2 km: Sheep Pasture Incline. This is the steep incline met immediately after High Peak Junction. See (2) Sheep Pasture Engine House.

1½ miles, 2.5 km: The Black Rocks. These are over to the left of the Trail. A fine crag which was developed at an early stage in the gritstone era.

2¾ miles, 4.5 km: Middleton Incline and Engine House. There is a car-park, cycle-hire centre, picnic area and Information Centre at the Engine House. See (3) The Middleton Top Engine House.

4 miles, 6.5 km: Hopton Incline. See (4) below.

6½ miles, 10 km: Longcliffe Station. A shed, loading bay and the station master's house are still in existence.

8 miles, 13 km: The two round brick structures to the L of the Trail were kilns used last century in the production of bricks. The hill top over to the R, crowned with trees, is Minninglow, the largest chambered barrow in the Peak District. Constructed 2500–2000 BC, it was robbed in Roman times.

9.5 miles, 15 km: Car-park and picnic area about ½ mile (800 m) south of Pikehall. There is a very impressive stone embankment just before.

12 miles, 19 km: Car-park and picnic area at Friden. This was originally a small shunting yard.

The High Peak Trail enters the National Park near Minninglow Hill. Note the small millstone to the left of the track.

14½ miles, 23 km: Parsley Hay. The junction with the Tissington Trail is just before the station.

17½ miles, 28 km: The Trail ends at a rough lane. Turn R in the lane and go up to the A515. Go R for the lay-by.

(1) *The High Peak Trail*

The Cromford and High Peak Railway was unusual in that it was built as a link between two canals: the Cromford and the Peak Forest. The former, opened in 1794 as a branch from the Erewash Canal, ended at Cromford Wharfe; while the latter, built by Benjamin Outram and in use – although not fully completed – in 1799, ended at Whaley Bridge (actually this was a branch with the real terminus at Bugsworth – later Buxworth – Basin). As canal construction across the limestone area of the White Peak, which separated the two canals, would have been difficult, the junction was made by a railway line. Built by Josias Jessop, the first section from Cromford to Hurdlow opened in May 1830 and the second section to Whaley Bridge in 1831. The total length was 33 miles (53 km). Initially, horses were used for haulage – with steam winding engines to pull trucks up the inclines – but these were replaced by steam locomotives after 1841.

As an independent concern the line was not particularly successful and it was leased in 1861 to the London and North Western Railway Company, who carried out some work along the line with a view to improving its viability. Even after these improvements, however, a journey along the Cromford and High Peak was still a slow affair, taking about sixteen hours to travel the 33 miles (53 km). Passengers were carried from 1833 until 1877, but the main use was always commercial and included the transport of limestone from quarries and dairy products from farms. The Buxton to Ashbourne Railway, which used a section of the Cromford and High Peak line from Parsley Hay to near Harpur Hill, was completed by 1899; this made the northern part of the Cromford and High Peak Railway redundant and it was dismantled beyond Ladmanlow. In 1963 the Middleton Incline towards the southern

Sheep Pasture Engine House.

end of the track was also closed, breaking the railway into two separate parts. With that move early closure of the entire line became almost inevitable, and the last scheduled service ran on 21 April 1967.

Part of the track was acquired in 1969 – 10½ miles (17 km) by the Peak Park Joint Planning Board and 7 miles (11 km) by Derbyshire County Council – and converted into the High Peak Trail. The Trail may be used throughout by walkers, cyclists and horse riders.

(2) *Sheep Pasture Engine House (119-301562)*
Two lines ran up the 1:8 Sheep Pasture Incline, each carrying a steel cable down its centre (see next entry). A steam engine, built by the Butterley Company, was housed in the building at the top of the incline. This engine house was opened on 20 May 1830.

(3) *The Middleton Top Engine House (119-276552)*
An endless steel cable ran down from the engine house at the top of the incline and around a wheel set in a pit at the bottom – which is still there although in a poor condition. Between the rails the cable was carried on rollers. Wagons were attached to this cable and hauled to the top or lowered to the bottom. The engine house holds a beam winding engine operated by steam (the boiler house is next to the engine house). This was also built by the Butterley Company in the period 1825–9.

The engine house is open to the public each Sunday from 10.30 a.m. to 5 p.m.; on the first Sunday only of each month the engine can be seen in operation.

(4) *The Hopton Incline (119-257546)*
This incline was nearly ¼ mile (400 m) long. Originally, trucks were hauled up the incline by a steam winding engine, but this became redundant in 1877 following improvements by the London and North Western Railway Company. From that date locomotives could ascend the line, although it was easily the steepest track climbed by locomotives in Britain.

Middleton Top Engine House.

Route 29 The Wye Valley

With the possible exception of Dovedale the Wye Valley between Buxton and Ashford in the Water is widely regarded as the most beautiful of all the Peak District valleys. It is very fortunate, therefore, that the best stretches of it can all be walked without recourse to metalled roads, due particularly to the Monsal Trail which runs along part of it and to the creation of several concessionary footpaths. This route follows the Trail as far as Monsal Head and then leaves it down Monsal Dale to the A6 road. The link between the two ends of the valley – a large proportion of the total – crosses the limestone plateau to the south via Taddington and Chelmorton. By the sound of it, a very pleasant walk in delightful surroundings. But make no mistake about it: although this route is in the 'soft' south of the Park, the distance to be covered is considerable and in cold, wet and windy weather the plateau – well over 1000 ft (305 m) in height – can be a challenging place.

Length: 16 miles (26 km).

Ascent: 1450 ft (450 m).

Starting and finishing point: White Lodge car-park on the A6, Bakewell-Buxton road, at the end of Monsal Dale (119-170706).

Maps: Landranger 119; Outdoor Leisure The White Peak (East and West Sheets).

Route description (Maps 29A, 29B, 23A, 23B, 6)
Leave the car-park over a stile in the fence which is on the opposite side from the main road. Pass through a broken wall and on to an intact wall. Do not go through the stile in the wall (marked '3.8'), but keep to the R going into a narrow wooded ravine. On emerging at the far end of the ravine continue on a path to the L of a wall which goes through a dry valley (Deep Dale). After about ¾ mile (1.2 km) at a wall corner go through a small gate to continue on the

R-hand side of the wall. Reach a lane and turn R uphill. Pass a farm (Over Wheal) and 200 yds (180 m) later at a crossroads turn L up another walled lane.

The walk up this lane on a pleasant day will be highly enjoyable – on the way, note the close field systems on the R. After nearly 1 mile (1.6 km) reach a road and turn R. Ignore the junction to the L and follow the road down into the village of Taddington. At the bottom of the hill you will reach a T-junction. To visit the church turn R for a short distance to a gate on the L which leads into the churchyard – see (1) Taddington, for information on the church and village. Otherwise, just *before* the junction go L over a stile and along a path which leads into a field. Go half R up the field to reach a higher road. Cross to a stile opposite and then up to a gap in a wall. Go slightly L through a second gap and then across the large field beyond aiming for a few trees at the top. Cross the wall there at a gap just to the R of the trees and head across the next field towards the L-hand side of a reservoir. Go through a stile to the L of a gate and then across the next field, passing a trough, to a stile in the far R-hand corner. (There is an OS obelisk over the wall to the R – it is difficult to realise how high you are at this point, but this is Sough Top, 1437 ft (438 m) above sea-level.)

Follow the footpath to the L of the wall crossing a series of walls at stiles. After 500 yds (460 m) cross a walled lane and shortly afterwards pass Fivewells Farm (the farm is to the R). One of the large fields behind the farm contains a stone tomb in which several skeletons were discovered (this is on private ground, however). Soon after the farm, where the wall ends at a corner, go through a stile and cross a field to a road.

Turn R and then after 45 yds (40 m) L through a small gate (PFS). Keep in the same direction as before with walls on each side and alongside an irregular trench (this is the worked line of an old mineral rake). Eventually, at the end, descend on a clear path down to the village of Chelmorton, reaching it at a bend in the road. The church on the L has a highly unusual weathervane – see (2) The church at Chelmorton.

Just *before* the bend turn to the R up a farm road (PFS 'Old Coalpit Lane') soon crossing a cattle grid. (Before leaving

MAP 29A

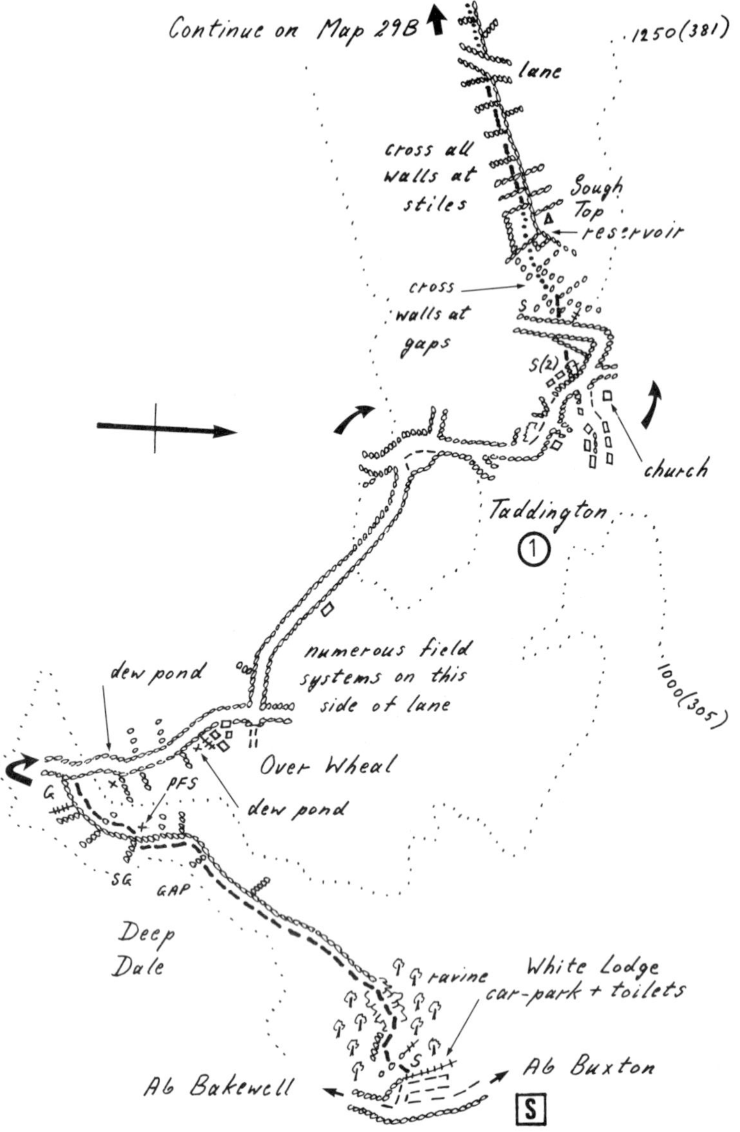

Continue on Map 29B
1250(381)
lane
cross all walls at stiles
Sough Top
reservoir
cross walls at gaps
S
S(2)
church
Taddington
1
numerous field systems on this side of lane
1000(305)
dew pond
Over Wheal
G
PFS
dew pond
SG
GAP
Deep Dale
ravine
White Lodge car-park + toilets
S
A6 Buxton
A6 Bakewell
S

MAP 29B

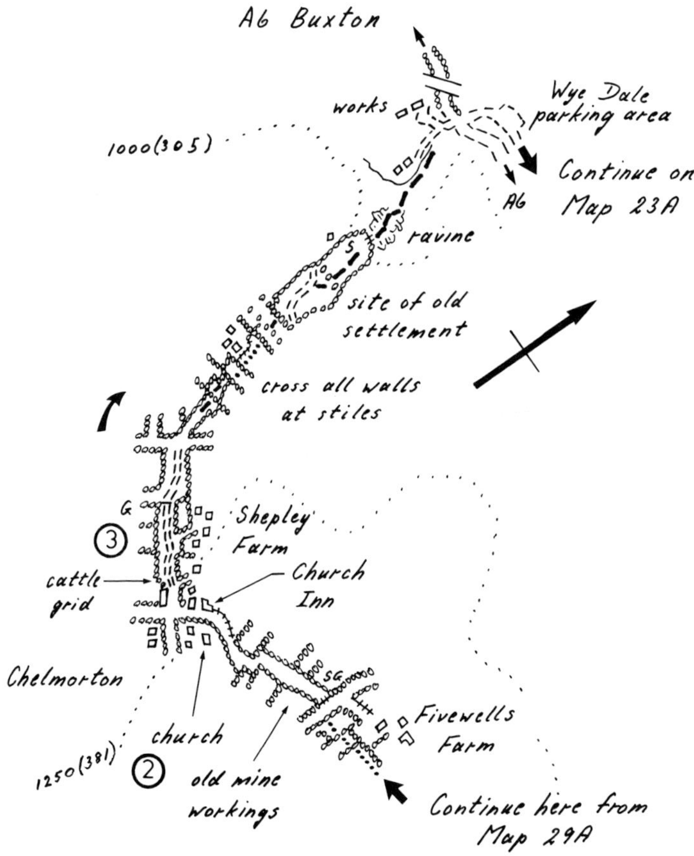
A6 Buxton
works
Wye Dale
parking area
1000(305)
Continue on
Map 23A
A6
S
ravine
site of old
settlement
cross all walls
at stiles
G
Shepley
Farm
3
cattle
grid
Church
Inn
SG
Chelmorton
Fivewells
Farm
church
1250(381)
2
old mine
workings
Continue here from
Map 29A

Chelmorton have a look at the fields to the L of the lane; the closely spaced walls trace the outlines of the old medieval field strips which once surrounded the village – see (3) The 'fossilised' landscape of Chelmorton.) At a farm the farm road bends to the L and then goes on between walls. Reach a road, cross and continue down the lane half R. Where the lane branches go down to a stile in the bottom R-hand corner of the field. Keep descending to rejoin the lane. At the bottom go over a stile and cross the field ahead to a further stile to the R of a farmhouse. Keep in the same direction over three more stiles to a farm road crossing a large area of rough ground – this is the site of a long-vanished settlement. Where the farm road turns L up to a gate leave it, keeping in the same direction, to pass a large concerete slab and down the valley with a wall to the R. Cross a stile by some trees and enter a narrow ravine. Follow this down to a large cement works. Just before the works the path turns R and goes along the R-hand side of the valley with a stream and a works road to the L. The path joins the works road just beyond two ponds. Turn R and at a T-junction R again to continue down to the main road (A6). Cross the road and go down to the Wye Dale car-park opposite.

The route from here to Monsal Head follows the route of the Monsal Trail. For full details see Route 23.

At the start of the Monsal Head viaduct go L through a small gate and down half L to reach the river by a footbridge. Do not cross but turn R along a clear path which goes under the viaduct. Keep on the path to the R of the river for 1¼ miles (2 km) to the A6. Cross and go up to the car-park where you started.

(1) *Taddington (119-142711)*

The village is mentioned in Domesday Book when it was known as Tadintune, probably derived from 'The Tun of Tata's People' (*tun* is an Old English word meaning village or town).

The first positive evidence of a church at Taddington dates from the early thirteenth century when King John granted the church at Bakewell to the Dean and Chapter of Lichfield along with chapels at Taddington and elsewhere. Near the door of the choir vestry is an old font, possibly Norman, which was found in a public house near the church fixed to the wall by a fireplace. It is said that it was used there for 'ordinary culinary purposes', which included the washing of beer glasses. Fortunately, it was rescued in 1939 and placed in the church porch before being set into its present position on a new base. In All Saints Chapel there is the tomb of Sir Richard Blackwall, who died on 8 March 1505; Sir Richard and his wife, Agnes, were responsible for a family of eleven, six sons and five daughters, who are shown on their brass.

(2) *The church at Chelmorton (119-116703)*

In the gospel according to Matthew it is written that '. . . John the Baptist came to the desert of Judaea and started preaching . . . John's clothes were made of camel's hair; he wore a leather belt round his waist, and his food was locusts and wild honey.' It is appropriate therefore that the spire of the church at Chelmorton, which is dedicated to him, should be topped with a weathervane in the form of a golden locust. A moulding a few feet down the spire indicates the point of repair when the top was blown down some 200 years ago.

It is known that a church existed in Chelmorton in 1256 for in that year five local inhabitants were granted permission to add a perpetual chantry, i.e. a small chapel, to it. (It was common practice for wealthy individuals – or small groups of the not-so-wealthy – to build chantries on to existing churches; an endowment would provide the salary of a full-time priest who prayed daily for the souls of the departed to ease their way in the next world. It was a perpetual chantry because it was intended to last for ever.) It is likely, however, that a building was there at the beginning of the century or even a hundred years earlier. The present building is the result of that work and of several major restorations and additions.

Built into the walls of the south porch are several grave-covers, the profession of their original owners marked by emblems – a sword for a soldier (by far the most common), keys for a blacksmith and shears for a wool stapler. The octagonal font contains letters on each of its faces whose meaning is still obscure and in the south transept there is a box carved with the words '1630 RAPH. BUXTON OF FLAGG GAVE THIS'. There is also a memorial cross to Sergeant Joseph

Pickford of the Notts. and Derby Regiment who was killed in action at Neuvilly on 12 October 1918 aged twenty-six years.

(3) *The 'fossilised' landscape of Chelmorton*

No visitor to Chelmorton can fail to be impressed by the close-packed multiplicity of drystone walls to the south and east of the village, similar to those around Flagg and Taddington a few miles away across the plateau. The character of these field systems is shown far more clearly however by the briefest examination of the White Peak sheet of the Ordnance Survey Outdoor Leisure series. On this map the long narrow fields around the village stand out in sharp contrast to the much larger square or rectangular fields further away. It is likely that the former were medieval while the latter were marked out very much later under the great Enclosure Acts around the end of the eighteenth century. In some cases the narrow strips have ends curving to the left – this device was used in medieval times when the ploughs were pulled by teams of eight oxen yoked in pairs. These curved ends permitted a narrower headland for turning resulting in a lower loss of productive land.

Route 30 The Western Moorlands

For many walkers the Western Moorlands are one of the most attractive regions of the Park, offering peace and quietness well away from the hurly-burly of such popular tourist spots as Edale, Castleton and Chatsworth. There is also, some have suggested, more than a touch of magic about them. I would agree. This route offers a wide variety of walking: moor, forest and pasture land with a section of the Gritstone Trail. It is likely, however, that your most vivid memory will be the sight of the Cat and Fiddle Inn, seen from afar, holding forth across the moor a promise of much-needed refreshment. Macclesfield Forest Chapel, the lovely packhorse bridge at Three Shire Heads and the view from Shutlingsloe are some of the other attractions.

The close-packed drystone walls around Chelmorton follow the original lines of medieval field boundaries.

Length: 16 miles (26 km).

Ascent: 2450 ft (750 m).

Starting and finishing point: A parking place (small lay-by) on the road running to the south-west of Wildboarclough (118-980681).

Maps: Landranger 118 and 119; Outdoor Leisure The White Peak (West Sheet).

Route description (Maps 30A, 30B, 30C)
Walk up the road with the stream on your R. After ½ mile (880 m) turn R over a bridge and follow the road uphill through the small hamlet of Wildboarclough. Several features of interest are passed in rapid succession as you climb. The very imposing building set back from the road by the telephone kiosk on your L was at one time the largest sub-post office in the country. Further up the hill is the church, also on the L – see (1) St Saviour's Church, Wildboarclough – and finally there is a large hall near the top.

At a road junction at a large grass triangle keep in the same direction. Where the road bends to the R go ahead down a grassy path (PFS 'Three Shire Heads'). Go through a gate and then in the same direction to the R of a wall. Where the wall swings to the L go ahead to the L of a barn by some trees and then on across a short stretch of moor to a stile in a wall which leads into a lane. Cross the lane to a stile opposite and then across the next stretch of moor, heading towards a farm.

At the farm go into the road and turn R, immediately leaving it down a farm road half L. The farm road gradually descends down the hillside to a lovely bridge which spans the river to the R – this bridge is very old, the meeting point of three counties and in days gone by of several packhorse trails – see (2) Three Shire Heads. Do not cross but instead continue along the L bank of the stream. Just after a ruin at a fence corner go R over a stile and keep in the same direction. Where the stream bends to the R cross a wall at a stile and head across a field (no path) to a further stile in the far R-hand corner (there is a farm to the L). After rejoining the stream, keep

MAP 30A

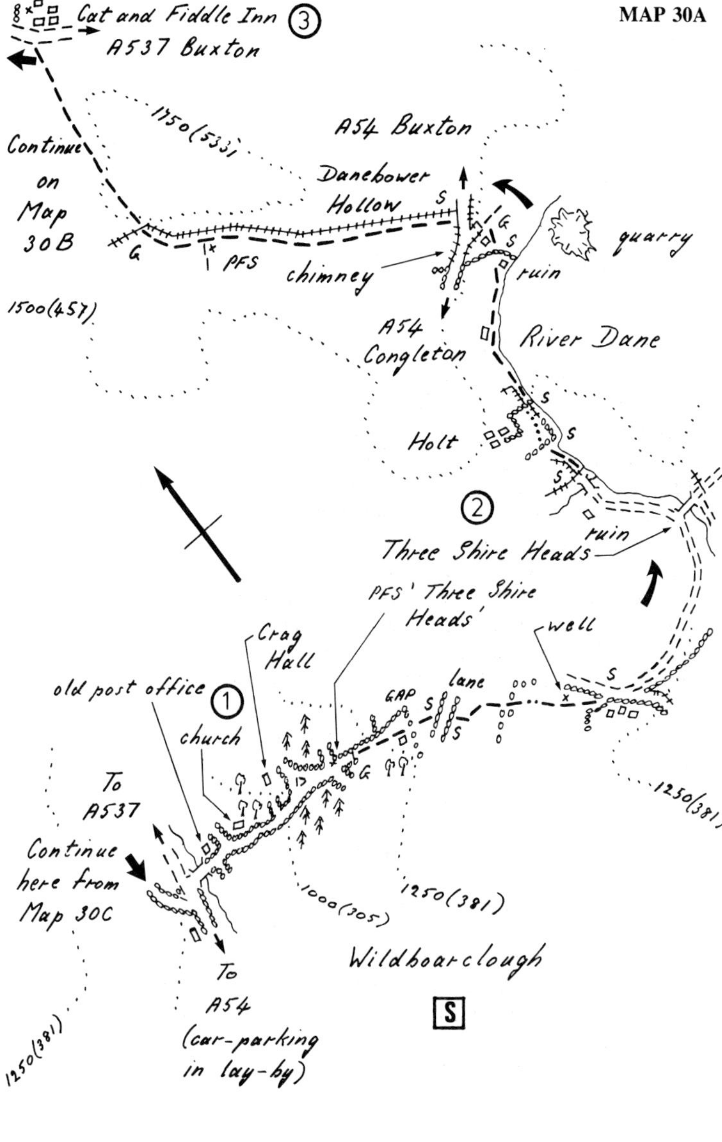

Cat and Fiddle Inn
3
A537 Buxton
1750(533)
A54 Buxton
Continue on Map 30B
Danebower Hollow
S
G
S
quarry
G
PFS
chimney
ruin
1500(457)
A54 Congleton
River Dane
S
Holt
S
S
2
ruin
Three Shire Heads
PFS 'Three Shire Heads'
Crag Hall
well
lane
old post office
1
GAP
S
S
S
church
G
To A537
Continue here from Map 30C
1000(305)
1250(381)
1250(381)
Wildboarclough
To A54 (car-parking in lay-by)
1250(381)
S

MAP 30B

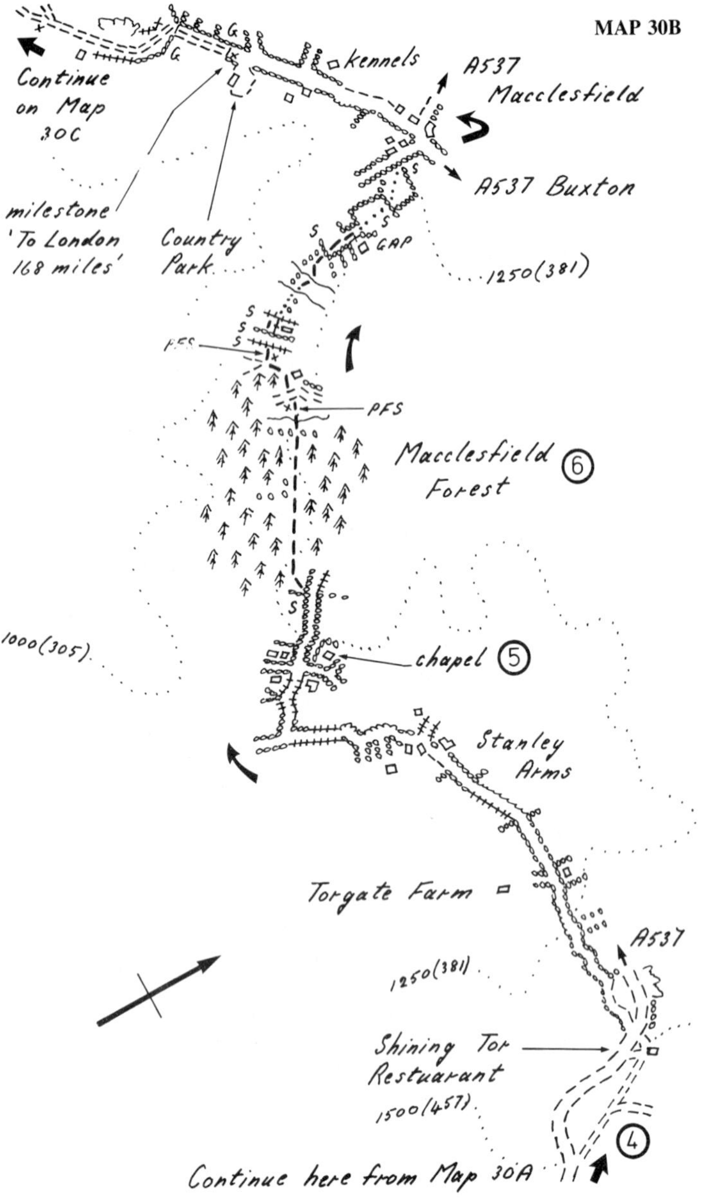

Continue on Map 30C

kennels

A537 Macclesfield

A537 Buxton

milestone 'To London 168 miles'

Country Park

GAP

1250(381)

PFS

PFS

Macclesfield Forest ⑥

1000(305)

chapel ⑤

Stanley Arms

Torgate Farm

A537

1250(381)

Shining Tor Restuarant

1500(457)

④

Continue here from Map 30A

on its L bank, soon passing another ruin, to a stile below a chimney. Go half L up the steep hillside past the chimney to a gate. Go L through it and along to a road. Turn R.

200 yds (180 m) later, just after a bend in the road, go L through a stile. Follow the clear path to the L of a fence for nearly 1 mile (1.6 km). The path then leaves the fence at a gate and heads straight across the moor towards a building in the distance – this is the famous Cat and Fiddle Inn – see (3).

Cross the road (A537) at the inn and turn L. After 250 yds (230 m), where the main road swings L, keep ahead along a rough road over the moor. The surface of this moorland road is unusual – see (4) The Stonyway. Rejoin the main road by the restaurant and after a few yards leave it again down a minor road half L. After about 1 mile (1.6 km) reach the Stanley Arms public house and at the road junction take the minor road to the L. At a junction go R (i.e. to 'Forest Chapel') and at a second junction turn R uphill. At the top the road bends to the L by several houses – go to the R for a few yards to a very interesting chapel – see (5) Rushbearing at Macclesfield Forest Chapel.

Return to the road and go R. After 400 yds (370 m), where the forest begins on the L, go into it over a stile. Follow the clear path through the forest to reach a forest road after about ⅔ mile (1.1 km). Go straight across and along a footpath to the L of a barn. 180 yds (160 m) beyond the barn reach a crossing track (PFS 'Walker Barn') and turn R up to a road. Turn L and then R over a stile after a few yards. See (6) The Forest of Macclesfield, for information about the forest area.

Keep by the fence on the R as you pass some buildings (Ashtreetop) to a stile. Beyond continue in the same direction to the L of a broken wall (no path) soon dropping down to a marshy area. Climb over the hill on the opposite side, now to the R of a broken wall, and down to a second marshy area. Climb again and on to a stile at a corner. Continue, still keeping in the same direction, but now to the L of a wall, to pass a farm. After the farm go through a gap and then head straight across a field (no path) to a ladder stile, beyond go down half L to a ladder stile leading into a lane. Turn R to a road (the A537, met earlier at the Cat and Fiddle).

MAP 30C

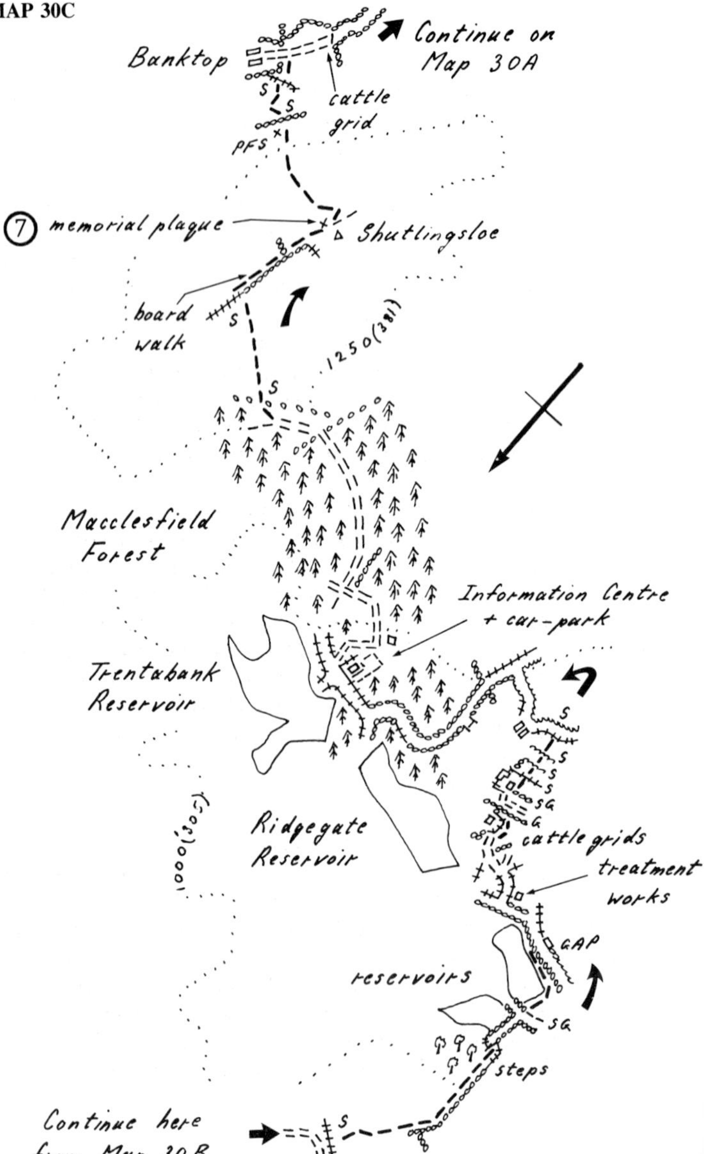

Continue on Map 30A
Banktop
cattle grid
S
S
PFS
7 memorial plaque
Shutlingsloe
board walk
S
1250 (381)
S
Macclesfield Forest
Information Centre + car-park
Trentabank Reservoir
S
S
S
S
SG
G
Ridgegate Reservoir
cattle grids
1000 (305)
treatment works
GAP
reservoirs
SG
steps
Continue here from Map 30B
S

Turn L and immediately L again at a junction (sign 'Tegg's Nose'). Pass the entrance to the country park on your L (toilets and café). Immediately afterwards, where the road bends R, keep ahead. Go through a gate and then on to a second gate, there turn L. You are now on the Gritstone Trail – see page 308 – which will be followed for about 2 miles (3 km) to beyond Ridgegate Reservoir.

Soon reach the steep edge of the hill, curving to the R past some quarries (and a small display area). At the end of the ridge the path curves to the R by a fence. Go over a stile on the L (Gritstone Trail sign) and drop down a field towards the R-hand side of two reservoirs. Soon meet a wall and descend with it, finally going down some steps on to the first reservoir, Teggsnose Reservoir. Cross the dam. At the end go half L to a small gate and descend to the dam of the second reservoir (Bottoms Reservoir). At the end of that dam turn L, along the reservoir embankment, to finally reach a road. Go L.

Immediately after a treatment works turn R along a lane. At a cattle grid take the L fork. Soon reach a house and pass it on its R-hand side going alongside a fence (PFS). At the end of the fence go through a gate and turn L along a farm road. This soon bends to the R towards a farm. Do not enter the farmyard, but instead use the small gate just to the R of the first barn thus passing the farm on its R-hand side. At the end go over a stile and then ahead across three fields to a lane. Turn L, after ¼ mile (400 m) turning L again at a T-junction. The road soon bends R into a coniferous forest. At a further T-junction go R.

Soon you will reach a large car-park and Information Centre on the R-hand side of the road (opposite the dam of a further reservoir, Trentabank). 70 yds (65 m) later, leave the road half R (following 1,2,3 signs) into the forest. After ½ mile (800 m) reach a cross-track and turn R (there is a wall to the R). Keep climbing until an open area appears to your R. Continue in the same direction past this for a further 250 yds (230 m) until another open area appears on the R and the path forks. Go R. Leave the forest area at a stile and follow the clear path up the open moor (duck-boards later). Cross a fence at a stile and turn R. Climb to the L of a wall up to the summit of Shutlingsloe (OS obelisk). Notice the small plaque just to the L of the obelisk – see (7) Memorial plaque on Shutlingsloe.

Take the obvious path which descends half L from the summit and across the moor. Lower down cross a wall at a stile (PFS) and continue in the same direction to a stile in a fence. Go half R around a wall corner and down to a farm road. Turn R and follow the farm road down into the valley to join a metalled road. Turn R back to the lay-by.

(1) *St Saviour's Church, Wildboarclough (118-985688)*
This small church, with a square tower and low nave, was built by Frederick Arthur Stanley, 16th Earl of Derby, as a thanksgiving for the safe return of his sons from the South African War. The foundation stone was laid in September 1901 and consecration took place on St Peter's Day, 1909 in the presence of the Countess of Derby (Frederick Stanley had died on 14 June 1908 and therefore never saw his work finished). The church was largely built from local stone.

(2) *Three Shire Heads (119-009685)*
The beautiful old bridge which spans the River Dane at Three Shire Heads was originally a packhorse bridge which was probably built some 300 years ago. There are clear indications under the bridge that it was widened on the upstream side by about 3 ft (1 m) at some time in the past. The bridge was an important meeting point of five packhorse trails. The pool just below the bridge is still called Panniers Pool and perhaps marks the site of an earlier ford or drinking point.

Up to the development of the turnpikes in the eighteenth century travel over any distance was both slow and uncomfortable. For goods, the main – and, on the whole, the sole – means of transport was the packhorse train. A typical train might consist of up to fifty horses (probably Galloway or Jaeger-pony), travelling in file, carrying two panniers each and with bells to warn of their approach. From the early Middle Ages up to the middle of last century, a mere 150 years ago, packhorse trains were used extensively throughout the Peak District. It is scarcely surprising therefore that they have

The packhorse bridge at Three Shire Heads.

left their mark upon it: packhorse bridges (narrow, humpbacked, low-parapeted), hollow-ways carved out of hillsides by constant use, paved 'causeways' and finally place-names such as Jaggers' Lane or Jagger Way. This form of transport was used throughout the British Isles, but it is in hilly regions such as the Peak District where the signs are now the clearest.

The bridge is at the meeting point of three counties (Staffordshire, Cheshire and Derbyshire), hence its name.

(3) *The Cat and Fiddle (119-001719)*

This remote inn lies on the A537, Buxton-Macclesfield road, where it crosses the high ground at the head of the Goyt valley. At 1690 ft (515 m), it is the second highest in England, beaten only by Tan Hill Inn on the northern extremity of the Yorkshire Dales National Park. It was built by John Ryle of Macclesfield on the new turnpike which was completed in 1823 – see (4) The Stonyway below. On the front of the building is a stone tablet of a cat playing a fiddle. Walkers approaching the inn over Danebower Hollow will be pleased to know that they will be made very welcome.

(4) *The Stonyway (118-998723)*

Observant walkers cannot fail to notice the unusual surface on the short length of moorland road which cuts across a corner of the A537 soon after leaving the Cat and Fiddle. It was originally part of a turnpike from Macclesfield to Buxton which was constructed in 1759 and which is still substantially in its original condition. It was superseded in 1823 along almost its entire length by an improved turnpike – now the A537 – which used the contours cunningly, but at slightly greater length, to avoid some of the steep ascents and descents of the earlier road. The Cat and Fiddle was built to serve the second turnpike which went past the door, the earlier one crossing the moor behind. As turnpikes were private roads – although authorised by Parliament – travellers had to pay a toll for their use; one tollgate was situated at the Stonyway.

(5) *Rushbearing at Macclesfield Forest Chapel (118-974722)*

It was a common practice in early churches to cover the floor with a layer of hay or rushes in order to reduce cold and damp. With use

The Cat and Fiddle.

THE CAT & FIDDLE.

this covering would become soiled and downtrodden and would then have to be replaced, the ceremony of replacement – usually carried out annually – being referred to as a Rushbearing. The custom for practical purposes has now, of course, completely died out, but it still remains in a few churches as a tradition. One of these is St Stephen's Church on the edge of Macclesfield Forest, more usually referred to as the Forest Chapel. There the annual Rushbearing Service is held on the nearest Sunday to 12 August. The path from the churchyard gate to the porch and the floor inside the church are strewn with rushes, whilst bundles of rushes and flowers are used for decoration both inside and out. A service is held at the church in the afternoon.

(6) *The Forest of Macclesfield*

The Forest of Macclesfield occupied a much larger area than the present Macclesfield Forest which is a coniferous plantation on the gathering grounds of the Ridgegate and Trentabank Reservoirs. Bounded on the east by the Goyt valley and on the south by the Dane, the Forest extended in the other two directions up to the towns of Macclesfield and Marple. It was probably used for hunting in Anglo-Saxon times, but was established after the Norman Conquest as a Royal Forest to which the harsh forest laws applied. The word 'forest' is misleading in this respect as it does not necessarily imply dense woodland: in fact in this case it is more likely to have been an area of waste land with scattered trees. It was reserved exclusively for hunting, not just for recreational purposes but also as a valuable source of fresh meat, particularly in the winter months when salted meats were the only alternatives available. Two kinds of deer are known to have occupied the forest area and probably wild boar, all of which were eaten.

(7) *Memorial plaque on Shutlingsloe (118-976696)*

A few yards from the obelisk on the summit of Shutlingsloe is a small plaque in memory of Arthur Smith.

Previous pages

Left: Macclesfield Forest Chapel decorated for the annual Rushbearing Service in 1986.

Right: A distant view of Shutlingsloe from Macclesfield Forest.

Very Strenuous Routes

Route 31 The Kinder Round

The objective of this walk is to make a complete circuit of the main Kinder Scout plateau using convenient paths across adjoining areas of moorland. As the plateau covers an area some 4 miles in length and nearly 1½ miles in width (6.5 × 2.5 km) it will be appreciated that the distance covered is bound to be considerable, particularly as the walker is always pushed some distance away from the base of the plateau in his search for suitable ways. The result, however, is a route of the highest quality. Do it in one go if you can, but in two or three easy-paced expeditions if you can't, calling upon long-suffering wives, husbands or friends to provide the necessary transport to the beginning and to the end of each stage. The route keeps generally to fairly low ground, the highest point being the crossing of Ashop Head at 1700 ft (510 m).

Length: 20 miles (32 km).

Ascent: 3550 ft (1080 m).

Starting and finishing point: The car-park at Edale (110-124853).

Maps: Landranger 110; Outdoor Leisure The Dark Peak.

Route description (Maps 14, 13, 31A, 31B, 31C)
The route to Ashop Head has already been described. To avoid duplication, therefore, use (a) Route 14 from Edale to Edale Cross (page 153), (b) Route 13 from Edale Cross to the Kinder Road (page 148), and (c) Route 13 from the Kinder Road to Ashop Head (page 146).

Cross straight over at the Head. The path gradually descends and shortly reaches a stream; from there it follows the L bank for about 3¼ miles (5 km) to a stream meeting point and a footbridge. Cross the footbridge and turn L. Follow the path to the R of a stream through a wood. Shortly pass a bridge to the L and reach a small stream coming in from the R. The path bends to the R on the R-hand bank of this side stream; where the stream goes into a tunnel, cross and go over a ladder stile. On the other side rise up to the road.

Turn R and go along the road for about 350 yds (320 m) and then take a track which goes into the wood on the L. Follow the path through the forest slowly rising until you eventually leave it at a stile in a corner. The path crosses the hillside ahead still rising to meet the wood again at a further corner. Continue along the side of the wood boundary until it turns to the R and descends steeply. Go with it until you reach a wall. Turn L and follow the wall down to a small stream, then rise up on the other side still keeping by the wall. Go through a gate by a sheepfold and on to a gate and stile in a fence. In the large field on the other side the path swings to the L to eventually reach a stile in a fence. Continue now in the same direction over three fields (keeping by or near to the wall on the R) crossing intervening walls at stiles. In the fourth field still continue in the same direction, but now with a fence to the R, until you reach a farm. Pass the farm on the L alongside a fence to a ladder stile. There go half R to the farm road. Go L and after a short distance where the fence on the R bends R turn with it and go down to a stile and then more steeply to a road (A57).

Cross the road and go down to a gate to the R of the stream. This leads to a ford which can be crossed if safe (if not, use the footbridge nearby). Follow the rough farm road which goes off to the L. After ¼ mile (400 m) cross a ladder stile by a gate to the L of a farm, Upper Ashop. The farm road now swings L to join another coming in from the farm. Shortly, keep in the same direction at a fork, i.e. go to the R, climbing slowly up the hillside. At the top go around a clough, Blackley Clough, crossing a stile just before the stream. Keep in the same direction to leave the access area at a further stile. 300 yds (275 m) later reach a gate at a PFS.

Do not cross the gate, but instead turn R (i.e. to Clough Farm). Go over a stile by a gate and continue down into a deep clough (Jaggers Clough). Cross and go through a small gate. Turn R, then

MAP 31A

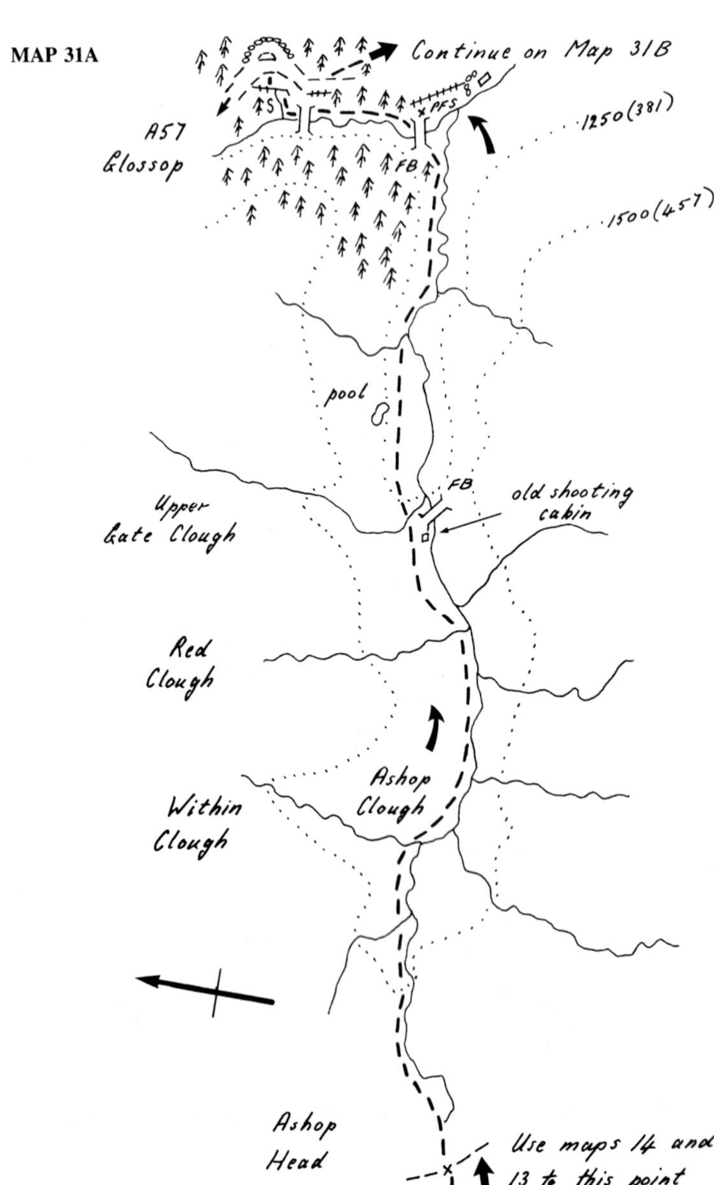

Continue on Map 31B
S
PFS
1250(381)
A57
Glossop
FB
1500(457)
pool
FB
old shooting
cabin
Upper
Gate Clough
Red
Clough
Ashop
Clough
Within
Clough
Ashop
Head
Use maps 14 and
13 to this point

MAP 31B

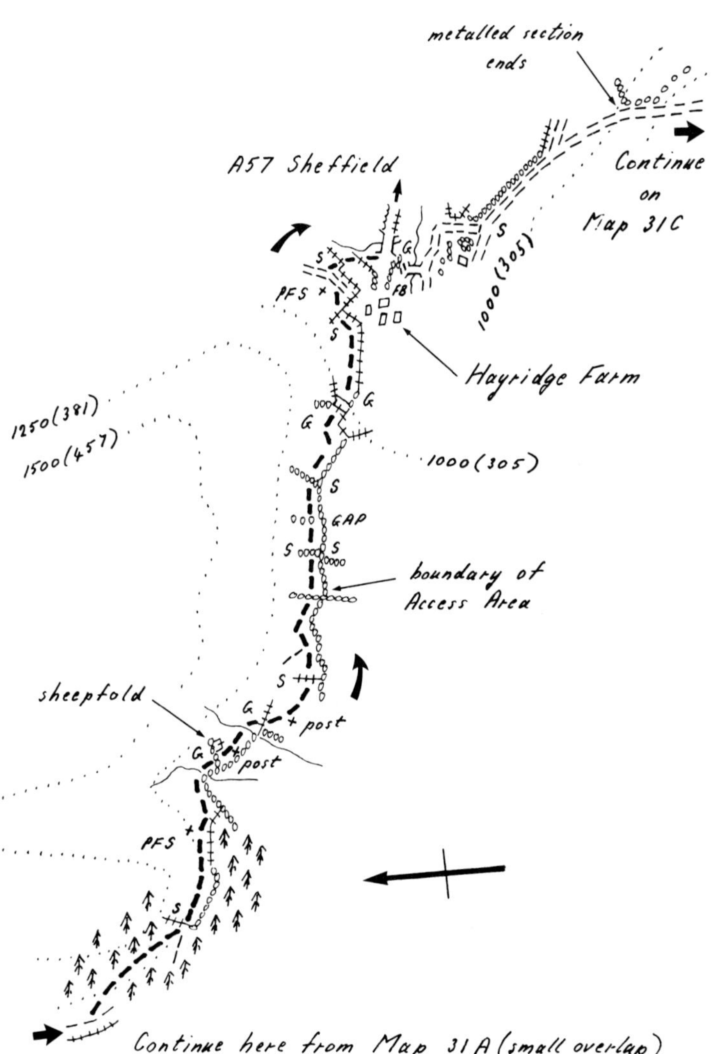
metalled section ends
A57 Sheffield
Continue on Map 31C
S
G
PFS
FB
1000 (305)
S
Hayridge Farm
1250 (381)
1500 (457)
G
G
1000 (305)
S
GAP
S
S
boundary of Access Area
sheepfold
S
G
post
G
post
PFS
S
Continue here from Map 31A (small overlap)

MAP 31C

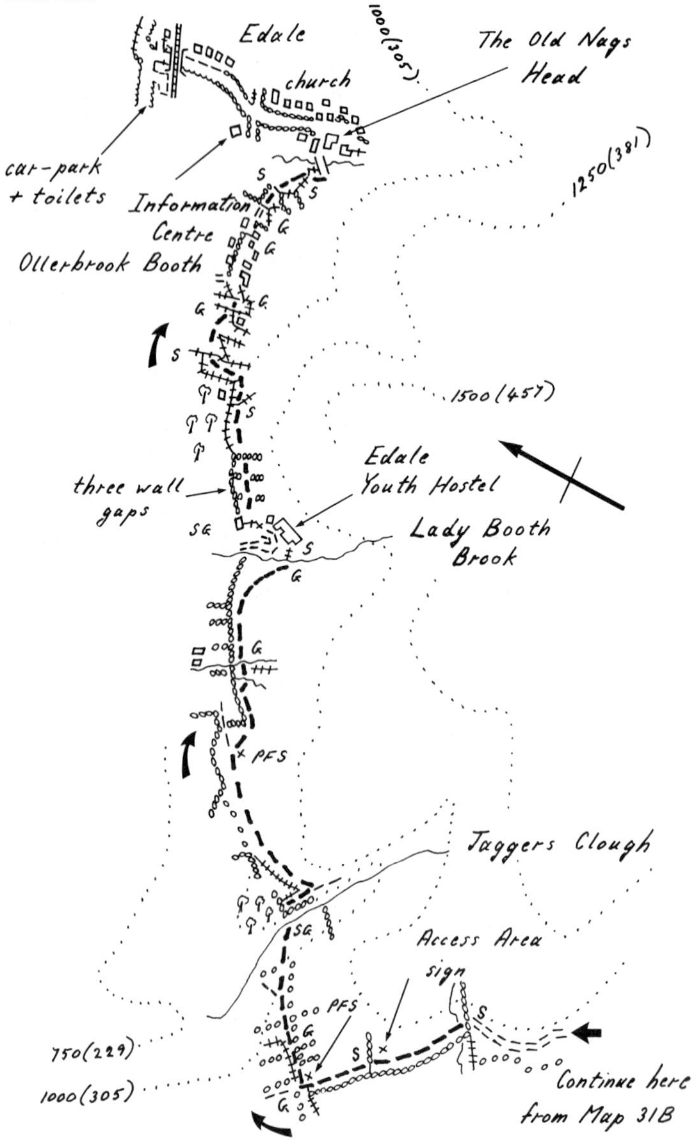

Edale
1000(305)
The Old Nags Head
church
1250(381)
car-park + toilets
Information Centre
Ollerbrook Booth
1500(457)
Edale Youth Hostel
three wall gaps
Lady Booth Brook
PFS
Jaggers Clough
SG
Access Area sign
PFS
750(229)
1000(305)
Continue here from Map 31B

at the end of a fence go up the path back half L to climb out of the clough. Follow the path until you reach a junction (PFS). Take the R-hand fork which soon goes round a wall corner and alongside a wall. Keep along this until you reach a further clough. Go through the stile by the gate in the clough. On the opposite side go up by a wall; the path soon bends to the R away from the wall and drops down into a third clough in front of a large building. Go through a gate and rise up L to a stile. Pass along the front of the building (Edale Youth Hostel) to the far end of the parking area.

There go through a swing gate and along a lovely green track. Follow the very clear path through three wall gaps to reach a stile by a wood. Beyond follow a fence until it swings to the L; here turn half L across a large field to a PFS on the opposite side. At the sign continue down by the fence to another PFS in the bottom R-hand corner of the field. In the corner go through a stile on the R and across a field to a fence corner, then half R to a gate in front of a farmhouse.

Cross the field beyond to enter a farm road. Follow this between several farm buildings and through several gates to another farm road on the opposite side. Go along this to a gate and then along a footpath to a stile in a corner. Continue ahead across a field and then down to an old packhorse bridge. Go up the street on the opposite side to reach the road by the Old Nags Head. Then continue down the road back to the car-park in Edale.

Route 32 The Eastern Edges Walk

Running down the eastern side of the National Park, from the Howden Moors to Chatsworth, is an almost continuous line of superb gritstone edges which face inwards towards the limestone area of the Peak. They provide one of the finest walks to be found anywhere. It is not one, however, which should be undertaken lightly. 26 miles (42 km) and 2550 ft (780 m) of climbing are not everybody's idea of a good day out. But the wonderful walking and the magnificent views are; and whether taken in one fell swoop or on several expeditions – knocking off a little at a time – this is one walk that everybody should do at some time. Either way one important ingredient will be the provision of transport to the start and from the finish or at strategic points along the way.

Length: 26 miles (42 km).

Ascent: 2550 ft (780 m).

Starting point: The Flouch Inn at the junction of the A616 and A628 (110-198016). An alternative starting point for those who would really like a long walk is Salter's Brook Bridge on the A628 (110-137002).

Finishing point: The Robin Hood Inn on the A619 about 1½ miles (2.4 km) east of Baslow (119-279722).

Maps: Landranger 110 and 119; Outdoor Leisure The Dark Peak and The White Peak (East Sheet) – part only.

Route description (Maps 32A, 32B, 32C, 32D, 32E, 11,4)
A number of features of interest will be passed along the way but it is assumed that you will be far too busy with the demands of this long walk to have much time for them.

From the crossroads walk along the A628 towards Glossop. Immediately after a bungalow on the L-hand side turn L (PFS) down a footpath. At the end at a stile take the footpath to the L. This soon bends to the R to a forest road. There keep straight ahead to a further forest road. This goes through the forest and shortly drops down to a bridge. Over the bridge continue along the forest road (not directly ahead!). The forest road climbs steeply, bending to the R and then to the L. Soon it leaves the forest area and strikes across the moor. Towards the top of the moor cross a broken wall and continue in the same direction, ignoring a branch to the L.

Continue to follow this excellent moorland road (Cut Gate) as it goes across the moor past several broken walls. Soon it drops steeply down and goes to the edge of a clough (Mickeldon Beck). Follow the path for nearly 2 miles (3 km), first alongside the stream and then up the open moor. At the top of the moor leave the path to

MAP 32A

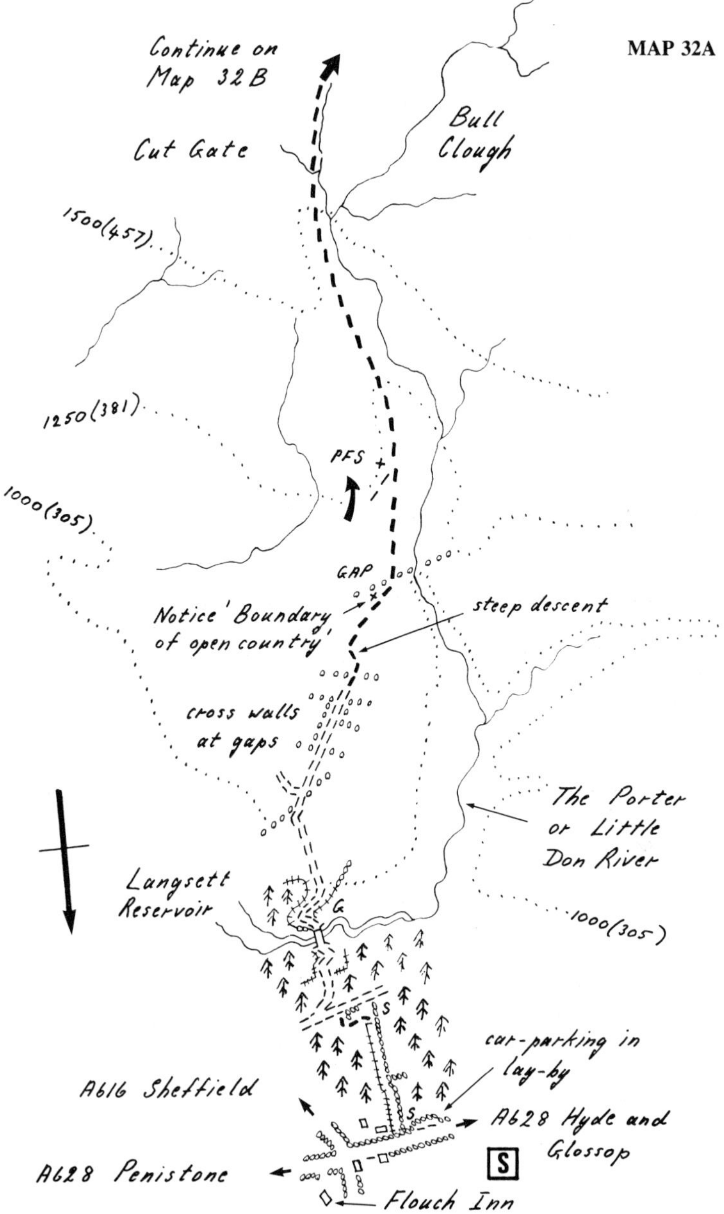

Continue on Map 32B
Cut Gate
Bull Clough
1500(457)
1250(381)
PFS
1000(305)
GAP
Notice 'Boundary of open country'
steep descent
cross walls at gaps
The Porter or Little Don River
Langsett Reservoir
G
1000(305)
S
car-parking in lay-by
A616 Sheffield
S
A628 Hyde and Glossop
S
A628 Penistone
Flouch Inn

MAP 32B

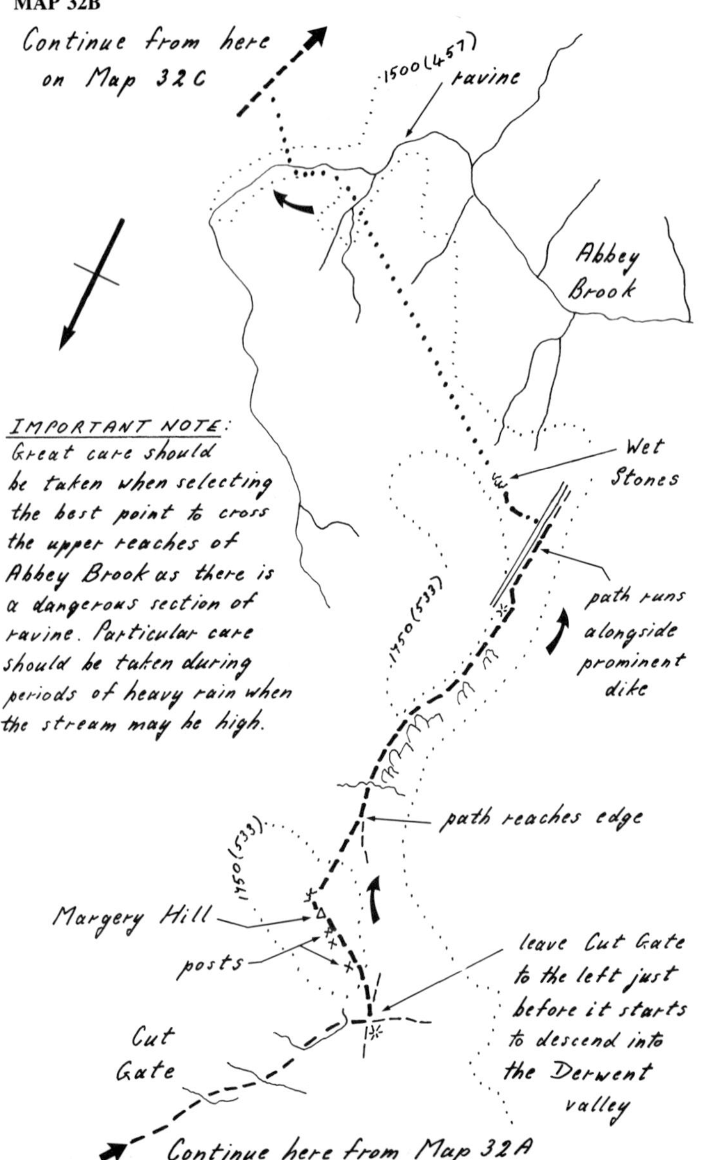

Continue from here on Map 32C
1500(457)
ravine
Abbey Brook
IMPORTANT NOTE:
Great care should be taken when selecting the best point to cross the upper reaches of Abbey Brook as there is a dangerous section of ravine. Particular care should be taken during periods of heavy rain when the stream may be high.
Wet Stones
path runs alongside prominent dike
1450(533)
path reaches edge
1450(533)
Margery Hill
posts
leave Cut Gate to the left just before it starts to descend into the Derwent valley
Cut Gate
Continue here from Map 32A

MAP 32C

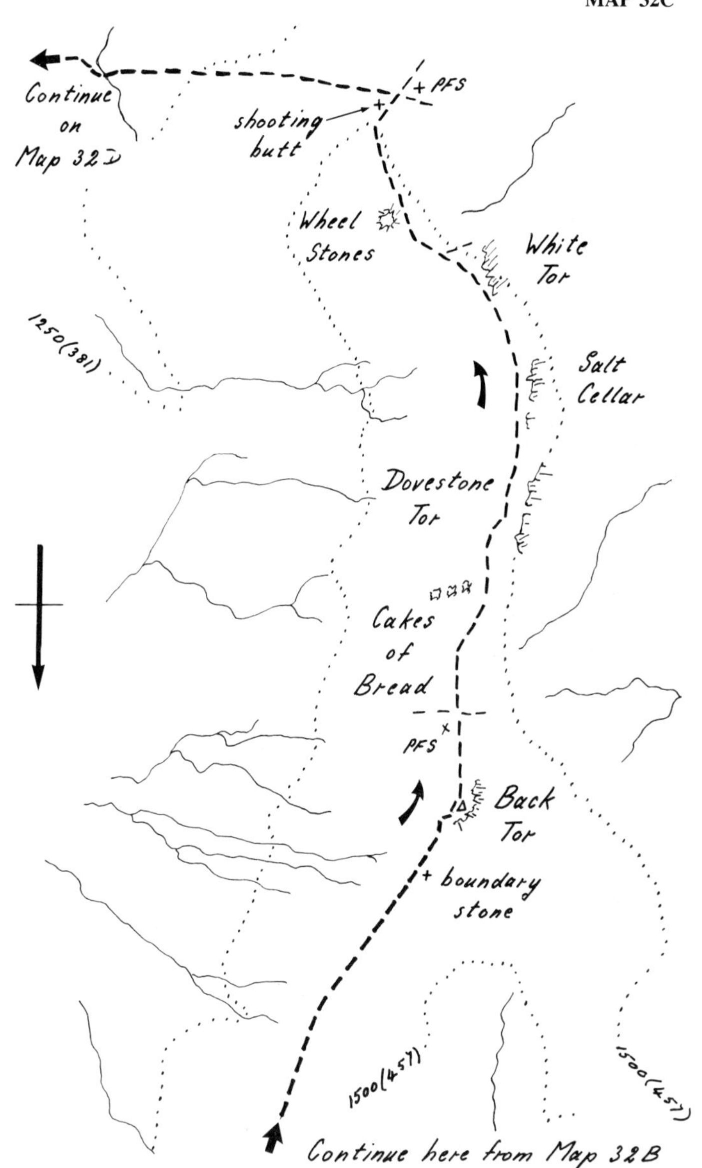
Continue on Map 32D
+ PFS
shooting butt
Wheel Stones
White Tor
1250(381)
Salt Cellar
Dovestone Tor
Cakes of Bread
PFS
Back Tor
+ boundary stone
1500(457)
1500(457)
Continue here from Map 32B

MAP 32D

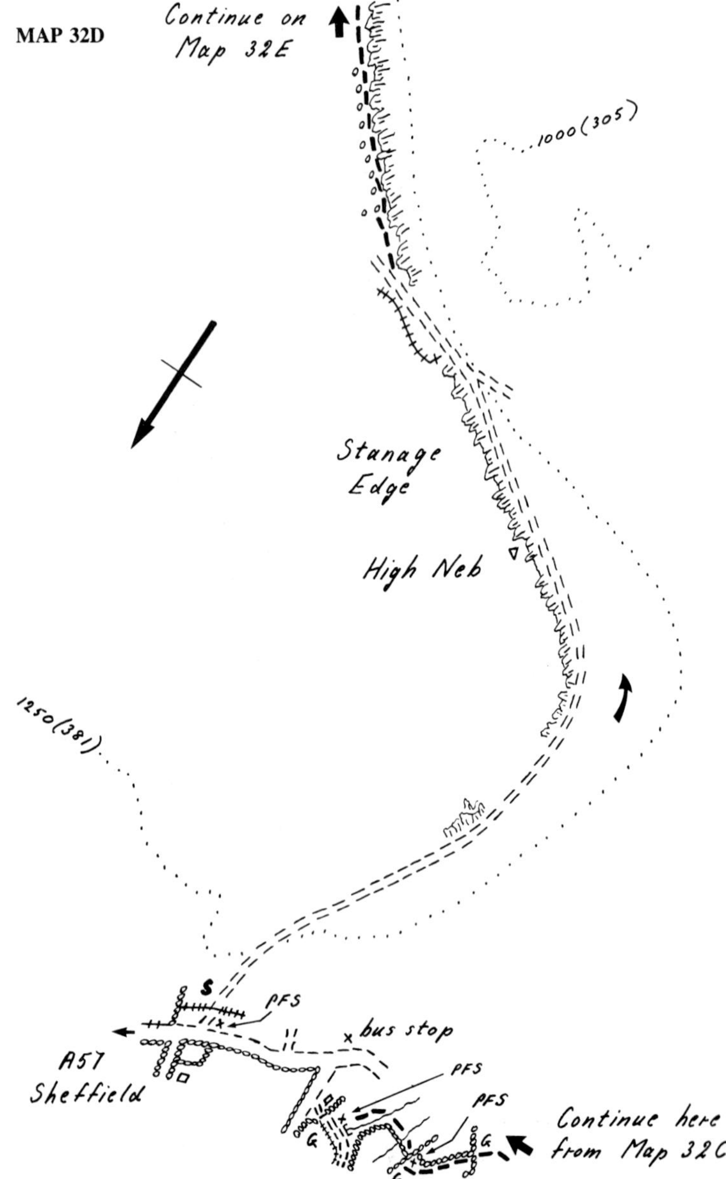
Continue on
Map 32E
1000(305)
Stanage
Edge
High Neb
1250(381)
S
PFS
bus stop
A57
Sheffield
PFS
G
PFS
G
G
Continue here
from Map 32C

MAP 32E

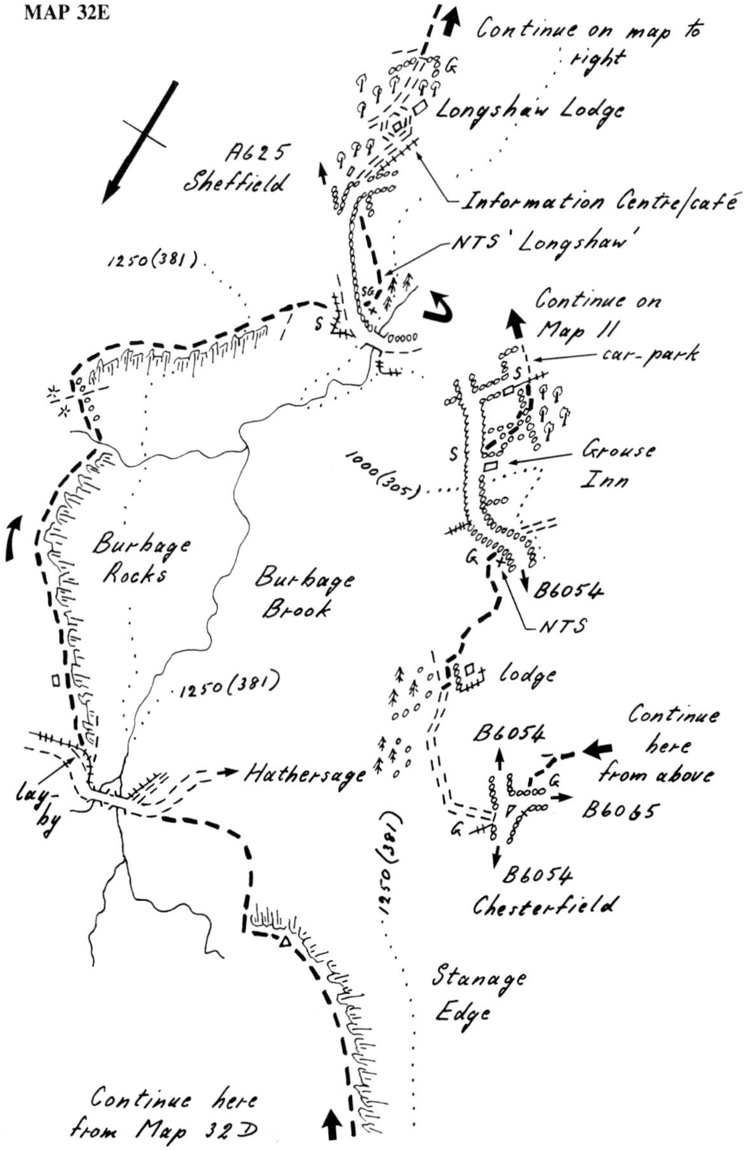

Continue on map to right

Longshaw Lodge

A625 Sheffield

Information Centre/café

NTS 'Longshaw'

1250(381)

SG

S

Continue on Map 11

car-park

Grouse Inn

1000(305)

B6054

NTS

G

Burbage Rocks

Burbage Brook

1250(381)

lodge

Continue here from above

B6054

B6065

lay-by

Hathersage

B6054 Chesterfield

1250(381)

Stanage Edge

Continue here from Map 32D

the SE climbing slowly up to an Ordnance Survey obelisk about ½ mile (800 m) away. This is Margery Hill. Continue beyond the obelisk to some boulders, then half R on a path which eventually reaches an edge. Turn L along the edge, later slowly climbing. After about ½ mile (800 m) go over a top and on to a long shallow groove coming in on the L. Follow this down on its R-hand side for about 500 yards (450 m) from the top, then cross it to the L to pick up a path which heads towards some prominent rocks (Wet Stones).

Cross the open moor (there is no path) on a bearing of 130° magnetic to eventually cross Abbey Brook (*see important note on Map 32B*). Rise up on the opposite side to reach a clear crossing path on the ridge top. Turn R and follow this to Back Tor.

From Back Tor follow a path which runs generally to the south with the steep edge of the moor to the R for nearly 2 miles (3.5 km) to a crossing track at a PFS and by a shooting butt. Here turn L. Descend the moor on the clear path passing a number of shooting butts. After ¾ mile (1.2 km) cross a stream and rise up to a gate in a wall. Cross and go down a field keeping to the R-hand side by a wall. Lower, curve to the R with the wall to a corner (PFS and gate). Go through the gate and continue in the same direction with the wall to the L. Where the wall bends to the L go with it and cross a small stream. Keep by the stream until you reach a farm road. There turn R and go up to a house and a road. Turn R to the main road (A57).

Turn L and go up the A57 for about 350 yds (320 m) to the top of the hill, there turn R off the road at a PFS. Follow the clear path which crosses a stile after a few yards and goes up the moor. After about 1¼ miles (2 km) the rock edge of Stanage begins on the L. Either (a) continue along this path which later rises up to the top of the rocks, or (b) choose a suitable point to climb up where the rocks start. In either case follow the edge for its full length of about 2 miles (3 km). Just beyond an O S obelisk (this is the second on Stanage Edge) the edge bends to the L. 200 yds (180 m) later bend down to the R with the path and cross the moor to reach a road.

Turn L and go along the road, soon crossing two bridges close

Stanage Edge.

together. Immediately after the second bridge turn R through an opening on the R at the *far* end of the small parking area. Follow the clear path which keeps above the crag (Burbage Rocks). Where the cliff on the R fades away the path bends L and rises to the start of a second line of rocks; there it bends R to resume its original line along the edge. Eventually at the far end of the rocks follow the path down to a road.

Cross the road and go through a small gate on to a path. After a few yards the path bends L to run parallel with the road. Shortly rejoin the road and cross half R to a drive entrance. About 125 yds (115 m) down the drive you will reach a NT Information Centre/café before a large house. Just before the Centre turn L and after a few yards R to go behind the house. Go up through a wood to reach a gate. Continue in the same direction up the estate road, later going L at a junction to a road. Turn R for a few yards then L across the island at a roundabout to the R side of the Chesterfield road. Go through a gate (NT sign 'White Edge Moor') and along the farm road beyond. At a tall building (White Edge Lodge) bend to the R to a wall just in front of it, then turn L and follow a farm road across the moor leaving the lodge behind. Eventually reach a road (B6054) and turn L. Immediately after the Grouse Inn turn R over a stile and cross a field half L to a gateway. Continue across the next field in the same direction to a gap in a broken wall and then on to a further gap which leads into a small wood. Turn L and follow the wall to a stile which leads into a car-park.

The remainder of the route has already been described: (a) For the section from the car-park to Wellington's Monument see Route 11 (page 135); (b) For the route from Wellington's Monument to the end at Robin Hood Inn see Route 4 (page 80).

Discarded millstones below Stanage Edge. Renowned for their hard-wearing properties, 'Peak Stones' were manufactured here and at other sites in the area.

Appendix

Appendix 1 Other recommended walks

Long-distance routes

The Cal-Der-Went Walk
A 30-mile (48 km) route from Horbury Bridge near Wakefield on the A642 to the Snake Road where it crosses Ladybower Reservoir over the viaduct. The name of the walk was derived from the names of the rivers at the start and end of the route, i.e. Calder and Derwent, using the common three letters 'der' to join them.

Guide: *The Cal-Der-Went Walk*, Geoffrey Carr, Dalesman.

Cestrian Link Walk
A 112-mile (180 km) link between the southern end of the Pennine Way at Edale and the northern end of Offa's Dyke Path at Prestatyn in Clwyd. The route runs southwards before leaving the Park and therefore takes in more of it than might be expected.

For details of the route see *A Cestrian Link Walk* by John N. Davenport published by Westmorland Gazette.

The Derbyshire Gritstone Way
Not to be confused with the Gritstone Trail (see below) which is in Cheshire. This route of 56 miles (90 km) starts at Derby and runs up the eastern side of the Park before turning west along the Great Ridge to Mam Tor and Edale.

See *The Derbyshire Gritstone Way*, S. Burton, M. Maughan and I. Quarrinton, Thornhill Press.

The Gritstone Trail
A trail of 17 miles (27 km) from Lyme Park, south of Disley, to a junction with the Staffordshire Way, north-west of Rushton Spencer (118-930634). It runs north to south along the western boundary of the National Park where the hills drop down to the Cheshire plain. As might be expected from such a situation the views are superb, as is most of the walking.

A guide, *Gritstone Trail Walker's Guide*, is available from the Director of Countryside and Recreation, Cheshire County Council, County Hall, Chester, CH1 1SF.

John Merrill's Peak District Challenge Walk
A 25-mile (40 km) circular walk starting from Bakewell which visits Rowsley, Robin Hood's Stride, Monyash and Monsal Dale.
Guide: *John Merrill's Peak District Challenge Walk*, John N. Merrill, JNM Publications.

The Limey Way
A north to south route from Castleton to Thorpe across the White Peak which traverses a number of the most beautiful dales of the area. It is 40 miles (64 km) long and was inaugurated by John Merrill.
Guide: *The Limey Way*, John N. Merrill, JNM Publications.

The Peak District High Level Route
Another circular route in the Peak District which, as its name implies, keeps to high ground. The Roaches and the Shining Tor ridge to the west, the Kinder Edges to the north and the eastern gritstone edges are all on the route which is 90 miles (145 km) long.
Guide: *The Peak District High Level Route*, John N. Merrill, JNM Publications.

The Peakland Way
A circular walk of 96 miles (154 km), devised by John Merrill, which starts and finishes at Ashbourne. The route goes up the Manifold valley to Longnor, then via Blackwell Peak Forest and Barber Booth to Kinder which is skirted on its western and northern flanks to the Snake Inn. The Woodlands valley is followed to Hagg Farm and then Win Hill. The return route is via Hathersage and the eastern edges to Baslow, Rowsley, Birchover and Parwich.
See *Peakland Way Guide*, John N. Merrill, JNM Publications.

The Pennine Way
At Edale, the Pennine Way begins its long, long trek up the backbone of the Pennine hills towards the distant goal of Kirk Yetholm which lies just over the Scottish border. 250 miles (403 km) of glorious walking, most of it over high and lonely moorlands. Take no notice whatsoever of the critics. By any standards it is superb.

The route leaves Edale up Grindsbrook Clough, crosses the Kinder plateau to the Downfall and on to Mill Hill and the Snake Road. Devil's Dike leads to Bleaklow Head, then Torside Clough to Longdendale. Crowden Great Brook and Laddow Rocks take the Way to the bare peat top of Black Hill from where a descent can be made to the north-west to the A635. The final stretch within the Park is across White Moss and Black Moss to the A62 south-west of Marsden.

Guides are *Pennine Way Companion*, A. Wainwright, Westmorland Gazette; *The Pennine Way*, Tom Stephenson, HMSO and *A Guide to the Pennine Way*, Christopher John Wright, Constable.

Ramblers Way

38 miles (61 km) from Castleton to Hathersage. The route was inaugurated as a memorial to those ramblers who were involved some fifty years or so ago in the struggle for access to the moors of the Peak District. A considerable amount of climbing is involved in this route which keeps to the Dark Peak area of the Park. A badge is available for anyone completing.

See *Ramblers Way*, Andrew Newton and Paul Summers, from Mountain Peak Climbing Club, 17 Humberston Road, Wollaton, Nottingham, NG8 2SU.

The Rivers Way

A route of 40 miles (64 km) which follows the principal rivers of the Park – the Noe, Derwent, Wye, Dove and Manifold – from Edale to Ilam.

Guide: *The Rivers Way*, John N. Merrill, JNM Publications.

The White Peak Way

A circular route of 80 miles (130 km) from Bakewell which links seven youth hostels mainly in the White Peak area of the Park. The hostels visited are Bakewell, Hathersage, Castleton, Ravenstor, Hartington Hall, Ilam Hall and Youlgreave. A certificate and badge are available to those who complete the walk.

Guide: *The White Peak Way*, Robert Haslam, Cicerone.

Nature, town and forest trails

The Forestry Commission
Woodland Walk. A trail (with information plaques) of about 1¼ miles (2 km) has been laid out in the grounds of Errwood Hall in the Goyt valley; this starts from Errwood Hall car-park by Errwood Reservoir (119-012749). Leaflets are available in the car-park.

The National Trust
Ilam Hall Country Park. Although not a definite trail, a walk of about 1 mile (1.6 km) can be worked out in the grounds of the Park. A guide, *Ilam Hall Country Park*, obtainable from the National Trust shop and Information Centre at the Hall, shows the footpaths and features of interest.

North-West Water Authority
Macclesfield Forest (a coniferous forest 3½ miles, 5.5 km ESE of Macclesfield). Three forest trails have been prepared which start from the Information Centre by Trentabank Reservoir (118-964712). The trails, which are numbered and waymarked, are 1, 3 and 5 miles (1.5, 5 and 8 km) respectively. Guide, *Macclesfield Forest Visitors' Guide*, from the Information Centre.

Peak Park Joint Planning Board
Bakewell Town Trail. A trail, about 1 mile (1.6 km) in length, starts at the Information Centre, Old Market Hall (119-218686) and visits features of interest in the town. A guide, *Bakewell Town Trail*, Peak Park Joint Planning Board, is available at the Information Centre.
'Routes for People' Scheme. A number of routes have been chosen as part of this scheme which is operated jointly by the Board and Derbyshire County Council. The routes vary in length from 1 to 6 miles (1.6 to 10 km) and are waymarked with numbered yellow arrows. Currently leaflets are available from the Board's Information Centres describing routes from Bakewell, Friden, Minninglow, Monyash, Moor Lane and White Lodge.

Peak Park Joint Planning Board/Sheffield University
Roystone Grange Archaeological Trail. The trail, 4 miles (6.5 km) long, starts at the Minninglow car-park about ½ mile (800 m) south of Pikehall which is on the A5012 Cromford-Newhaven road (119-194583). It was produced by co-operation between Sheffield University and the Peak Park Joint Planning Board and takes the visitor past Roman and medieval farms and field systems, as well as the remains of Victorian quarries and brickworks. The trail is marked by yellow arrows with the letter 'R'. Guide: *Roystone Grange Archaeological Trail.*

Appendix 2 Addresses of useful organisations

Camping and Caravanning Club, 11 Lower Grosvenor Place, London SW1W 0EY. Telephone: 01-828 1012/7.
Council for National Parks, 45 Shelton Street, London WC2H 9HJ. Telephone: 01-240 3603.
Council for the Protection of Rural England, 4 Hobart Place, London SW1W 0HY. Telephone: 01-235 9481.
Countryside Commission, John Dower House, Crescent Place, Cheltenham, Gloucesterhsire, GL50 3RA. Telephone: Cheltenham (0242) 521381.
English Tourist Board, Thames Tower, Blacks Road, Hammersmith , London W6 9EL (postal enquiries only).
The Forestry Commission, Public Information Division, 231 Corstorphine Road, Edinburgh EH12 7AT. Telephone: 031-334 0303.
The Long Distance Walkers' Association, Membership Secretary, Lodgefield Cottage, High Street, Flimwell, Wadhurst, East Sussex, TN5 7PA. Telephone: Flimwell (058 087) 341.
The National Trust, 36 Queen Anne's Gate, London SW1H 9AS. Telephone: 01-222 9251. (East Midlands Regional Office, Clumber Park Stableyard, Worksop S80 3BE. Telephone: Worksop (0909) 486411.)
Peak National Park Study Centre, Losehill Hall, Castleton, Derbyshire, S30 2WB. Telephone: Hope Valley (0433) 20373.
Peak Park Joint Planning Board, The National Park Office, Peak District National Park, Aldern House, Baslow Road, Bakewell, Derbyshire, DE4 1AE. Telephone: Bakewell (062 981) 4321. For free list of publications, send a SAE.
The Ramblers' Association, 1/5 Wandsworth Road, London SW8 2XX. Telephone: 01-582 6878. The RA has a number of local Groups around the area of the Park; the addresses of Group Secretaries change frequently but an up-to-date list can be obtained from the Head Office.
Youth Hostels Association (England and Wales), Trevelyan House, 8 St Stephen's Hill, St Albans, Hertfordshire, AL1 2DY. Telephone: St Albans (0727) 55215. (Peak District Area Office: 38 Bank Road, Matlock, Derbyshire, DE4 3NF. Telephone: Matlock (0629) 4666/7.)

Appendix 3 Glossary

Bog-trotter: a specifically Peak District term for a hard walker who enjoys long walks on the rough and boggy moorlands of the Dark Peak.

Brook: a stream

Buttress: a prominent rock face standing out from a hillside

Cairn: a heap of stones marking a mountain summit or a hilltop or part of a route.

Cloud: corruption of Old English *clud* which means rock, but used also in the sense of 'hill', e.g. Thorpe Cloud, Hen Cloud.

Clough: a valley cut into a moor by a stream. In very common use throughout and also to the north of the Peak District.

Col: a dip in a ridge between two hills, sometimes offering an easy way from one valley to the next.

Crag: a cliff.

Dale: a valley; a term widely used throughout the Pennines and Lake District.

Dike: a stream.

Edge: further north in the Lake District this term is used to denote a narrow mountain ridge. In the Peak District, however, the term is used in a different way to describe the edge of a moor where it drops steeply away into the valley, usually marked by a long thin line of gritstone crag. Examples are Derwent Edge, Curbar Edge and Froggatt Edge.

Fell: used throughout the Lake District and northern Pennines for areas of high moorland. Also used in a more general way, e.g. fellwalker.

Grain: a small tributary stream, meeting another at a fork. Derived from the Old Norse *grein*. For example, Grains-in-the-Water.

Gritstone: a dark rock which forms the characteristic 'edges' of the Peak District; holds a long and important place in climbing history.

Grough: a channel cut into the soft top surface of peat moors by running water. A very common feature on the moors of the Dark Peak. Pronounced 'gruff'.

Gully: a wide and steep cleft down a rock face. The few in the Peak

District tend to be very short compared to those in the mountain areas of the Lake District and Snowdonia.

Gutter: a stream.

Hag: an isolated grassy topped mound with walls of bare peat. A common feature on the northern moors.

In-by: improved moorland around a hill farm.

Moss: a very common name on the northern gritstone moors. Describes a particularly marshy area, probably because sphagnum moss grows – or, more likely, once grew – there, e.g. Featherbed Moss.

Pass: a relatively easy passage with high ground on each side, perhaps from one valley to the next, e.g. Winnats, Snake Pass.

Pike: a hill or mountain with a sharp, well-defined appearance, e.g. Winhill Pike.

Pot-hole: a large vertical shaft in limestone, e.g. Eldon Hole.

Ridge: used in several slightly different ways. A narrow buttress of rock, a spur of a mountain, or a long and substantially horizontal felltop, perhaps with several summits and cols, e.g. The Great Ridge.

Scramble: a climb up fairly broken rock requiring the use of hands for balance purposes, but not difficult enough to justify the use of a rope even for a fairly inexperienced party.

Scree slope: a slope covered with a layer of small rock fragments, produced by the weathering of higher cliffs.

Sough: underground tunnel cut in lead mines for drainage purposes. Pronounced 'suff'.

Stones: probably derived from Old English *stan*. Used on the northern moors of the Peak District for small shapely outcrops of gritstone, e.g. Crow Stones, Wain Stones.

Swallets: solution holes or cavities in limestone down which streams flow and disappear. (Also known as 'shack-holes' and 'swallow-holes'.)

Tor: a hill; derived from the Old English word *torr*. An example is Mam Tor. Also used for gritstone outcrops, e.g. Nether Tor.

Traverse: a movement across a rock face or fellside without any loss of, or gain in, height.

Water: a stream, e.g. Peakshole Water near Castleton.

Watershed: a ridge separating river basins so that the streams on opposite sides – even though they rise very near to each other – flow in different directions.

Index

Illustrations are indicated by *Italics*. With a few important exceptions place names have only been included if they are on or near to the routes described.